WITHDRAWN

The Geography of Risk

The Geography of Risk

Epic Storms, Rising Seas,
AND THE *Cost* OF *America's Coasts*

Gilbert M. Gaul

SARAH CRICHTON BOOKS

Farrar, Straus and Giroux

New York

Sarah Crichton Books
Farrar, Straus and Giroux
120 Broadway, New York 10271

Copyright © 2019 by Gilbert M. Gaul
Maps copyright © 2019 by Jeffrey L. Ward
All rights reserved
Printed in the United States of America
First edition, 2019

Grateful acknowledgment is made for permission to reprint photographs and
charts from the following: pp. 18, 25, 42: courtesy of Herbert Shapiro; pp. 79, 247:
photograph by Ray Fisk / The SandPaper Inc.; pp. 90, 148, 164: courtesy of the
Event Database; p. 238: courtesy of Dave Rinear.

Library of Congress Control Number: 2019011314
ISBN: 978-0-374-16080-7

Designed by Richard Oriolo

Our books may be purchased in bulk for promotional, educational, or business
use. Please contact your local bookseller or the Macmillan Corporate and
Premium Sales Department at 1-800-221-7945, extension 5442, or by e-mail at
MacmillanSpecialMarkets@macmillan.com.

www.fsgbooks.com
www.twitter.com/fsgbooks • www.facebook.com/fsgbooks

10 9 8 7 6 5 4 3 2 1

For Xander, Violet, and Rowan
Little Stars of the Sea

I have frequently been asked: What are the possibilities of our Atlantic coast resorts being submerged? In answer to this I will say that it is more than a possibility that great disasters may come to populous centers located directly on the Atlantic coast that are unprotected by breakwaters and that have flimsy building foundations placed almost at sea-level.

—WILLIS L. MOORE, *MOORE'S METEOROLOGICAL ALMANAC AND WEATHER GUIDE*, 1901

CONTENTS

The Geography of Risk

Introduction:
The Old Man and the Sea

The definition of insanity is doing the same thing over and over again and expecting a different result.

—AUTHOR UNKNOWN

A WEEK BEFORE CHRISTMAS IN 1999, I met the acclaimed coastal geologist Orrin H. Pilkey on the Outer Banks of North Carolina, a more or less continuous spit of sand extending along half of the state's four-hundred-mile coast. We had come to talk about erosion, hurricanes, and the relentlessly defiant pace of development along the state's once-pristine shore. Billions of dollars of property now perched in harm's way. Parts of Kitty Hawk, Kill Devil Hills, and Nags Head had lost entire rows of beach houses to the sea. Dozens of other houses now wobbled on stilts in the surf. Some industrious owners had placed mesh bags filled with giant boulders around the pilings. But these makeshift attempts at engineering provided only so much help. One by one, the houses toppled into the ocean or were condemned by the towns—"red-tagged," in the parlance of local zoning officials.

"It's madness," Pilkey exclaimed as we examined a sliver of beach where two rows of homes were now underwater. "I am sometimes condemned for saying this, but that's what it is—madness and hubris of unbelievable proportions."

Pilkey is a short, square hobbit of a man, with an unruly gray beard and a disarming sense of humor. Depending on your point of view, he is either a prophet or the Antichrist of the coast. For more than half a century, he has been churning out scientific papers (more than 250) and books (45 and counting) spotlighting the immeasurable beauty of barrier islands and the illogic of building houses on them. The mayor of a beach town in New Jersey once blurted, "I hate him, hate him, hate him," after Pilkey pointed out that his shoreline was rapidly washing away. In 1991, the town of Folly Beach, South Carolina, passed a resolution condemning Pilkey's studies as "insulting, uninformed and radical." Pilkey framed the resolution and hung it on his office wall at Duke University, where he ran the marine geology program.

Now eighty-four, Pilkey is retired, yet he's still challenging the often reckless development of the coasts and the billions in government subsidies and bailouts that normalize risks and encourage rebuilding in harm's way after hurricanes and floods. "The mayors and politicians like to call hurricanes 'natural' disasters," he said. "But in my opinion, there's nothing natural about them. They are man-made. Barrier islands are always moving. Beaches are always eroding. It's only a problem when you put a house there."

This is a book about water and risk—that is, how Americans live with water and accommodate its beauty, power, and fury. It grew out of my longstanding love affair with the ocean and what I have watched occurring at the coast over nearly seven decades. It isn't enough to say that rising seas and larger, more ferocious storms threaten trillions of dollars of property. What is equally critical to understand is how we arrived at this point, with so much at stake and so few good choices. Which human and economic forces propelled Americans to build in one of the most ecologically fragile and dangerous places on earth—coastal floodplains—and then reward those decisions without truly apportioning the risks?

What we think of as the coast is a relatively modern phenomenon. True, ancient peoples ferried across the bays and sounds to fish and hunt. And Gilded Age industrialists built Victorian mansions, hotels, and hunting clubs along the Atlantic and Gulf Coasts. However, developers didn't turn to the coast in earnest until the last century, when postwar prosperity enabled Americans to indulge themselves after years of sacrifice. Over the next few decades, a surge of second homes filled beach towns and communities along the ocean, gulf, and bays. That wave of development has only accelerated since, backed by an array of federal and state programs that provide inexpensive financing and tax breaks; offer heavily subsidized flood insurance; underwrite roads, bridges, and utilities; and distribute billions more in disaster aid to help beach towns rebuild after hurricanes and floods—setting the stage for a seemingly endless loop of government payouts. It isn't an exaggeration to say that without the federal government, the coast as we know it simply wouldn't exist.

One can fairly argue that it was an unintentional policy. After all, there was never a national debate about whether to develop the coasts. Critical choices were left to beach-town politicians, who controlled land-use, zoning, and building decisions and, unsurprisingly, favored development. Later, when state and federal officials tried to slow the unrestricted building, politicians and developers stiff-armed them aside. The result, this book argues, is one of the most costly and damaging planning failures in American history, with at least $3 trillion worth of property now at risk of flooding and catastrophic storms, and the U.S. Department of the Treasury serving as the insurer of last resort.

The costs are multiplying each decade. Hurricanes and coastal storms now account for sixteen of the twenty most expensive disasters in U.S. history, with well over half a trillion dollars in damage in the last two decades alone— far more than the damage caused by earthquakes, wildfires, and tornadoes combined. Worryingly, the pace of destruction is accelerating, with seventeen of the most destructive hurricanes in history occurring since 2000. In 2017, Harvey, Irma, and Maria resulted in over $300 billion in losses, the most in a single year. As I write, Florence is bearing down on an area of North Carolina that has been repeatedly pummeled by storms, yet is rapidly adding houses and people. No doubt the damage will cost taxpayers billions. Meanwhile, federally subsidized flood claims at the coast have increased twentyfold in the last two decades and account for three-quarters of all flood losses nationwide, effectively leaving the government's insurance program insolvent. Now, with rising seas, warmer oceans, and more property than ever before at risk, even more calamitous storms—and government payouts—are inevitable.

The most pressing question is, why do we keep repeating the same mistakes over and over? The development of the coasts is a peculiarly American expression of optimism, commerce, and defiance—even willful blindness. After each hurricane, Americans keep rebuilding, normalizing their risky choices. At least two million houses have been erected on low-lying barrier islands and bays in recent decades, many of them vacation homes and investment properties insured by the federal government. Surprisingly, some of the riskiest properties benefit from the most generous taxpayer subsidies, despite flooding repeatedly. Yet half a century after the government got into the business of insuring vacation homes at the beach, no one can explain how it happened, let alone whether it is an appropriate role. One can fairly argue it was an unintentional policy, and that the costs have been, and will be, astounding. Researchers have estimated that even a relatively modest one-foot rise in sea level will nearly double the nation's flood losses in the coming decades. A more likely three-to-six-foot rise will bury over one million homes underwater, leaving them inaccessible, if not modern-day versions of the mythical sunken city of Atlantis.

In 2017, politicians in Texas dismissed climate change as pseudoscientific opinion even as Houston was drowning in epic rainfall from Hurricane Harvey, flooding more than 300,000 properties. Now, without so much as a trace of irony, they are pleading for billions in federal aid to save them from their own arrogance and mistakes. And Congress is going along. It has awarded nearly $130 billion so far in disaster aid and billions more to armor the Texas coast. Meanwhile, the Trump administration is gutting scores of regulations aimed at slowing the looming threats, freeing coal-fired power plants and manufacturers to spew carbon dioxide and methane into the already oversaturated atmosphere. In March 2018, the Federal Emergency Management Administration (FEMA) even dropped any mention of "climate change" from its strategic plan.

Leaders from New York City to Miami to Galveston, Texas, have been left to devise their own solutions. Some are thinking deeply about what it means to live with rising water, torrential rain bombs, and staggeringly destructive hurricanes. Yet far more are still in denial or focusing on temporary measures, including pumping sand in front of million-dollar beach houses, only to watch it wash away in the next storm. There is a startling gap in their reasoning. Instead of thinking in geologic time, they are measuring time in days, months, and years, until the next hurricane or nor'easter inundates their towns and they again turn to federal taxpayers for help. Social scientists refer to such short-term thinking as the Tragedy of the Commons, in which people and politicians favor temporary solutions over their own long-term interests—only in this case, the decisions are subsidized by the U.S. Treasury.

The Geography of Risk is, in part, a meditation on the question of risk: How much should be private; how much public? The cost of storm damage, once borne by beach towns and homeowners, is now largely paid for by federal taxpayers. Most of them live far from the coasts and can only dream of owning a house at the beach, let alone an oceanfront mansion.

In the 1950s, the federal government covered just 5 percent of the cost of rebuilding after hurricanes. Today, it pays for 70 percent. And in some cases, it pays for 100 percent. It is no accident that the federalization of disasters coincided with the explosive development at the coasts. As coastal property values soared, the expectations of politicians and homeowners shifted dramatically as well, and the nature of risk with it, from private to public. Now, with government payouts for coastal disasters rising precipitously and beach-town politicians clamoring for even more money to protect their towns, the question of who pays is more important than ever.

Recently, the U.S. Army Corps of Engineers unveiled a series of proposals to protect New York Harbor and Lower Manhattan from hurricane surge. One idea calls for building a massive hurricane barrier from Sandy Hook to the Rockaways, in Queens. The barrier and surge gates would be similar to ones in the Netherlands, which can be closed during storms. The estimated cost is $20 billion, but even that may be low. Hundreds of millions more would be needed to operate the gates. Federal taxpayers are likely to cover the cost.

Strikingly, that's just one project. Texans want $61 billion to protect their coast from hurricanes and floods. That includes a $31 billion barrier and levee to protect Galveston and the Houston Ship Channel, which is lined with oil refineries and petrochemical facilities. The huge project is backed by the state's senators, Ted Cruz and John Cornyn, both reliable critics of federal spending and climate change. Neither has mentioned the controversial role of the oil industry in global warming or suggested oil titans pay for some of the cost.

Altogether, there are thousands of miles of heavily developed shoreline, barrier islands, and estuaries along the Atlantic and Gulf Coasts. The challenge of scaling up to protect all the property would be monumentally difficult, not to mention prohibitively expensive. Will we build a wall around the entire Florida peninsula? Put gates and barriers along hundreds of miles of New Jersey bays? Backers of these projects talk about building resilient, sustainable coasts. But even then, they acknowledge that the barriers, levees, and sand dunes will not eliminate flooding. Given time, they allow, water will always win out.

Decades ago, Orrin Pilkey made the case for a slow, managed retreat from the coast. No one listened. Developers called Pilkey naive. Homeowners will never leave, they said. There is too much money and property at stake. Instead, they successfully lobbied for billions in aid and crowded the shores with larger and more expensive homes.

"We are going to have to retreat at some point," Pilkey continues to insist. "And it will be sooner than later. There is no question about that, with the seas rising, warmer oceans, and more catastrophic storms. One of the reasonable ways would be, don't allow people to repair destroyed homes. But people insist, storm after storm, time after time. It's mind-blowing, really."

Building the Modern Coast

And as the moon rose higher the inessential houses began to melt away until gradually I became aware of the old island here that flowered once for Dutch sailors' eyes—a fresh, green breast of the new world.

—F. SCOTT FITZGERALD, *THE GREAT GATSBY*

Troubled Waters

October 29, 2012

AFTER THE WIND CAME THE FLOOD, a roaring, fitful sheet of water capped by frothing waves. It spilled across the low-lying barrier islands, leveling the sand dunes and anything else in its path. Then it poured through the inlets connecting the Atlantic Ocean and the narrow bays that line the New Jersey coast. The bays were already swollen with rain. Now they bulged dangerously as billions of gallons of water washed over the salt marshes everyone imagined would save them, but didn't. Afterward, survivors would say the flood seemed to come in pulses—not a tsunami exactly, but a wall of water that filled every corner of their blackened world, making what was once whole invisible.

From the window of her one-story ranch house on Mystic Island, a sprawling grid of retirement bungalows and pricier waterfront homes along

Barnegat Bay, in Ocean County, Lisa Stevens nervously studied a shadow. At first, she imagined it was a bear. But what would a bear be doing by her lagoon? Then she saw it wasn't a bear; it was her dock, tossed on its end by the flood. Lisa yelled to her partner, Kathy, to grab the dogs, and then climbed on top of a couch, spinning and spinning as water sloshed inside.

Over the next few hours, Lisa and Kathy's house filled with three and a half feet of brackish water. Lisa was certain they were going to drown. A day before, a local policeman had knocked on their door and advised them to leave. It was going to be bad, he'd warned, and no one would be able to rescue them if there was trouble. But Lisa and Kathy had been through other storms and opted to stay. "It was the worst, dumbest decision I ever made," Lisa said.

The next morning, a chalky blue sky and bright sun revealed towering piles of sand, debris, and sewage. Lisa's house was still standing. But the foundation had shifted and cracked, and the inside was ruined. Entire neighborhoods were gone; family histories as well, washed away in the deluge from Hurricane Sandy, the most catastrophic storm in the state's history. The sour tang of tide and mud mingled with venting gas. In the nearby sedge, fishing boats dangled from cedar trees like Christmas ornaments. Hundreds had been swept from their winter moorings and pitched into the roaring current. One, a twenty-four-foot speedboat named *Plan B*, had crashed into Dave Rinear's cottage on nearby Cedar Bonnet Island, a tiny knob of sand and sedge in Barnegat Bay. "It raced up the bay like a laser-guided missile with my name on it," the retired professor and active waterman said.

Dave's hundred-year-old cedar-shake bungalow had survived other storms, large and small. But it faced the wrong direction during Sandy, south, as the worst of the surge spilled up the bay. Now it was listing sideways and stuffed with sand and seaweed, one of thousands of houses along the state's coastal waterways flooded or wrecked by Sandy. Many were old and low, like Dave's, but not all. Huge multimillion-dollar beach houses wobbled on stilts at the edge of the Atlantic Ocean. The hurricane had sliced open their bottom floors as if they were fish, and now electrical wires and appliances swayed below in the gusting breeze.

At the southern tip of Long Beach Island, the largest and richest barrier island in New Jersey, just a short boat ride from Dave's cottage, the damage was apocalyptic. The shoreline there had been eroding for decades and was largely defenseless. Sandy's towering waves crashed through the meager sand dunes and across a two-lane blacktop road along the southern end, toppling dozens of nearby trailers as if they were Legos. The trailers that weren't smashed were flooded and uninhabitable. For more than half a century, the scrubby, four-acre Long Beach Island Trailer Park had been home to a quirky collection of bohemians, artists, and sun-worshippers. As land values soared and beach houses grew ever larger and more lavish, the trailer park had assumed a revered status as one of the last affordable places on the island. Now it was gutted, along with the simple, stripped-down lifestyle the residents had enjoyed.

Still, one of the paradoxes of hurricanes is that they both destroy and renew. Instead of homeowners retreating out of harm's way, they build back, often in the same dangerous locations. Insurance money and federal aid fuel building booms. Speculators and developers bid up prices. Land rushes follow. Perfectly fine humble old cottages and bungalows are torn down and replaced with towering beach palaces. People of modest means are priced out.

It was no different after Sandy. The southern tip of Long Beach Island quickly shifted from a bohemian enclave to an upscale resort. Virtually overnight, houses doubled and tripled in size. Some had entertainment centers. Others came with pocket pools built right into the decks. The number of million-dollar houses increased more than tenfold. Most were second homes, owned by absentee investors.

In the midst of the land boom, the empty, disheveled trailer park sold for $12 million. The only mild surprise was the price. But that is how the inflated economics at the beach work now, with land more valuable than gold. Three million an acre for a scruffy lot that had recently flooded in a historic storm was considered reasonable, if not precisely a bargain.

The Deal of the Century

1

ON A WARM SUNDAY MORNING IN AUGUST 1926, Morris L. Shapiro climbed into his new Willys-Knight sedan and started alone down the New Jersey coast. The idea was to break the car in slowly by taking it out for short drives, until the odometer reached one hundred miles. At that point, he could drive as often and as far as he liked.

The Shapiros—Morris; his wife, Jennie; their sons, Jerry and Herb; and their daughter, Muriel—were spending the month of August in a large Victorian rental on Fourth and Ocean Streets in Bradley Beach, a popular summer resort along the northern New Jersey shore, an hour's drive from the bustling cities of Newark, Elizabeth, and Irvington. It was an extravagance, to be sure, but one Morris could afford. He owned the largest shoe store in Elizabeth, near the busy port, and recently had ventured into real estate, buying and selling land and building single-family homes in the Elmora section of the city.

Morris was supposed to go only a short distance that morning, but the ride was so pleasantly distracting that he didn't notice the miles slipping by. Soon, he was in Ocean County, on Route 9, a winding two-lane blacktop then no wider than a farm road. Ocean County was one of the largest in the state. But it was far from the cities and isolated, with small fishing villages shouldering Barnegat Bay, blueberry and cranberry farms squeezed inside a sprawling forest of pygmy pines and cedar creeks, and black-water rivers and bogs spilling into lush salt meadows. Many of the towns and crossroads appeared to Morris to have more in common with the sleepy Deep South than the busy Northeast.

When he reached Manahawkin, a fishing colony located on the southernmost edge of Barnegat Bay, Morris saw a wooden sign advertising Long Beach Island and on a whim turned left onto a rickety wooden bridge only a foot or two higher than the water. It is unclear whether Morris had ever heard of the slender barrier island before, but he probably hadn't. It was a slow, nerve-wracking drive across the bay, but the view was spectacular. The vibrant colors exploded at Morris—the blue-green swirl of the shallow bay, no more than six feet deep in most places; the golden ridge of sand dunes across the water; and the even deeper chromatic blue of the Atlantic Ocean limning the horizon. The popular beach resorts at the time, including Asbury Park and Long Branch in North Jersey and Atlantic City to the south, were small cities, with redbrick hotels, crowded boardwalks, and amusement piers projecting dangerously over the ocean. By contrast, Long Beach Island was nearly virgin and empty. Morris didn't see any boardwalks, piers, or tall buildings. In fact, other than a small cluster of cedar-shake bungalows at the end of the wooden causeway connecting the island to the mainland, he didn't see any houses at all.

Morris turned right and drove four or five miles along a sand-and-gravel road toward an area of the island now known as Beach Haven Park. What he saw was a flat, windswept space with rolling sand dunes along the ocean and clumps of bayberry, ivy, honeysuckle, and wild blackberries near the bay. The island itself was eighteen miles long from tip to tip, but low-lying and narrow. Morris guessed it couldn't be more than a half mile at its widest. In any case, it wasn't so wide he ever lost sight of the ocean or lush salt meadows bordering Barnegat Bay.

Morris slowed his sedan, enthralled and curious. At a certain point, he encountered a man standing outside a humble plywood office. As best as anyone can recall, the man's name was Renaldo Kenyon. He was the owner of one of the few hotels on the island and, like Morris, fancied himself a developer on the side.

Without trying to appear too eager, Morris inquired whether Kenyon knew of any land for sale.

As a matter of fact, Kenyon replied, he happened to have a fifty-three-acre plot available, and Morris was standing on it. Best of all, Kenyon added, it stretched from the ocean to the bay, nearly one square mile of prime real estate.

Kenyon was asking $1,000 an acre—or $53,000 altogether. It was a lot of money even for someone as relatively well off as Morris Shapiro. But Morris did some quick math to determine how many lots he could fit on fifty-three acres, and decided it would be enough to double or triple his investment. But before he purchased anything, he informed Kenyon he needed to talk to his wife, Jennie. She was his partner in everything he did, smart, with her own knack for numbers. Morris told Kenyon he would return in a week. He wanted to bring Jennie to show her around. If she approved, he would buy the land.

\\\

A week later, Morris and Jennie Shapiro made the long drive to Long Beach Island. Initially, Jennie was unimpressed. She was used to the busy North Jersey beaches, which filled with visitors on weekends. The scruffy, narrow island was wild and remote. The streets were gravel and sand, and there were hardly any houses or businesses, as far as she could see. She asked Morris who would want to travel all the way out here, miles at sea, so far from the cities.

It was a good question, and Morris didn't have a ready answer. Long Beach

In 1926, Morris Shapiro and his wife, Jennie, bought fifty-three acres from ocean to bay on Long Beach Island for $53,000. Today, that same tract is worth about $400 million.
(Courtesy of Herbert Shapiro)

Island was located midway along the 141-mile-long New Jersey coast, with no major highways connecting it with the cities. The nearest resort, Atlantic City, was an hour's drive to the south; the urban centers of Philadelphia, Newark, and New York City were hours away by train.

According to the U.S. Census, the year-round population of Long Beach Island was fewer than seven hundred people in 1920. Half lived in Beach Haven, an established resort near the southern end of the barrier island. It had several large hotels that catered to Philadelphia patricians eager to escape the summer heat and enjoy a few weeks of cool ocean breezes. Another small hotel straddled Tucker's Island on a wild, migrating spit of sand across from the Beach Haven Inlet, also near the southern tip of the island. It had been developed by Quakers in the 1800s but was now being reclaimed by rising water, and would soon vanish entirely. Most wealthy industrialists of the day headed to Atlantic City, with its notable hotels, glitzy boardwalk, and Jazz Era speakeasies. Or, if they preferred a quieter setting, they might travel to Cape May, with its stately Victorians and deep Quaker influences, or the equally historic Methodist camp of Ocean Grove, in North Jersey. Altogether, the few thousand houses and businesses on Long Beach Island were worth just $3 million when Morris Shapiro arrived, real estate records from the day show. A single city block in Atlantic City was worth more.

And yet, Morris saw a unique opportunity in the pristine but hard-to-get-to island. Sure, most of it was wild now, he told Jennie, but it wouldn't always be like this. The American economy was strong; people had jobs and money. The beach resorts were growing. Look at Miami and Charleston, South Carolina. Even Galveston, which had been flattened by a hurricane in 1900, was booming. With the resorts close to the big cities already crowded, vacationers would soon begin to look elsewhere to escape. Why not Long Beach Island? It was beautiful and unspoiled.

As it happened, a handful of developers were already advertising the charms of Long Beach Island in the Philadelphia and Camden newspapers. "For sale: 240 splendid seashore lots $40 each," one advertisement read. "And they say money won't buy happiness. Well, they'd better guess again," exclaimed another. The way Morris figured, it was only a matter of time until state officials built a highway from the more populous northern counties to open the island up to development. The smart choice was to get in early. And so, he made his case to Jennie: "I have a good feeling," he said. "People are going to want to come here. You'll see."

Morris Shapiro had a gift when it came to real estate. A few years earlier, he'd begun buying empty lots in Elizabeth for $100, and then quickly turned them around for $200. Morris used the profits to build single-family houses and a commercial office building in downtown Elizabeth with half a dozen tenants. Soon, he had a steady stream of rents and cash. It was a lot easier and far more lucrative than selling rubber boots to dockworkers for 99 cents a pair.

"My father was a smart man. I think he saw right away he was in the wrong business. Real estate was the business to be in," recalled Morris's son Herb, now ninety-six but still possessing a subtle memory. "I remember the first time I came here to the island. I was probably four years old. There was nothing here. It was desolate, with wild blackberries growing in the streets. But my father had a vision. He could see opportunities no one else saw."

Eventually, Jennie saw it, too. The more she listened to her husband, the more she warmed to the idea. Morris had brought along a check for $53,000 made out to the Highland Beach Corporation, Kenyon's company. It was an interesting name, given that the island was only seven feet above sea level at its highest point. Not that Morris was worried about elevation or storms at that moment. That was a concern for the distant future, for his children and their sons and daughters.

Today, the fifty-three acres that Morris Shapiro purchased in 1926 would be worth around $400 million, according to my analysis of property records. That's an appreciation of over 7,500 percent in ninety years—or a 530-fold increase, after adjusting for inflation.

Still, even as inspired an investor as Morris Shapiro couldn't possibly have imagined the extraordinary land rush that would one day transform Long Beach Island from a humble fishing village and blue-collar resort into an increasingly lavish confection for the rich. Today, nineteen thousand houses and businesses crowd the low, slender barrier island. Vacation houses sell for an average of $1 million, with oceanfront houses topping $10 million. There are traffic jams, floods from overwhelmed sewer and stormwater systems, and barely a whisper of air between the ever-larger beach houses stacked side by side in many neighborhoods.

The story of Long Beach Island mirrors the larger narrative of America's coasts, now congested with trillions of dollars of lavish yet astoundingly vulnerable property. The slim barrier island has been wrecked twice by storms, bookended almost fifty years apart, with about a billion in damages in Sandy alone. Yet officials and developers ignored the palpable risks and built back after each storm, aided by government disaster dollars and federal flood payments. That, too, mirrors the larger, often contradictory narrative of America's coasts, conceived in modesty by men such as Morris Shapiro, but now gilded with entitlement.

\\\

Even as Morris Shapiro was discovering Long Beach Island in 1926, America was already experiencing a real estate bubble at the coast. But instead of

New Jersey, it was in swampy Florida, 1,200 miles to the south, where a mix of entrepreneurs, real estate wildcatters, hucksters, and con men were hawking owning beachfront property as the next American dream. Most of the action was in the fledgling developments of Miami Beach, Fort Lauderdale, and West Palm Beach. But the land fever extended as far west as Sarasota and Tampa, and as far south as Key West, thanks to an overseas railroad built by the industrialist Henry Morrison Flagler, John D. Rockefeller's longtime business partner in Standard Oil.

Flagler was already a successful entrepreneur and investor when he met Rockefeller in the mid-1800s. In 1863, he helped secure a $100,000 loan so the then cash-strapped Rockefeller could fund his fledgling oil business. Flagler received 25 percent of the new company, which quickly became the leading oil refinery business in America. But in time, Flagler grew bored with the oil business, and in the 1880s shifted his attention to Florida, which he believed would one day attract large numbers of tourists seeking to flee the harsh northern winters. Flagler built hotels in Daytona, Palm Beach, St. Augustine, and Miami, and purchased a railroad that eventually traversed the state's eastern coast. But Flagler wasn't done. He was intent on linking Key West to Miami, and eventually with the Panama Canal, establishing trade routes with Cuba and other Caribbean outposts. His extended railroad ran from the small city of Homestead, about forty miles southeast of Miami, through the Everglades and across twenty-five miles of open water at Big Pine Key, down to the Lower Keys. Built at an astonishing cost of $50 million (nearly $800 million in today's dollars), it was sometimes referred to as the Eighth Wonder of the World.

The speculative frenzy reached such heights that *The New York Times* saw fit to start a stand-alone real estate section chronicling the Florida land rush. But land rushes come and land rushes go. This one had already begun to wane when a devastating hurricane slammed into Miami in 1926, the same year Morris Shapiro arrived on Long Beach Island. The storm caused over $100 million in damage, an extraordinary sum for the time, marking it as one of the most catastrophic hurricanes in history. Only a few years later, two more hurricanes killed thousands of Floridians and swamped Flagler's railroad, by then in bankruptcy, effectively popping the nation's first coastal real estate bubble. Both the speculative land rush and the hurricanes foreshadowed what would become a familiar script at the coast—a loop of intense development followed by ruinous storms, followed by costly rebuilding, followed by yet more storms and then even more building.

Florida is perhaps the best example of unchecked development at the coast. In 1920, fewer than one million people lived along the state's fifty barrier islands and scores of canals, swamps, and bays. Only three decades later, the population had swelled threefold. Not content to build solely along the shoreline, developers began to fill thousands of acres of wetlands, mangrove swamps, and tidal creeks for thousands of houses for retirees fleeing cold-weather states in the North. By 1980, the population had soared to nearly ten million. Today, it is over twenty million, with six million alone in the congested Miami-Dade metropolitan area. Most live atop porous limestone outcrops or canals that are ready-made conduits for floods and storm surge. Especially during king tides, full moons, and heavy downpours, residents are sometimes trapped in their low-lying bungalows by rising water, with nowhere to go. The city of Miami itself hasn't been hit directly by a major hurricane in decades. But it is only a matter of time. Researchers estimate that a storm as powerful as the Great Miami Hurricane of 1926 would cause $250 billion in damage today—more than Hurricanes Katrina and Sandy combined.

2.

Blue-Collar Houses

MORRIS SHAPIRO WASN'T WORRYING about hurricanes when he purchased the fifty-three acres on Long Beach Island in 1926. The island seemed safe enough to him. It was protected by sand dunes along the ocean-front and salt marsh on the bay. Besides, storms were considered part of living on a barrier island. If your small bungalow got knocked down, you replaced it with another simple cottage. It wasn't like Asbury Park, Atlantic City, or Miami Beach, for that matter, with their expensive hotels and big Victorians. Most of the houses on the island were tiny, and there weren't nearly enough for a hurricane to do much damage.

Long Beach Island consisted of six towns—Barnegat Light, Harvey Cedars, Surf City, Ship Bottom, Long Beach Township, and Beach Haven. Beach Haven Park, where Morris now owned nearly a square mile from the ocean to the bay, was more of a notion than an actual place. Many of the towns had similar communities and neighborhoods, highlighting the highly local, if not parochial, nature of the island. You didn't own a beach house in Long Beach Township. You owned a beach house in Brant Beach or Beach Haven Crest or Loveladies, all communities within the larger legally designated community. It could be confusing. For example, Beach Haven Park, Morris's budding community, didn't have legal ties to Beach Haven, the most populous town on the island. Instead, it was part of Long Beach Township, the largest of the six island towns in terms of geography, accounting for almost twelve of the eighteen miles and many different local communities.

Even today, politics on Long Beach Island are intensely local. The six towns operate independently and only occasionally share services, leading to costly duplication. There are separate police, fire, and emergency services, and two distinct school systems. Children who live on the southern end of the island in Holgate, part of Long Beach Township, aren't allowed to attend grade school in Beach Haven, even though it is the closest school and barely has enough students to fill a single classroom. Instead, they are bused up the island to another school in Surf City, a dozen miles away. Attempts to consolidate the two systems have failed. "They are constantly fighting over territorial issues," observes Bernie Haney, a tax assessor for several island towns. "Believe me, there will be dead bodies in the street before they merge."

Morris Shapiro filed a map with Long Beach Township identifying his future development as Beach Haven Park by the Sea. It was literally true and made at least as much sense as any other name. At the time, there were few rules governing zoning and very few building codes. Developers were left to decide things themselves. How many bungalows could they squeeze onto a lot? How wide should the lots be—twenty feet, forty feet, or more? How deep should they be? Should their houses have one floor or two?

Although he now owned potentially valuable property, and had a plan to develop it, Morris was in no particular hurry to begin building. His principal business—and income—remained in Elizabeth, where he continued to buy and sell land and build much-admired residential neighborhoods. But it was also likely that Morris was waiting for a new highway to make the island more

Morris Shapiro built a small bungalow on Long Beach Boulevard to house his new real estate business. M. L. Shapiro Co. played a major role in developing Long Beach Island, now the largest and richest barrier island in New Jersey. (Courtesy of Herbert Shapiro)

accessible. He also may have been concerned about the economy, which began to falter not long after his purchase, and collapsed in 1929, remaining in a calamitous downturn for the next decade. In any case, Morris waited, studying his empty tract and thinking about the best way to develop it.

Morris did build four beach houses in the early 1930s. They were small capes with modest living areas and knotty-pine paneling, efficiency kitchens, and one or two bedrooms. He sold two to family friends and one to a business executive, and he held on to one for his family. Separately, Morris built a bungalow to serve as the offices of M. L. Shapiro Co., the business he incorporated a few years later when he began building in earnest. According to his son Herb, Morris viewed the simple white cottage as a form of advertising. He even painted the name M. L. SHAPIRO on the north-side exterior, which fronted the gravel road visitors used to get from one end of Long Beach Island to the other. "It was so no one could miss it as they were driving down the road," Herb Shapiro said. Morris didn't spend a lot of time at the office in the early days; there wasn't enough business. But if he was at the family bungalow and heard a car slow down, he would sprint up the street to meet with the potential customer.

According to Herb, his father was an astute businessman—attentive to details, disciplined financially, wary of debt, yet also a visionary when it came to creating a future market at the beach. "He did not have a lot of education, but he was smart, especially when it came to numbers," Herb said. "He could sit there and in a few moments add up all of the numbers in his head and figure out if it was a good deal or a bad deal." It was how Morris had decided to buy the fifty-three-acre tract. "He quickly realized the land was potentially worth a lot more—maybe not right then, but that it would be."

\\\

Morris Shapiro arrived in America on July 18, 1899, after a long journey that began in his birthplace of Kupiskis, in central Lithuania. The small city was located along the Kupa River and divided into six districts, including one populated by Jews. The family fled to America amid a Russian pogrom that eventually emptied the district. Morris's father, Solomon, had seventy-eight dollars in his pocket, not a fortune but enough for a start. Shortly after debarking at Ellis Island, the Shapiros settled in Elizabeth, then a thriving port and industrial hub in North Jersey. Morris was eighteen and, like so many other immigrants, eager to make his mark in the vast new world. He quickly found work and, later, used his savings to open a shoe store serving dockworkers at the port.

Elizabeth was a busy, wildly diverse place, with a sizable Jewish population. A family acquaintance introduced Morris to a beautiful young woman, Jennie Rebecca Block, and he asked for her hand. According to Herb, Jennie's father wanted to check out Morris before he gave his daughter permission to marry. So one day he visited Morris's shoe store on East Jersey Street, near the water. Apparently satisfied, he agreed to the marriage.

Morris was friendly, humble, and generous, according to his son. He was of average height, with hazel eyes and dark hair that turned milk-white at an early age. "He was a good listener, although hard of hearing, and had a fine sense of humor—a basic good, slow-talking salesman who loved his product," Herb Shapiro recalled. "He often traveled to Philadelphia to visit prospective home purchasers, often returning with dents in the fenders of his car when brushed by Philly trolleys."

Conscious of making a good first impression, Morris always wore a suit, tie, and hat, even keeping his suit jacket on while napping on an office cot. He was curious and not afraid to try new things, Herb said. The family's home was kosher, "but he was inquisitive enough to eat six clams [non-kosher] at a local clam bar because everyone was talking about clams." Instead of joining an all-Jewish Masonic lodge in Elizabeth, he chose a lodge with mixed religions "because he wanted to be around all kinds of people." On fall weekends, he often headed to Penn or Princeton for the football games.

Morris split his time between Elizabeth and Long Beach Island throughout the Great Depression, working in Elizabeth during the week and traveling to the island on weekends. Sometimes he would bring along his sons, who would drive the family car up and down the gravel road, taking turns standing on the running board and shouting "Lots for sale! Lots for sale!" while handing out company circulars.

In the late 1930s, with the economy finally showing signs of recovering, Morris began building summer homes along the oceanfront, selling them for as little as $3,000—$100 down and $10 a month. He named the streets after his wife, Jennie, and children, Jerome, Herbert, and Muriel. The first street he built was Herbert Avenue, across from the present-day Acme supermarket. Surprisingly, a few of Morris's original bungalows can still be found, although they have been updated and expanded over the years. When he ran out of family names for his streets, Morris began naming his streets after the states, starting with Alabama and California and working his way to Nebraska before he ran out of land.

M. L. Shapiro didn't sell many houses at first—probably fewer than a hundred throughout the decade-long Great Depression. Having no debt saved the company, Herb said. At one point, Morris was forced to choose between paying taxes on a property he owned in Hillside, in northern New Jersey, or his land on Long Beach Island. Even with slow sales, he opted to hold on to the land in Beach Haven Park and give up the Hillside property. Another year, it appeared that his older son, Jerry, would have to drop out of Harvard Law School because Morris couldn't afford the $350 tuition. It was touch and go. But at the last minute, Morris sold an oceanfront lot to an executive of a telephone company, and Jerry returned to school.

After graduating from Harvard Law in 1935, Jerry began practicing law in Elizabeth, handling all the legal work for M. L. Shapiro. But he wanted to be a developer, and a few years later joined his father, proving to be a genial salesman with a talent for making and closing deals. Herb, ten years younger than Jerry, graduated from Penn and served in the Navy in World War II. Following the war, he earned a law degree from Rutgers University–Newark. Then, like his brother, Herb joined the family business. "There was never any question," he said. "It was considered automatic I would join." When Herb married, Morris gave him and his new wife, Selma, ten oceanfront lots as a wedding gift.

\\\

By the 1940s, the market for beach houses was improving. Morris added a large tract adjacent to his original fifty-three acres in Beach Haven Park. A few years later, he acquired two entire blocks from Long Beach Township for $1,000 each. It was a remarkable deal, considering that the two streets could each hold up to a hundred houses, selling for thousands of dollars each.

M. L. Shapiro now owned well over one square mile from ocean to bay. Meanwhile, the company added a lumberyard on the site of the old Peahala Gunning Club, near the northern border of the original fifty-three-acre tract. Morris could now sell himself lumber at a discount and also service the growing number of builders on the island, reducing his costs while adding an important new revenue stream. Other changes quickly followed as the firm looked for ways to standardize its operations and grow the business. In the early 1940s, Morris began to take out full-page advertisements in the Philadelphia and Camden newspapers, offering "Fully Improved Oceanside Lots with gas, electric, city water and gravel streets for $150." If a buyer wanted to place a modest two-bedroom Cape Cod cottage on the lot, M. L. Shapiro would build it for $2,475. The monthly payment on a fifteen-year mortgage was just $18, thanks in part to the advent of government-backed Federal Housing Administration mortgages.

Unlike many developers, the Shapiros were willing to take calculated risks. For example, if a bank didn't want to take on the entire mortgage, M. L. Shapiro would finance the balance at a modest rate. The idea was to entice potential buyers, Herb said, and sometimes that meant taking chances. If buyers occasionally fell behind on their monthly installments, the company would carry them until they got back on their feet. Even so, they rarely lost money.

After the war ended, in 1945, there was a nationwide surge in demand for homes, which spilled over to the market for second homes. According to Dennis J. Ventry, an expert in tax law at the University of California, Davis, the national rate of homeownership increased from 43 percent to 55 percent, with most of that gain occurring between 1945 and 1950. The postwar economy boomed as soldiers returned to the factories and the demand for new cars, state-of-the-art appliances, and a startling array of new consumer goods (from electric can openers to gasoline-powered lawn mowers) reached previously uncharted levels. The tight labor market and the advent of labor unions helped push up wages and create an exuberant middle class hungry for the good life. Americans' purchasing power swelled by nearly a third. Each August, an auto plant in Edison, in North Jersey, would shut down for two weeks, and the workers eagerly looked for a place to escape the heat with their families. Those lucky enough headed to the popular beach resorts of Asbury Park, Long Branch, and Point Pleasant. But there were never enough bungalows to meet the growing demand. What the families needed was a building boom at the beach—and it was about to happen, thanks to Morris Shapiro and a handful of other prominent developers.

\\\

Morris Shapiro studied the transformative shifts of postwar American life and had a novel idea. Instead of building large Victorian homes and hotels for the wealthy, what if he built a new kind of beach house that teachers, plumbers, factory workers, and other ordinary Americans could afford? He could charge a few thousand dollars for his simple bungalows, with $100 down and $20 or $30 in monthly installments. The houses didn't need to be big or luxurious—a small square frame with a couple of bedrooms and an unfinished attic, where owners could put a mattress for the kids, or finish themselves if they liked. After all, it was a beach cottage; the point was to own a small piece of paradise, not a mansion. If someone insisted on a little more room, M. L. Shapiro Co. could add a bedroom or build a small deck and an outdoor shower.

At first, the company used local contractors to build their capes and ranches. But later on, Jerry and Herb began hiring their own carpenters at an hourly rate and subbing out the electrical, plumbing, and other trades, lowering their expenses in the process. Profit varied according to the size of the house. An oceanfront Cape Cod—616 square feet altogether—cost about $6,000 to build, or roughly $10 per square foot, Herb Shapiro said. The cost of the land added about $500 to the purchase price. If the Shapiros charged $8,000, the company made a profit of about $1,500.

Morris's vision of a new market at the beach for ordinary Americans worked. By the end of the 1950s, M. L. Shapiro had redrawn the geography of Long Beach Island, lining street after street with small, affordable bungalows from ocean to bay. The exact number is unclear, but Herb Shapiro estimated the figure at two thousand, give or take. The pace of building only accelerated in the following decades, with scores of modest capes and ranches rising each year. After Jerry and Herb assumed control of the company, around 1950, they bought large tracts of land in Holgate, then a remote two-mile stretch of sand and dune at the southern end of the island, and began laying out new streets and planning a big future development. One builder who worked for the Shapiros said M. L. Shapiro Co. was so efficient it could "put up a bungalow in one day." He was exaggerating, but only slightly. Houses went up in weeks, from pouring the concrete slab to finishing the A-frame attic. "Our approach was always to build for a mass market," Herb said. "It was a volume business, not a custom-home business, like today."

Some property owners looked down their noses at the small cottages as cookie-cutter and cheap. They likened the Shapiros' developments to Levittown, the sprawling planned community on Long Island built for returning veterans in the 1940s.

"When they first went up, we said it was like Levittown on Long Beach Island," recalled Richard Plunkett, the unofficial architectural historian of the island and the owner of a popular antiques shop, now shuttered, called the Wizard of Odds. "We couldn't deal with it. It was cookie-cutter. Now they are viewed as charming. It shows how your point of view changes."

Today, many longtime residents and visitors fondly refer to the dwindling supply of bungalows as "Shapiro shacks," posting pictures on Facebook and pining for the lost innocence of the island as it increasingly becomes an exclusive province of the wealthy.

It is impossible to overstate the importance of Morris Shapiro and the market for second homes he helped create. His simple, affordable cottages opened an entirely new experience for thousands of American families that had previously been reserved for corporate tycoons, Gatsby-era financiers, and other moneyed elites. Almost anyone could afford to escape the summer heat for a few weeks at the Jersey Shore. Over the decades, families passed their Shapiro bungalows from generation to generation, and for decades that was all you saw along the side streets and oceanfront of Long Beach Island: Morris's signature capes, ranches, and cottages tucked among the dunes and grass.

3

Manufacturing Dirt

ONE DAY IN 1947, Herbert Shapiro and his father were driving back from a shopping trip in Manahawkin when Morris pointed to a sprawling salt meadow bordering Barnegat Bay.

"You should buy that," Morris told his son.

The marsh stretched from the shallow mudflats beneath the wooden bridge connecting Long Beach Island to the mainland all the way to the Revolutionary-era seaport of Tuckerton, miles to the south. Herb had to admit it was beautiful, a wave of emerald grass and cattails shimmering in the warm summer breeze. But what would he do with it?

"You can build on it," Morris said.

"No one will want to buy here," Herb said.

"You'd be surprised," Morris replied. "One day they will."

The Shapiros already had their hands full on Long Beach Island. They were buying more land, building bungalows, planning new developments.

But Morris in his own quiet way was relentless. "Every time we drove across that bridge, he would point and tell us we should buy that land," Herb recalled. "He saw something we didn't see until much later."

What Morris saw was the future. He knew that one day they would fill up Long Beach Island with bungalows and need somewhere else to build. After all, the barrier island was only eighteen miles long and a half mile wide. There were only so many houses they could put there. The salt marshes along the back bays, located between the barrier islands and the mainland, were replete with coves, nooks, and other indentations. The shoreline curved in and out, a watery greensward. Best of all, the marsh—or wetlands, as it is known today—was empty. Other than a hunting shack or two, there was nothing but grass and sedge. Manahawkin, one of the larger fishing villages in Ocean County, had only a thousand people, and most lived in the town center, away from the water. Apparently, no one thought Barnegat Bay was valuable. If they hurried, Morris said, Herb and Jerry could buy the meadow for a good price.

Many states, including New Jersey, would one day pass laws to protect their wetlands, which serve as buffers in hurricanes, helping to absorb surging water, while also providing critical habitats for birds, fish, and other wildlife. But that was still decades in the future. At the time, in the 1940s and 1950s, there were no environmental rules, let alone building codes or master plans to guide development. If a developer had a few dollars (it literally required only dollars), he could buy the rights to the land beneath the marsh, fill it with mud and dirt, and erect a house on top. Small fishing villages like Manahawkin were looking for ways to grow and needed cash. Building, even on salt marshes, meant jobs and taxes.

Local watermen and hunters understood that the salt marsh was essential to the health of Barnegat Bay. The water, sea meadows, and mud were home to a breathtaking array of waterfowl and migrating birds—plovers, red-breasted mergansers, Atlantic brant, peregrine falcons, great blue herons, bald eagles, nesting osprey, buffleheads, terns, and black skippers, among many others. Some arrived in late fall and wintered over. Others fed a while and flew on to warmer climates. The monarch butterflies that arrived each October to feed on the seaside goldenrod rode the wind all the way to Mexico.

Long and narrow, Barnegat Bay was no deeper than a few feet in many places. It stretched the entire length of Ocean County, forty-four miles in all, funneling water from Tuckerton in the south to Bay Head in the north. Twice a day the briny ocean tides poured through the inlets: Barnegat Inlet, a dozen miles to the north, near the historic lighthouse, Old Barney; and the unruly Little Egg Inlet in the south, across from Mystic Island and Tuckerton. Tidal creeks and freshwater rivers drained from upland forests dense with sumac, wax myrtle, pitch pine, white cedar, and oak. In the fall, cranberry bogs, hidden among the pines just behind the bay, bled onto the rumpled forest floor, turning it scarlet.

The stew of water, seagrass, and mud made for one of the richest habitats on earth. The bottom crawled with blue claws, fiddler crabs, and terrapins. Thick beds of oysters and clams tucked among the channels and shallow-bottom ridges. Closer to shore, the grassy creases served as spawning grounds for killifish and sheepshead minnows. Meanwhile, croakers, eel, bluefish, black sea bass, mackerel, and summer flounder filled the shadows. When the water cooled in the fall, waves of migrating stripers turned the surface of the Barnegat Bay into a glittering jewel. The weight of the fish—twenty, thirty, forty, even fifty pounds—cracked the simple wood poles of the day. If you were lucky, a short-eared owl might greet you at dawn.

But the watermen were too few in number and lacked the political power to stop the crush of development that would over time fill the shoreline of Barnegat Bay and the state's other bays with hundreds of thousands of houses. Meanwhile, for developers, the salt meadows were an opportunity to build homes. "It was a different era," Herb Shapiro said. "No one was thinking about storms or floods back then. We thought we were doing a good thing. We certainly didn't think we were doing any harm."

Altogether, between 1940 and 1970, developers dredged and filled tens of thousands of acres of wetlands along the back bays in New Jersey, an area equal to one-third of all the coastal wetlands. In Ocean County alone, more than 400 communities and 13,000 lagoons were built along

Barnegat Bay. More than 100,000 houses were stacked on or near the water.

Of course, New Jersey wasn't the only state to destroy its fragile wetlands. A kind of sublime ignorance prevailed at the time. Coastal communities in South Carolina, Florida, Mississippi, and Texas gutted and filled thousands of acres of salt marsh. Low-lying Louisiana erased upward of 90 percent of its coastal wetlands, cutting channels and passes for ships, oil rigs, and pipelines, and is now drowning as the Gulf of Mexico rises around it. Altogether, millions of houses and summer cottages currently sit on top of man-made fill where wetlands once sprawled, including suburbs that spill out from Charleston and Houston along the bays, rivers, tidal creeks, old rice fields, and coastal prairies. Many now routinely flood in hurricanes and nor'easters, sometimes epically, such as in Hurricanes Harvey and Florence. Some even flood at high tide. Developers weren't just erasing sensitive habitats for wildlife when they carved up the marsh and estuaries for houses; they were—even if inadvertently—creating the conditions for future catastrophes in an age of rising water and storm-driven surges.

"It was a mistake to build there," the Charleston mayor John Tecklenburg told me after a flood in 2017 inundated his postcard-pretty city, the third flood in a handful of years, resulting in millions in damage.

Tecklenburg showed me a photograph of a ranch home in a nearby subdivision along the Ashley River that had flooded ten times in the last decade. He kept it as a reminder. The owners, a young couple with three small children, wanted to move to higher ground but couldn't sell their house. The city didn't have the money to buy it from them and was waiting to hear from FEMA if the agency could help with a buyout.

"The idea is, it is an area where we can let nature take over," said Tecklenburg, "where marshes can evolve and take back the land."

\\\

A year after their father died, in 1949, at the age of sixty-eight, Herb and Jerry Shapiro decided to follow Morris's advice and purchased five hundred acres of salt marsh on Barnegat Bay for $25,000—or $50 an acre. The area was known locally as the Remsen Meadow. It was owned by Stafford Township, the small, historic community that includes Manahawkin. The meadow was located across Barnegat Bay from the town of Ship Bottom on Long Beach Island and bordered on the north by the wooden bridge that connected the island to the mainland.

The Shapiro brothers decided to call their development Beach Haven West, after Long Beach Island's largest and best-known resort, Beach Haven, even though it was much closer to Ship Bottom. "We were going for the name recognition," Herb Shapiro said. "People knew the name Beach Haven. We thought it would be good for marketing."

At the time, Stafford Township was leasing the Remsen Meadow to a local hunter named Kingsley, who kept a duck blind on Mill Creek, one of the freshwater creeks that drain into Barnegat Bay from the upland forests. To boost their offer, the Shapiros agreed to build $25,000 worth of property within two years. Stafford Township was then land rich but cash poor. The Shapiro brothers figured that township officials would be eager to strike a deal, and they were right. They won the meadow and in short order built ten cottages, satisfying their promise. A few years later, they bought another five hundred acres from the township, giving them most of the salt marsh along the Manahawkin portion of Barnegat Bay.

Why did the brothers change their minds? In part, it was to honor their father's legacy. But they also slowly came to realize that Morris was right. There was only so much oceanfront on Long Beach Island, and one day they would need more land to build on. Why not build along Barnegat Bay? It was waterfront. And water views always carried a premium.

"Good real estate developers tried to be way ahead of the times. My father was always looking forward well into the future and tried to install that trait in Jerry and me," Herb said. Just as their father had invented a market for affordable beach houses, they would create a market for second homes along the bay.

It would prove to be a deft strategy. In the 1950s, the economy was booming, and the suburbs outside New York and Philadelphia were expanding ever closer toward the coast. Instead of a five- or six-hour trip, families could now get to the beach in one or two hours. The idea of a summer home by the water seemed more reasonable.

Automobiles were also quickly becoming a mainstay of modern American life, with three of every four American families owning a car, a sharp increase from only a decade earlier. Highways were expanding as well. New Jersey was close to finishing the Garden State Parkway, a major 140-mile road extending from the New York border in the north to Cape May in the south. It would help to popularize Long Beach Island and other resorts in the heretofore hard-to-reach southern beaches. Meanwhile, the rickety wooden bridge linking Manahawkin and Long Beach Island was being replaced with a soaring new concrete span, making the island easily accessible from the Shapiros' planned development on Barnegat Bay. Now all the brothers had to do was figure out how to build a bungalow on top of a marsh.

Up until that point, in 1950, the Shapiros hadn't dug any lagoons, and didn't own a dredge. But shortly after they bought the Remsen Meadow, Herb traveled to North Carolina with Reynold Thomas, the mayor of Harvey Cedars and himself an instrumental figure in the development of Long Beach Island. Thomas owned a small dredging company and went along as an adviser. Herb wound up purchasing a dredge with an eight-inch nozzle and hired a tugboat to haul it up the coast to New Jersey.

Before they could begin work, the Shapiros first had to secure the rights to the land beneath the Barnegat Bay marsh, known as tidelands, or riparian lands, because streams, creeks, and waterways once flowed there—in this instance, Barnegat Bay. The state of New Jersey owned the legal rights to the tidelands, held in trust for the people of the state. And while obtaining the rights was considered virtually automatic, it did take time. Finally, after months of waiting, the Shapiros and their crew began cutting ten-foot-deep lagoons out of the sedge and marsh, sucking up mud from the bottom of the bay with their newly acquired dredge, piling the mud into huge mounds, and finally shaping the mounds into parcels where bungalows could be built.

It was unimaginably tedious, dirty work and yet, in its own way, brutally creative. A reporter from one of the Newark newspapers called the process "manufacturing dirt." The brothers liked the description so much they

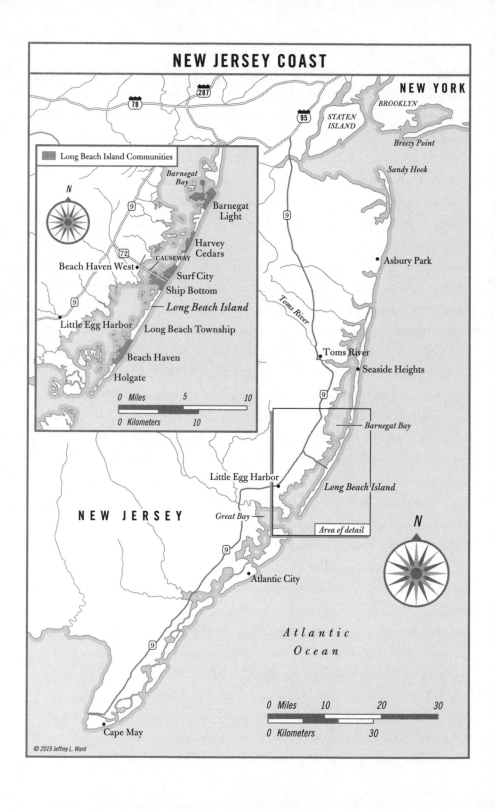

NEW JERSEY COAST

NEW YORK

BROOKLYN

STATEN ISLAND

Breezy Point

Sandy Hook

Long Beach Island Communities

Barnegat Bay

Barnegat Light

Harvey Cedars

CAUSEWAY

Beach Haven West

Surf City

Ship Bottom

Long Beach Island

Little Egg Harbor

Long Beach Township

Beach Haven

Holgate

0 Miles 5 10

0 Kilometers 10

N

• Asbury Park

Toms River

• Toms River

• Seaside Heights

Little Egg Harbor •

Barnegat Bay

Long Beach Island

Area of detail

N

NEW JERSEY

Great Bay

• Atlantic City

Atlantic Ocean

0 Miles 10 20 30

0 Kilometers 30

Cape May

© 2019 Jeffrey L. Ward

adopted it. Once the lagoons were cut and the marshes filled, crews constructed wooden bulkheads to hold the dirt and mud in place. Then they drove cedar pilings into the spongy turf to secure the foundations and poured a concrete slab for the bungalows.

There were no sewers in the area, so each house had its own cesspool. No doubt some of the waste found its way into Barnegat Bay, polluting it. But as Herb noted, there was "no zoning and very few municipal rules at the time." The brothers worked with Stafford Township to create a local sewer authority and the first sewers were installed in 1958. Today, a countywide sewer serves the region.

The Shapiros showcased their first model in Beach Haven West in the early 1950s, an eight-hundred-square-foot two-bedroom cape with an unfinished attic that could be converted into additional living space. It sold for slightly under $7,000. Like all the other cottages they would build in Beach Haven West, it fronted Barnegat Bay and offered access to the water. The tiny lots were an added advantage, Jerry Shapiro told potential buyers, because they required little maintenance.

In 1963, the brothers negotiated an unusual deal with Bamberger's, then a thriving chain of department stores in New Jersey, to construct a full-scale walk-through model of one of their Beach Haven West bungalows. It was featured on the seventh floor of the retailer's flagship store in downtown Newark.

"WHAT A CHRISTMAS GIFT FOR YOUR ENTIRE FAMILY," a full-page advertisement in *The Newark Evening News* exclaimed. "Only 5 minutes to free Atlantic Ocean beaches. Tie up your boat right in your own backyard. For as low as $890 down . . . you can buy a 3-bedroom house, waterfront lot and furnishings—as little as $8,990."

The advertisement ran on November 17, 1963. A week later, Herb and his wife, Selma, were driving up to Bamberger's when word came over the radio that President John F. Kennedy had been shot and killed. "I thought, that was that—no one would ever come. The nation would be in mourning," Herb said. Yet over the next five weeks, thirty-five thousand curious onlookers walked through their model. "It was a great success from that perspective. And people became familiar with the Shapiro name, and it had a spillover effect on [the brothers' sales on] Long Beach Island. But we didn't sell a single house in Beach Haven West. The reason why was because Bamberger's insisted that if you bought a house, you had to buy three thousand dollars' worth of furnishings from them. And their furnishings were junk. Nobody wanted it. So we didn't sell a single house, and they pulled the ad after five weeks."

\\\

Even though Jerry was ten years older than Herb, the brothers were unusually close and worked well together. At least on the surface, Jerry was quiet and easygoing, while Herb was more serious and detail-oriented. Jim Nobel, a contractor who did work for the brothers, recalled that they set up their office desks diagonally "so you were doing business in a crossfire. Jerry was smooth as silk, a real quiet gentleman. Herb was the tough one. They'd put you in a crossfire. So you went out of there with no idea of what you'd get."

Herb didn't dispute the characterization. "Was it a bit of the good-cop, bad-cop routine? I suppose it was," he said.

In 1952, Jerry built a large colonial-style home with a partial stone facade along the oceanfront on one of the tracts of land that the brothers owned in Beach Haven Park, on Long Beach Island. "He was a foodie, so he had a cold-storage room in the cellar where he hung meat to age and kept winesap apples at the right humidity so they would not become mushy," Herb said. "He had five children, so he had a full soda-and-ice-cream bar that was a meeting place for LBI kids."

Herb began work on his own house the following year. It overlooked Barnegat Bay at the opposite end of the tract, with empty field in between. "Jerry and I joked that we could stand on our porches and shout at one another," Herb said.

Herb and Selma hoped to have Frank Lloyd Wright design their house, but the famed architect wasn't available. Instead, they chose Abraham Geller, a well-known New York architect, who designed a postwar American beach villa for the couple. It was sleek and modern in all respects, with towering glass windows framing the bay. A 140-ton stone fireplace highlighted the bottom floor. Mack trucks hauled the stone to Long Beach Island from Pennsylvania quarries. Outside, an artist created a dramatic thirty-two-foot mural made of stone, concrete, and shells along an entryway to the garage. Herb paid to ship Douglas fir beams from Oregon to adorn the ceiling in the spacious living area. Many years later, when Herb and Selma sold the house, a local woodworker acquired the beams and repurposed them into tables and other sculpted pieces that he sold to wealthy homeowners in Loveladies, an exclusive enclave of doctors, lawyers, artists, and financiers on the northern end of the island, and part of Long Beach Township.

Herb and Selma's house quickly became a showcase. A saltwater pool faced Barnegat Bay. In the winter, Herb filled the pool for skating parties. A light shined across the bay as on Jay Gatsby's fictional East Egg mansion. "The residence has the crisp, tensile quality of much of modern architecture," observed the noted architecture critic Paul Goldberger. *House and Garden* and *Architectural Digest* ran full-page spreads. The front door alone was a conversation piece. One side was teak, the other birch. It weighed over eight hundred pounds.

I once asked Herb why the brothers—who made their fortune building small, affordable bungalows—would themselves build large, ostentatious homes. At first, Herb objected to the characterization, maintaining that their homes weren't *that* big. But then he said something revealing. He and Jerry viewed the homes as a form of advertising, he said. "We figured people would see them and say that's where the Shapiros live." He wasn't wrong. In the 1960s, island visitors would often pull over to gawk at the homes.

Tellingly, Herb said that he never felt safe in his bayfront home. Rain leaked between the cracks, and the wind rattled the windows in nor'easters. The sprawling home was hard to heat in winter and even harder to cool in the blazing summer months. "It was a spectacular house, but always needed attention from day one," he would write in a self-published memoir. "We lived there for 40 years never convinced we were home safe."

Instead of a small bungalow, Herb and Selma Shapiro built a modern showcase on Barnegat Bay. In the winter, Herb transformed the saltwater pool into an ice-skating rink for the kids. (Courtesy of Herbert Shapiro)

\\\

By the 1960s, Herb and Jerry were well on their way to building a prototypical postwar suburb on Barnegat Bay that would eventually include 4,500 bungalows, from the water's edge to the upland pine forests. In the process, they would help quadruple the size of sleepy Stafford Township and add significantly to its tax base.

Yet, even as the brothers were rising as the predominant builders of second homes along the bay, they weren't immune from competition. About ten miles south of Beach Haven West, midway between Long Beach Island and Atlantic City, another development team was building a huge lagoon-style colony on Great Bay called Mystic Island. The project spilled along the bay in Little Egg Harbor Township, near Tuckerton, and included a massive network of finger-shaped canals connecting the bungalows to the water. Like the Shapiros, the brothers Lewis and Isidore Glorsky were targeting the newly emerging middle class, not the rich.

The Glorsky family had also emigrated from Russia, initially settling in Brooklyn before moving to Toms River, in Ocean County. But unlike Jerry and Herb Shapiro, the Glorsky brothers battled over business and later refused to even speak with each other. "They were definitely opposites," recalled Lewis's daughter, Maxine Glorsky, a theater and dance producer in New York City. "My uncle was rather severe. My father, I would say, was more fun-loving."

Lewis Glorsky was short and heavyset, with a balding pate and steel-blue eyes. He was creative but undisciplined, bursting with ideas but hampered by a short attention span. "He was in a way a kind of P. T. Barnum character. He was very funny and enthusiastic, especially at the start of one of his projects," Maxine said.

At various times, the Mystic Island project called for a golf course and a boardwalk with amusement rides and arcades, fashioned after Atlantic City. There would also be a playhouse for entertainers and summer productions, a bathhouse, a canteen, and even a yacht club.

"The golf course was coming along fine," until a cloudburst washed away the newly seeded ground, Maxine recalled. "[My father] also wanted some sort of a zoo. I know there were sea lions. And I know he was getting a ship—a pirate ship. But it sank on its way from Alaska."

The Glorskys and their partners built 4,500 bungalows on top of the salt marsh. Lewis called one model the Catalina. He said it was named after a cathouse and meant to be a place where people had fun. The model included two small bedrooms, a utility room, and access to a canal. It was priced at $5,990, including the land.

Herb Shapiro said he never met the Glorskys. But the Shapiro brothers knew about Mystic Island and worried that the cheaper bungalows might cut into business at Beach Haven West. "We couldn't figure out how they were doing it," Herb said. One day, the Shapiros decided to go have a look. "My brother and I went down to Mystic with rulers and got in one of their houses and measured it," Herb said. "We started experimenting with their kind of house. That's how we got into smaller houses. It was what people wanted. We expanded into seven different models."

\\\

In April 1969, Jerry Shapiro died of a heart attack while playing bridge with friends in New York City. According to Herb, he was an accomplished, passionate player who'd paid for some of his undergraduate expenses at Harvard with his winnings. But the competition also caused "a lot of stress." It was the easygoing Jerry's third heart attack. "His doctor told him to give it up, but he wouldn't."

Jerry's death was crushing. Herb lost not only his brother but his trusted business partner. At the time, they had dug most of the lagoons and had built more than half of the eventual 4,500 bungalows at Beach Haven West. They were also moving ahead with a plan to build a 20,000-house, all-inclusive waterfront community called Dinners Point a few miles south of Beach Haven West, near the town of Eagleswood, on Barnegat Bay. It was going to include community pools and recreation centers, even its own grocery store.

"It would have been the largest self-contained waterfront development in the country," similar to Destin and other planned communities in Florida. "It would have everything right there, like a small city," Herb said.

If Jerry had lived, "I have no doubt we would have built it," he added. "But I couldn't do it on my own." So Herb and Jerry's family divided up the business and went their separate ways.

In 1970, another blow hampered Herb's plans along Barnegat Bay. That year, New Jersey lawmakers passed the Wetlands Act, a stringent if belated attempt to control development along the state's bays and save what remained of the coastal wetlands. The legislation called for the state to make a detailed inventory of all tidal wetlands, and it established strict, new controls over construction along the marshes. The act was too late by decades; a third of the coastal wetlands already had been destroyed. Still, the Wetlands Act of 1970 effectively put an end to any new lagoon-style developments like

Beach Haven West, Mystic Island, and the Shapiros' proposed Dinners Point development.

The Wetlands Act was signed by New Jersey's governor, William Cahill, a Republican and a personal friend of Herb's. "I knew him, visited him. I'm pretty sure I even hosted a fundraiser for him at our house," Herb said.

He never forgave Cahill. It felt like the state was picking his pocket, he said. Herb and Jerry had purchased over five thousand acres of salt marsh on Barnegat Bay before the Wetlands Act, with the expectation that they would be able to build there. In Herb's view, the state should have compensated them for their loss—what is known in legal circles as the Takings Clause.

During a 2015 interview, Herb pointed out a window to a large swath of marsh across Barnegat Bay where the Dinners Point development would have been built. "If we had developed all of that meadowland over there for people, affordable houses, it would have been an opportunity for people to participate in the American way of life. Instead, we are now keeping that empty for whatever reason. The question is balance. That is my thought."

Then he added: "Someday I hope a Republican president appoints property-rights justices and someone sues the state."

In 1973, Herb reached an agreement with Lincoln Properties, one of the nation's largest developers, based in Dallas, to buy his remaining land along Barnegat Bay. The deal included the last two undeveloped tracts in Beach Haven West and the Eagleswood marsh. The price was about $3 million. Herb distributed a share to Jerry's estate and invested the rest in tax-free securities, he said.

Lincoln Properties finished the last two sections of Beach Haven West, known as Village Harbour and Colony Lakes. The company donated the Eagleswood marsh to the nonprofit Nature Conservancy, which, in turn, gave it to the U.S. Department of the Interior. Today, the wetlands are part of the Edwin B. Forsythe National Wildlife Refuge, a pristine oasis along the highly developed bay.

The Shapiros, Glorskys, and other developers built 445 lagoon-style communities, including 13,000 canals in Ocean County, according to local records and the county historian. Only Florida, with its dramatically larger coast, has more lagoons. In all, 300,000 houses now line the back bays in New Jersey.

During Hurricane Sandy, billions of gallons of water poured into Barnegat Bay from the inlets, raising the water level by more than six feet. When the wind switched to the south, it pushed the water up the lagoons and into thousands of houses that had never flooded before. Nearly every bungalow in Beach Haven West and Mystic Island suffered flood damage, many beyond repair. Altogether, the insured losses in just those two communities totaled nearly half a billion dollars.

4

Five-High:
The Ash Wednesday
Storm of 1962

THE MORNING OF MARCH 5, 1962, was overcast and cold, with a hard wind blowing out of the northeast, kicking up the bay outside Herb Shapiro's celebrated home. Herb and Selma had only recently returned from a two-week vacation in the Bahamas and U.S. Virgin Islands, where they had played tennis and relaxed with friends. All in all, it had been a nice break. But now Herb was anxious to get back to work. There was land to buy and houses to build. Later that evening, he was scheduled to attend the regular school-board meeting at the high school across the new causeway, in Manahawkin. Herb had joined the board a few years earlier when his daughter and son were entering the local schools and he thought he might be able to help improve the education system.

Around midday, Herb drove up the island to check on a house he had built a few years earlier for a friend. The oceanfront cape was at the corner of Connecticut and Beach Avenues, not far from his office in Beach Haven Park. "For some reason, I had a feeling about that house," he said. "The beach wasn't as wide as up the island and, as I said, the wind was really howling."

Herb parked his car and hiked up the beach. What he saw unnerved him. Towering waves were heaving violently along the shore, one after another. Each wave seemed to inch closer to the dunes—and his friend's house.

Herb had lived through any number of nor'easters and storms, including a hurricane that had smashed the island's beaches. A day after that storm, he and Morris had driven down to a community known as Holgate on the southern end of Long Beach Island. There they'd seen crumpled cottages and cars buried in sand. The only bar on the island's southern end had been reduced to splinters. Years later, in 1960, Hurricane Donna had washed bungalows in Holgate from their cinder-block foundations and spun them sideways.

But this was no hurricane, Herb thought. It couldn't be. It was March. Hurricane season wouldn't start for months. The temperature was in the low thirties, more winter than spring.

Herb drove back to the office and told Jerry about what he'd seen. Then he got on the phone and began to make calls. One of the first people he reached was the head of the public maintenance yard where Long Beach Township kept its trucks and equipment, along with a collection of withered cars. Back then, it was common to use the rusted husks of old junkers to trap sand and build up protective dunes. Workers would position the cars at the toe of the dunes and bulldoze sand over them. In theory, the winter winds would add a few more layers of sand, so that by spring the dunes would look practically new— and the cars would be buried.

Herb explained his problem. A little later, he sent his construction foreman to the maintenance yard with a flatbed truck to load up some cars. Herb watched his workers scatter a dozen junkers in front of the endangered home on Connecticut Avenue. A bulldozer pushed sand around the frames, constructing a temporary seawall. It wasn't much, but maybe it would help.

That evening, Herb kissed Selma goodbye and drove to his school-board meeting. By the time he returned home, around eleven o'clock, the wind was blowing so hard that it nearly forced his sedan off the causeway. "I told Selma when I got home that I had a bad feeling about this storm," he said. "I told her I thought the island was in trouble."

The following morning, Tuesday, March 6, the ocean was washing over and through the sand dunes, slamming into the houses. It was a spring tide, which made the flooding worse. In a spring tide, the moon is closer to the earth, exerting its gravitational force against the ocean, adding inches or sometimes feet to the normal tide. The March 1962 tide measured eight and a half feet above mean low water at its peak—still one of the highest on record in New Jersey.

There was no sense going to the office. No one would be looking for beach houses in the storm. Herb listened to the radio instead. The weather forecasts confirmed his worst fears. It was a late-season nor'easter. Conditions were expected to get worse, with even bigger, lacerating waves. Herb called his brother, Jerry, and told him to bring his family over. Herb's house was on higher ground and safer than Jerry's oceanfront colonial. As he stared out the window at the leaden clouds and wind-chopped bay, it occurred to Herb that the Connecticut Avenue house was probably gone. The car frames, as well.

\\\

Afterward, reporters would call the punishing nor'easter the Great Ash Wednesday Storm because it began on the first day of Lent. It seemed appropriate enough. Lent was a time of fasting, repentance, and prayer—and there would be plenty of sacrifice and healing over the weeks and months to come.

To a great degree, the Ash Wednesday Storm is a forgotten event, outstripped by Katrina, Harvey, Sandy, and other calamitous storms in recent years. Since it occurred more than six decades ago, many Americans are simply too young to know about it. Yet for many years, the great nor'easter was one of the bellwether storms of the mid-Atlantic states, along with the 1938 New England Hurricane, which killed eight hundred. The Ash Wednesday Storm lashed beaches from northern Florida to the South Shore of Long Island, and it was larger than Sandy and Katrina, both epically large storms. It damaged or destroyed nearly seventy thousand houses in North Carolina, Maryland,

Delaware, New Jersey, and New York; swept away boardwalks and piers; crushed roads and bridges; and destroyed utilities.

Still, as unlikely as it may seem today, meteorologists didn't see the Ash Wednesday Storm coming. In the days leading up to the storm, they predicted a relatively short period of rain and sleet at the coast, with an inland blizzard at higher elevations in Pennsylvania and West Virginia. Instead, Long Beach Island and other coastal towns were blitzed by a brutal three-day onslaught, with hurricane-force winds and towering waves and surge. Like Hurricane Sandy, which bookended the Ash Wednesday Storm fifty years later, the giant nor'easter was anomalous—a huge late-season storm that reached the mid-latitudes only to find its path blocked by a ridge of high pressure to the north, near the coast of Labrador. With no way ahead, it stalled, relentlessly pounding the coast with twenty-to-forty-foot waves.

The meteorologists didn't have the science, tools, or data (computers, satellites, and Doppler radars) that help enhance modern forecasts. By Monday, March 5, they knew that a low-pressure system was forming along the northern coast of Florida and correctly predicted that it would merge with another storm moving across the Mississippi Valley. However, they didn't know how large or intense the combined storms would become, or that the newly merged storm would rapidly take on many of the characteristics of a hurricane.

The forecast in *The Newark Evening News* called for increasing clouds and continued cold in the metro area, and "for the shore: North to northeast winds about 10 m.p.h. through tonight, becoming northwest 15–20 tomorrow."

The following morning, gale-force winds were already pummeling the coast. The size and position of the storm, superimposed on the spring tides, led to unabated flooding. Normally, the storm surge in a hurricane lasts one or two tidal cycles. The Ash Wednesday flood lasted five cycles, each tide higher than the last. Long Beach Island was submerged under high water for nineteen hours—seven more hours than in Hurricane Sandy. M. P. O'Brien and J. W. Johnson of the University of California, Berkeley, likened the Ash Wednesday Storm to the calamitous 1953 North Atlantic storm that inundated the Netherlands and resulted in two thousand deaths.

Water piled on top of water. "The third high tide, on the morning of 7 March [Wednesday], generally overwhelmed the entire Middle Atlantic coast," the U.S. Army Corps of Engineers noted in its study of the Ash Wednesday Storm, known as the Five-High Report. "Coastal protective structures, man-made or natural, if still intact, were in seriously weakened condition at that point, and the recurrence of the attack of high water at tidal stages above normal literally leveled some communities."

"Leveled" isn't nearly strong enough. "Gutted" or "obliterated" seems more accurate. Waves and surge tore through the diminished sand dunes in six separate locations on Long Beach Island, allowing the ocean to merge with the bay. The small, historic borough of Harvey Cedars, on the north end of the island, lost four beaches. An eight-foot-wide hole near the center of town effectively isolated the borough from the rest of the island. Coast Guard helicopters had to fly over from the mainland to rescue residents stranded there.

Houses collapsed into the surf or were swept into Barnegat Bay. Months later, the rooflines could still be seen at low tide. Doors and windows jutted out of the sand like weathered dinosaur bones. Boris Blai, a sculptor and Temple University professor, reported losing $45,000 worth of art in the storm, including a bronze bust he'd made of the architect Frank Lloyd Wright. The bust miraculously surfaced several days later in a mound of ocean sand.

The raging ocean tore a hole through the dunes near a trailer park in Holgate, on the southern end of the island, stranding residents. Members of a local Coast Guard station made seven trips, using an amphibious vehicle known as a DUKW, to transport residents to higher ground. With night falling on March 6, they started on one last rescue, picking up two elderly couples and heading north to Beach Haven, about two miles away. Their rescue vehicle— thirty-two feet long and eight feet wide, with six wheels, a canopy, and a propeller—was built to navigate in rough surf zones. But it was swamped when a huge wave crashed through the dunes and across the road.

The seven occupants formed a human chain and struggled to make their way back to the Coast Guard station in Holgate. But the elderly couples were exhausted by the frigid ocean water, which at that time of the year would have been in the low forties. While the coastguardsmen worked their way south, the couples clung to a telephone pole. Hypothermia must have set in quickly, and the couples either let go or were swept away in the surge. The bodies of two of them were recovered the next day, forty-five miles away in Ocean City. Another washed up on a local beach. The fourth was never found.

Nearly all the 5,361 homes on Long Beach Island at the time of the Ash Wednesday Storm were damaged, including 1,000 that were severely impaired and 600 that were destroyed. Many communities along the back bays also flooded, including Tuckerton Beach, Mystic Island, Beachwood, Ocean Gate, and some of the larger lagoon developments in Ocean County. Altogether, the Ash Wednesday Storm caused about $2 billion in damage, measured in today's dollars. The only reason there wasn't more extensive damage was because the coast was far less developed in 1962 than it is today. The 141-mile New Jersey shore was worth about $1 billion in 1962. Today, it is worth over $100 billion. And all that property is vulnerable to storms.

\\\

Most of the discussion immediately following the Ash Wednesday Storm was around how quickly Long Beach Island and the other beach towns could rebuild. It was critical, insisted the mayors and politicians, for the towns to be back in business by Memorial Day, only a few months away.

"You must remember that the seashore is New Jersey's number one business, turning over $1 billion a year," the longtime state senator Frank "Hap" Farley, from Atlantic City, reminded his colleagues in a speech. "We must get ready for that business, and get ready mighty quick!"

The administration of Governor Richard J. Hughes was more circumspect. In late March, Hughes suggested that beach towns halt all new development for six months while the state drafted a long-range plan for protecting the coast. The governor's recommendation was seconded by the Army Corps of Engineers, which suggested that beach towns create a fifty-foot-wide buffer along the barrier islands to protect the sand dunes from development.

Hughes then proposed an even more stringent restriction: a ban on rebuilding along a one-hundred-foot-wide buffer along the beach, essentially shutting down the immediate oceanfront to development. But that moratorium shouldn't apply only to New Jersey, the governor said; it should extend the entire length of the Atlantic Coast. Beach towns "would be making a mistake in permitting private citizens to rebuild in the path of subsequent storms," Hughes explained. They should pull back and create what he called "a preservative zone," with no buildings. State and federal governments could use millions of dollars in state and federal grants to buy endangered property and turn it into public parks, he suggested.

It was a remarkably brave but unpopular idea. Hughes tasked Raymond F. Male with spreading his message. Male, a stick-thin bureaucrat with a degree from Princeton, was the commissioner of labor and industry, not an environmentalist. In his state role, he served as a cheerleader for business and development. Yet here he was, counseling the beach-town mayors to accept the governor's provocative proposal and pause in their rush to rebuild. It didn't make any sense "to return to a policy of helter-skelter private development of beach assets," he advised them. The state had $60 million in funds (equal to about $500 million in today's dollars) to buy flood-prone beach houses. It was also eligible for federal grants.

Two prominent geographers endorsed the state's approach. Rushing to rebuild would only add to the risks at the coast, leading to repeated coastal disasters, Ian Burton and Robert W. Kates wrote in the seminal 1964 study "The Floodplain and the Seashore." The future costs to the federal government would be huge, the authors declared, and Congress wouldn't be satisfied until it built an "Atlantic Wall . . . from Maine to Mexico" to defend coastal property.

Perhaps to appease builders and mayors, Hughes declared that his proposed building ban wouldn't apply to ordinary repairs. Instead, it would focus on new beach houses and properties that had suffered damage equal to more than 25 percent of the assessed value. Ideally, the preservative zone would cover the state's entire shoreline. But if that wasn't acceptable, it should include all the "severely damaged areas," the governor said.

Meanwhile, New Jersey officials were lobbying for $40 million in federal aid to repair their storm-scoured beaches and towns. Long Beach Island and other resorts had lost most of their oceanfronts. Many of their sand dunes had been flattened, leaving the towns defenseless. The state wanted to dredge the sand that had washed into Barnegat Bay and use it to rebuild the beaches and dunes.

The mayors liked the idea of widening their beaches, especially if the state was going to pay. But they hated Hughes's proposed ban on new development and giving large swaths of their beaches back to the public. There was too much money at stake, and restricting development threatened their tax bases. The debate shifted away from retreating out of harm's way to getting the federal government to pay as much as possible toward the recovery.

T. H. Bossert, the commissioner of revenue and finance for Long Beach Township, the largest of the island's six beach towns, wrote to Hughes that the beach towns were unable to contribute to their own recovery: "If you would take time to survey Long Beach Island, you would appreciate the extent of devastation and hardships necessitating the need of government grants."

On March 9, President John F. Kennedy issued a federal disaster declaration covering New Jersey and the other storm-damaged states, promising to send financial aid as quickly as possible. Congress passed a supplemental appropriation of $25 million as a recovery stopgap. Millions more poured into beach towns from the Department of Housing and Urban Development, Department of Transportation, Army Corps of Engineers, and other federal agencies. The Ash Wednesday Storm powerfully recast the politics of coastal disasters, sharply expanding federal aid and leading to the creation of new programs, including government-backed flood insurance several years later, not to mention helping to instill a growing expectation among Americans that the federal government would always be there to rescue them after hurricanes, floods, and other disasters, including aid for beach resorts and second homes. In this sense, the Ash Wednesday Storm represents a pivot point in the evolution of the nation's coasts, shifting some of the risk of rebuilding from private homeowners to the public, and encouraging a dangerous and costly pattern of building, damage, and rebuilding in harm's way.

\\\

Herb and Jerry Shapiro were convinced they would never sell another house after the Ash Wednesday Storm. "There was so much damage we were sure no one would want to come here," Herb said. Yet within weeks, speculators were prowling the damaged streets of Long Beach Island looking for bargains. And just a few months later, in June, the Shapiro brothers sold a house.

"We were back in business and never looked back," said Herb.

In the decade after the devastating Ash Wednesday Storm, Long Beach Island and other coastal communities saw a historic surge in development, adding thousands of houses and billions of dollars in property value. At the time, all the houses on Long Beach Island were worth less than $100 million. Today, they are worth more than $15 billion. Between 2000 and 2014 alone, housing values grew by an astonishing $10 billion.

M. L. Shapiro Co. reported record sales of 375 homes in 1963, the year after the 1962 nor'easter. It sold another 500 in 1965. "The demand for second homes on the New Jersey shore is stronger than ever," Herb told the *Asbury Park Press*. By 1971, he was able to boast that M. L. Shapiro had exceeded $50 million in sales.

It was a remarkable achievement—and yet not entirely surprising. Hurricanes and violent nor'easters have come to serve as market-clearing devices, weeding out older, more vulnerable homes while freeing space for the next wave of development. That was certainly true after the Ash Wednesday Storm, but it is also true generally. A form of reverse psychology appears to be at play. Instead of retreating after catastrophic storms, Americans move even closer to the water, in defiance of nature and risk.

"It is confounding and, in my opinion, incredibly dangerous and foolish," said Orrin H. Pilkey, the coastal geologist. For decades, he advised beach towns and coastal communities that they were tempting disaster and recommended that they slowly retreat to higher ground. The coasts are organic, he told the mayors. They are always shifting, growing here, eroding there. Building on low-lying floodplains was "just thumbing your nose at Mother Nature." But no one listened. The mayors dismissed Pilkey's message and filled their islands with even more houses.

After Hurricane Harvey flooded Houston and its suburbs in 2017, the *Houston Chronicle* reported that private-equity and hedge funds were buying up thousands of flood-damaged homes to renovate, flip, and sell at a quick profit. Local officials found themselves competing with investors for flooded properties that they hoped to set aside as open space. "All we're doing is perpetuating a cycle of flooding," the flood-control officer for Harris County told the newspaper.

Years before Harvey, I visited Pensacola Beach, on the Florida Panhandle. It was a year after Hurricane Ivan, a powerful Category 3 storm, had plowed into the coast there. I had come to the area to inspect the damage from Hurricane Katrina, a week earlier. The epic hurricane had obliterated the Mississippi coast, pitching homes a half mile into the pine forests behind the Gulf of Mexico. I was fairly confident it was as bad as it could get. Yet, here I was staring goggle-eyed at the bones and rubble of Pensacola Beach a year *after* Ivan. Apparently, it could get worse.

But when I suggested as much to Buck Lee, then general manager of the local government, he laughed at me. Lee could get away with laughing at a reporter. Tall, silver-haired, and perched high above the ground in a pumpkin-colored Hummer, he was clearly in charge. Pensacola Beach was doing just fine, he told me. What I was seeing was a few aftershocks. The recovery was well on its way.

"We've had speculators like you wouldn't believe," he rasped. "They ride around in their big cars with the windows rolled down, offering people cash on the spot. And a lot of people take it."

A short memory helps if you own a house at the beach. But it can also be a trap. For example, if you haven't suffered through a catastrophic hurricane, you may be inclined to think you never will. This is what behavioral economists call a favorable reference point. Given a choice between enjoying what's immediately in front of you, another beautiful day at the beach, or pondering the unthinkable, a major hurricane, who wouldn't opt for the mental shortcut? Why not assume you are immune?

Years after the Ash Wednesday Storm wrecked Long Beach Island, some homeowners had trouble remembering it. Even more improbably, they began to romanticize the nor'easter. "You heard people on LBI talking about it like it was the good old days," marveled John Weingart, a former coastal manager at the New Jersey Department of Environmental Protection. "They had been around and rebuilt. But they forgot how bad it actually was. That sort of thing happens a lot, I think."

In the 1990s, James J. Mancini, the longtime mayor of Long Beach Township, bragged to a reporter that Long Beach Island was now safe. The beaches were wider and the dunes were higher. A nor'easter like the Ash Wednesday Storm would barely make a dent today, he insisted.

Mancini explained that the 1962 nor'easter was a one-in-a-hundred-year event, the "storm of the century." What was the chance of another storm like that happening again in their lifetimes? Zero, said the mayor.

It was quintessential Jim Mancini: confident, enthusiastic, brash. Still, it was a remarkable claim, and naive, as events would later prove.

Perhaps the mayor didn't understand the math? He wouldn't be alone. Many homeowners think the term "hundred-year storm" means that a storm will happen only once every century. They don't realize that it is more of a term of art than of science. In fact, a storm like the Ash Wednesday nor'easter could occur more than once in the same year; it could even occur two or three times, as happened in 2004, 2005, 2017, and, most recently, 2018. Or a series of catastrophic storms could stack up, year after year, as they did in the 1940s and 1950s.

The term "hundred-year storm" was an accidental standard chosen in a rush to categorize the danger at the coast, not an accurate predictive measure of risk. Many scientists thought it gave homeowners and beach-town mayors a false sense of security. After all, what was a hundred-year storm in 1950 or 1960 might be a fifty-year storm in 2000 or 2010. The geography of risk was continually shifting as beaches eroded, sea levels rose, and storms became bigger, wilder, and more destructive. The Corps of Engineers disavowed the term after Hurricane Sandy in 2012. "It's not our term," testified John C. Becking, the former head of the Philadelphia office. "It's a convenient term to talk about, but that's not the term we would choose."

Possibly, Jim Mancini simply chose to ignore the math. It was easier. And if you told people often enough that their beloved island was safe, they would eventually believe you. Years later, even as he was recalibrating his thinking about development, Mancini continued to insist that Long

Beach Island was safe. He also dismissed sea-level rise as an opinion and a theory.

"That's absolutely ridiculous," the mayor exclaimed in 1990, when Jim Titus of the Environmental Protection Agency suggested that Long Beach Island would have to make drastic and expensive choices as the seas rose in the coming century. Titus, one of the nation's earliest leading experts on sea-level rise, estimated that it would cost $522 million to raise the island's profile high enough to protect its housing against a three-foot rise in sea level.

Mancini was unimpressed. "I know our beach is not getting small or eroding. It's getting larger," he told a local newspaper. "So I know we are not going to go out and get our people excited about the idea of building a . . . wall around the island. No one is going to do that. Why bring it up?"

Titus had more than a passing interest in Long Beach Island. His family owned a small, rustic cottage there. In 1962, water came up to the floor joists in the Ash Wednesday Storm. Afterward, the family added another layer of cinder blocks to the foundation. In Sandy, water once again came up to the floor joists but did not seep into the bungalow. Titus, who now owns the cottage outright, told me he thought about elevating the cottage on pilings but decided to leave that decision to his daughter, who will eventually inherit the house.

"Old man Mancini was interesting," he said. "He was harder to talk to than his son [Joseph H., the current mayor]. He gets it, I think. The old man didn't want to hear it."

Titus's study is now nearly three decades old. But using his assumptions and updating the data to reflect inflation and the dramatic increase in the cost of sand, I estimate it would cost at least $2 billion to $3 billion today to raise Long Beach Island high enough to protect it against a three-foot rise in sea level. That works out to an average of about $150,000 for each house.

Jim Mancini wore many hats. He was a developer, a builder, a tax assessor, an appraiser, and a self-described pro-business politician. He looked at Long Beach Island and saw only opportunities. Was there risk? Sure, it was a barrier island. But it wasn't like Orrin Pilkey or the pinhead environmentalists in Trenton believed. They wanted to shut down the barrier islands and leave them to the piping plovers and turtles. What about Oklahoma with its tornadoes and California with its earthquakes? Mancini sometimes asked. Why weren't they trying to shut down those places? Yes, every once in a while there was a hurricane or a winter gale. But most of the time, it was like paradise out here, miles at sea. Why do you think so many people loved coming here? They couldn't build houses fast enough. Go ahead, call him an incurable romantic; he didn't care. Just don't try to tell him what to do with his slender little island. And don't dare tell him he should think about retreating to higher ground. That was "preposterous" and was never going to happen, not as long as Jim Mancini was in charge.

PART II

The Political Economy of Water

From a basic knowledge of climatology of damage-producing storms, it should be possible to envision a more rational program of coastal occupancy and development and to establish effective zoning and protective ordinances that have some basis in fact.

—JOHN R. MATHER ET AL., *COASTAL STORMS OF THE EASTERN UNITED STATES*, 1964

We missed the opportunity. It's done. All of these opportunities to do new creative things, it's too late. We're done.

—MARK N. MAURIELLO, 2017, FORMER COMMISSIONER, NEW JERSEY DEPARTMENT OF ENVIRONMENTAL PROTECTION

5

The Bantam Mayor

THE BEST TIMES WERE WHEN he was outdoors in the warm sun framing a new house or slamming nails. Jim Mancini loved using his hands and building small bungalows for families to make memories at the beach. It was why he was always happiest at the start of a new project. He got to be outside, build something, and put smiles on peoples' faces. And, not unimportantly, he also made a little money. With a wife and four kids, and with another on the way, he needed every penny he could lay his hands on. (The Mancinis would have nine children. Jim often joked that if he had known how babies were made, he would have stopped sooner.)

At the moment, a few months after the Ash Wednesday Storm, money wasn't a problem. Jim Mancini couldn't believe all the orders he had. The backlog was fifty deep, and more seemed to come in every day. It felt like the start of a boom. He and his crew would be busy for months, maybe years.

It was shocking, in a way—or, if not shocking, certainly surprising. Like everyone, Mancini figured it would take years for Long Beach Island to recover. The day after the big storm, he had driven around on a bulldozer, taking Polaroid pictures of the damage. The pictures were to show how bad things were so that maybe President Kennedy would send a little money their way to help with the recovery. Jim didn't have to drive very far to see that the entire island was wrecked, especially along the oceanfront, where scores of houses had toppled into the surf.

After the storm, the governor had wanted to shut down any construction along the ocean. He had called for a buffer zone. But one man's buffer was another man's building moratorium. At least that's how it had sounded to Jim Mancini. If the politicians approved a buffer, there wouldn't be enough work. Jim would have to move back north to Irvington, his hometown, and go back to painting houses, which was what he'd done before moving to Long Beach Island. It was the last thing he wanted. He'd grown to love the island. It was beautiful and quiet, a great place to raise his growing family. It would crush him if he had to give all that up.

As it turned out, he didn't have to. The governor's proposal never went anywhere. And now the island was back in business. Mancini Company, which included Jim and his younger brother, Joe, specialized in building small capes and duplexes that sold for as little as $2,000 or $3,000. They built all over the island, but mostly near Brant Beach and Holgate, on the southern end, where they filled in the marsh by Barnegat Bay and were constructing a big new development called Sunset Harbor.

Like the Shapiros, Jim Mancini believed in keeping things simple and cheap. "Pop's vision was that this was a family resort. He was adamant that nothing be built over three stories and there were no boardwalks," recalled Jim's oldest son, Joe, himself a developer. "He felt very strongly that this was a family community. And he felt very strongly about mom-and-pop establishments."

Jim Mancini would later say that the two decades after the Ash Wednesday Storm, 1960 to 1980, represented the golden age of development on Long Beach Island. During that period, the number of houses and businesses doubled, to 12,000, and the value of property soared to about $2 billion, from $100 million. Mancini Company alone built 1,000 vacation homes. The national media, including *The New York Times*, among other publications, began to take notice, likening the slender barrier island to Cape Cod and the Hamptons.

"All Long Beach Island is divided into two parts," noted a writer for *Philadelphia Magazine*, "The Haves and The Have Mores." Loveladies, a one-mile swath of larger, more lavish and architecturally ambitious beach houses on the north end, overflowed with actors, artists, doctors, lawyers, politicians, and corporate titans. Parties stretched from dusk to dawn, and one famous writer was said to have stumbled into the lagoons in William Ludwig Ullman's bayside development, Loveladies Harbor. (Ullman himself was a story: a New Deal–era economist turned spy for Russia who fled to Long Beach Island while being pursued by the FBI and improbably became a major developer on the north end.) Where there was once a single house between the toe of the sand dunes and the road, there were now three or four stacked in a line, one more expensive than the next. Signs warned the public to stay away: PRIVATE. NO TRESPASSING. In another article, in 1988, a writer called the people on Long Beach Island "snobs. What's more, they admit it. They wallow in it. They love what the island has, and disdain what it doesn't have," he wrote.

Jim Mancini rankled at some of the characterizations. Long Beach Island wasn't the Hamptons, and never would be, he insisted. Yes, there was more money than there used to be, but there were still plenty of middle-class families enjoying their time in the sun. It wasn't all like Loveladies.

Politics came naturally to Mancini. He enjoyed talking with people and listening to their concerns, helping out when he could. He shook everyone's hand and gave the ladies a peck on the cheek. It was just the way he was. He'd grown up in the city and learned how to get along. After high school, he'd worked with his father painting houses in Irvington and Newark. Later, he'd served in the U.S. Air Force, though he never got to fly planes.

He returned to Irvington and painting houses, telling himself there must be a bigger canvas for him to paint.

Jim was dashingly handsome, like the actor Errol Flynn, with dark, wavy hair and a pencil-thin mustache. A cigarette dangled from the corner of his mouth; later, it would become a cigar. Although slight in build, he was bantam strong. When he walked into a room, Mancini bristled with energy, pumping his arms like a sprinter at the end of a hundred-yard dash.

One summer day, young Jim was visiting a friend in Keansburg, a modest beach town in North Jersey, when he spotted a beautiful girl lying in the sun. The way he would later tell the story, Mary Madeline Klass was the only one he noticed that day. "I saw this girl sunning herself on her stomach, and I liked her legs," he said. After they married, Jim built a house in nearby Union. But North Jersey was already built-up. Jim needed more room to make his mark. When a relative suggested he look into Long Beach Island, he found exactly what he wanted. It was 1950. The island was mostly empty. Jim looked at three lots near the ocean and bought them on the spot for $3,500. Then he built a small cape for his family.

At first, Mary wasn't so sure about life on a small island. While people were around in the summer months, after Labor Day you could drive up and down Long Beach Boulevard without seeing a soul. To make matters worse, there wasn't enough work at first. Half the year, Jim commuted two and a half hours to paint houses with his father to pay the bills. It would get better, he told his wife. And sure enough, it did.

After the storm, his business boomed. Mancini also took on side jobs as the township's building inspector and tax appraiser. The jobs didn't require a lot of effort. As long as developers followed the rules, they could build whatever they wanted. Jim would drive by, ask if they had a permit, and wave if they said yes.

Mancini took over as the township's mayor in 1964. After a full day of work, he would attend meetings well into the night. He was a tireless booster, and there wasn't a cause he didn't embrace: the Boy Scouts, the Chamber of Commerce, churches, hospitals, recreation centers, a new bank—anything that would make Long Beach Island a little more attractive. The joke was that he was out so often, his kids didn't recognize him. So Mary taped a picture of Jim to a chair and told them, "Look, it's your daddy."

"He loved being at the center of things," Joe recalled. "And there were many, many nights in which we wouldn't see him."

By 1970, Jim Mancini was a local political force. In addition to serving as mayor, he ran for the state assembly and was backed by the builders and developers: "Don't you think it's high time our clobbered industry wakes up and goes all out to help the man who wants to help us?" the builders asked in a political ad backing Mancini. Jim served two terms in Trenton but didn't like it, his son recalled. There was too much showboating and backroom trading. He saw himself as more clear-eyed and practical. Mancini was also elected to the Ocean County Board of Freeholders and held that post for over two decades.

In New Jersey, it isn't unusual for politicians to wear multiple hats. Leonard Connors, the longtime mayor of Surf City, also served as a county freeholder and state assemblyman. Together, he and Mancini used their influence to steer millions of tax dollars to Long Beach Island for sewers, roads, utilities, libraries, and a local hospital. "He loved the island," Joe said, and the island residents loved him back, repeatedly returning Jim to office over four decades.

\\\

With his business and political career thriving, Jim Mancini decided to expand. In the early 1970s, he and his brother purchased a bankrupt development for senior citizens in Manahawkin called Fawn Lakes. They paid $400,000 for the five-hundred-acre tract and announced plans to build more than two thousand condominium-style residences costing upward of $30,000 each.

It was, in hindsight, a terrible decision. The state was beginning to take a more active role in environmental issues, and it frowned on the idea of allowing thousands of additional septic systems so close to Barnegat Bay. The bay was already stressed from all the lagoon developments and building on the nearby barrier islands. Lawn fertilizer, waste, and runoff were leaching into the water, setting off algae blooms and fish kills. Some of the beaches were forced to close for days at a time. The clam and oyster beds were also in decline. And some popular fish had all but disappeared.

The solution, according to state and county officials, was to build a large new sewer system on the mainland, which would serve Long Beach Island, Beach Haven West, and the other communities along the bay in Ocean County. It was long overdue, they declared. But there was a catch. There would have to be a building moratorium on Long Beach Island while they constructed the system, which would take years.

Mancini's building company got hit hard on two fronts, with business on the island drying up and debts mounting from the ill-timed purchase of the Fawn Lakes development. Jim rushed to finish work on his major development, Sunset Harbor, on the southern end of Long Beach Island, taking out forty building permits in a single day.

But then things got even worse. In February 1976, Jim's brother and business partner, Joe, died of an aneurysm at the age of forty-four. Jim did his best to hide the pain and stress. He still wore a dark pinstripe suit every day, still shook everyone's hand, and still gave the ladies a kiss. But he was struggling, according to his son, and under a "terrible hardship," Joe said. Beneath the ever-present mask of optimism, Jim Mancini was worried. He began looking for a way to get out of the Fawn Lakes deal, finally arranging to sell his interest. But with the building moratorium still in place, his construction business was also moribund.

Jim blamed the state for his misfortune. In the early 1970s, the mood in Trenton had shifted from pro-business to pro-environment. First, there was the wetlands law, which was bad enough. Then there was the building moratorium for the new sewer. Now, they were talking about setting up a commission that would have control over the beach towns. Jim didn't have a problem with cleaning up the bay. Everyone wanted clean water. But this was too much. "Where does it stop?" he asked a reporter at the time.

6

A Brief Shining Moment

MANAGING DEVELOPMENT AT THE COAST has always been more of a goal than a reality. That's clearly the case in New Jersey, where local control, private property rights, money, and politics have frequently trumped public interests. An issue as simple as ensuring access to the beach has resulted in epic lawsuits over who owns the sand—the taxpayers who pay to widen and repair beaches after hurricanes or the millionaires who erect fences, gates, and signs to keep the public away? These issues aren't limited to New Jersey, of course. Questions about access, building, and environmental protections have surfaced in nearly every coastal state in recent decades, including Florida, Texas, and New York. On Sullivan's Island, a wealthy enclave near Charleston, South Carolina, homeowners even sued their town a few years ago, contending that a maritime forest was blocking their ocean views and, they argued, lowering property values. One homeowner took matters into his own hands and began cutting trees near his house. According to court records and newspaper accounts, the owner agreed to pay several thousand dollars in fines and leave the trees alone in the future.

But there was a time, albeit brief, when protectors of the coast thought they might be able to sensibly guide development and limit unchecked growth. In the early 1970s, public attitudes had shifted in a way that empowered environmental reformers with a newfound sense of purpose. At the federal level, Congress passed an array of new environmental legislation, including the Coastal Zone Management Act in 1972, intended to bring consistency and logic to how the states managed their coasts.

The new program was voluntary. However, a cluster of states, including New Jersey, signed up and then received millions in federal aid to hire consultants, create new environmental standards, and put together master plans guiding future development. "I was the program manager for that. I had to figure out what we were going to do and how we were going to do it," recalled David N. Kinsey, the former head of coastal programs at the New Jersey Department of Environmental Protection (DEP).

Kinsey welcomed the challenge. Growing up in South Jersey, he spent plenty of time at the beach, including on Long Beach and Island Beach State Park, one of the few undeveloped stretches on the 141-mile coast. His family owned a gentleman's farm in Moorestown, Burlington County, with fifty acres of Christmas trees. After earning a master's degree and doctorate in public policy from Princeton University's Woodrow Wilson School, Kinsey went to work at the environmental agency, tasked with helping to establish its first coastal division. There, he was joined by John Weingart and a small, ambitious group of planners and scientists who, like Kinsey, were eager to make their mark.

"The idea of environmental regulation and land-use regulation was so new it was scary," said Weingart, now a public policy analyst at the Eagleton Institute of Politics at Rutgers University. "We were all finding our way, with David as our leader."

"The thing that I remember about the earliest days was raising the level of expectation to unreasonable levels," said Lewis Goldshore, an attorney now in private practice. "We were very young. I think I was all of twenty-four. We passed lots of legislation . . . Our adversaries weren't very pleased with being told no."

The DEP opened for business on April 22, 1970, the initial Earth Day. Early on, the staff helped implement the Wetlands Act that so distracted Herb Shapiro and other developers. The law was cosponsored by a young, up-and-coming legislator, Tom Kean, who would go on to become governor. Kean came from strong Republican lineage but was an avowed environmentalist. In the early 1970s, he sponsored legislation to limit oil drilling and regulate large hotels and other developments along the coast. That was 1973, the year of the first oil crisis. Kean and other politicians were alarmed that proposals to drill for oil off the state's coast could threaten the fragile ecology, lead to spills, and damage the tourism economy.

That legislation was the Coastal Area Facility Review Act, or CAFRA, for short. The name was misleading because its regulations weren't limited to the coast but also covered large industrial development along inland water-ways. Nor did CAFRA infringe on the authority of coastal mayors, leaving them to exercise control over crucial land-use and building decisions at the beach.

"As with any law, there was a lot of wheeling and dealing with CAFRA," Kinsey said. "The state could not force changes to their zoning. The towns [still] have practically absolute discretion. They can zone for what they want."

Kinsey and the other reformers at DEP knew it would be political suicide to try to shut down development at the Jersey Shore. The mayors had too much power. But they thought they might be able to slow the pace of development enough to save the qualities that made the New Jersey coast so attractive in the first place. Developers could build smarter, safer communities while limiting building along the waterways and oceanfront. At least, that was the hope.

CAFRA focused on large developments with twenty-five or more units, including hotels, motels, and condominiums. Any developments below that threshold weren't subject to state review. Developers quickly found their way around the law. Thousands of new housing plans appeared on local dockets—all below the twenty-five-unit threshold. Planners jokingly referred to CAFRA as the "Rule of Twenty-Four" because so many projects were for exactly twenty-four units.

Environmental groups complained that the new law had exposed the coast to a new wave of development. They cited the surge in applications for condominium projects below twenty-four units. Thousands more permits for single-family beach houses were issued. It was a case of death by a thousand cuts, environmentalists contended.

Years later, in 1986, John Weingart told a gathering of coastal regulators that CAFRA had failed to make the New Jersey coast safe. "The strange result is that New Jersey's coastal management program is powerless to prevent developers from destroying oceanfront dunes to build one, five, or twenty-five houses," he said at a conference in Ocean City, Maryland. "The program has many strengths but dramatically limiting future storm damage is not yet among them."

\\\

In 2015, I met David Kinsey at his home in Princeton. Now retired, he is slight, with hawkish features and thinning gray hair. He told me that he is enormously proud of what he and his fellow reformers accomplished. They created a new department from scratch, drafted guidelines and rules, assembled a first-ever inventory of coastal assets, implemented CAFRA, and drafted New Jersey's initial coastal master plan.

"I think we accomplished a lot thinking of the coast as a system, from a scientific perspective as well as a planning perspective," Kinsey said. "I think that helped to guide actions for the long term—to think about regulation and planning and enforcement and education."

But when I asked Kinsey whether CAFRA had prevented unwise development at the coast, he hesitated, and then drew a sharp line between planning and oversight. "To some extent, CAFRA helped to preserve the low-rise nature of development," he said, referring to the height of buildings at the coast. "But we couldn't force the towns to change. That wasn't our role."

That raised a key question: Whose role was it? Was it the role of the land-use division? The federal officials who handed out the checks? Or was it the responsibility of the beach towns themselves?

Surprisingly, states participating in the federal Coastal Zone Management Program received little feedback on their efforts. The grant application was a cut-and-paste exercise. The states filled in the blanks and the feds sent the checks. John Weingart wasn't even sure the federal managers read what he wrote. So one quarter, he decided to test them, writing that New Jersey had purchased two elephants with some of its grant money. "They immediately called and said, 'You thought we didn't read these,'" he said, laughing.

Long before beginning work on this book, I interviewed the two top administrators of the federal coastal program. At that point, in 1998, it had existed for a quarter century, and I was curious what impact it'd had.

"It's just very difficult to evaluate this program—looking at whether things are getting better or getting worse," the director, Joe Uravich, explained.

"How do you define success when you are encouraging coastal development and preserving coastal resources?" wondered Bill O'Beirne, the assistant director.

While reading several of New Jersey's more recent reports to Washington, I noticed this disconcerting note: "Reconstruction of residential development and the conversion of single-family dwellings into multi-unit dwellings continue in hazardous areas, the value of property at risk is increasing significantly. With anticipated accelerating sea-level rise and increasing storm frequency and intensity, vulnerability to the risk of coastal hazard will not abate; it will only become more costly."

That was from a 2006 report. Two years later, the New Jersey Department of Environmental Protection issued an updated plan for the coast. Once again, it included no regulations, prompting Jeff Tittel, head of the Sierra Club's New Jersey Chapter, to respond: "We're still not really addressing the big issues that we have to," including overdevelopment and pollution.

Joseph Scarpelli, the mayor of Brick Township, a waterfront community on Barnegat Bay, complained that the state still was taking a "piecemeal approach" to the coast, and "it's not going to work because I think everything is interrelated."

Two years after his comments, Hurricane Sandy pushed six feet of water into thousands of homes in Scarpelli's town. Homeowners rebuilt. But in 2018, a torrential storm dumped over seven inches of rain on the town, flooding more than one hundred homes and prompting an emergency evacuation.

7

The Revolt at St. Francis

WITH THE FAILURE OF CAFRA, David Kinsey and John Weingart began searching for another way to manage risky development along New Jersey's oceanfront. The mayors would always argue that they—and they alone—controlled building and zoning decisions. But the state had its own legitimate interests, Kinsey and Weingart reasoned. Each year, New Jersey taxpayers provided millions of dollars to more than forty beach towns to maintain their roads and bridges and repair storm damage, among other benefits.

"It seemed crazy to rebuild in areas that were heavily damaged in storms," Weingart said. "There was a fair convergence of opinion among coastal scientists and bureaucrats that this was the right thing to do."

Still, what could they do? Their options were limited. The Department of Environmental Protection couldn't act on its own. The regulators needed political cover, someone in the state assembly, or even higher, to help clear a path. And they needed more science to back up their efforts, preferably from someone outside the department.

Kinsey and Weingart turned to Norbert P. Psuty, a respected marine scientist at Rutgers University who'd worked on the state's original Shore Protection Master Plan in 1980. No one knew more about the state's beaches, sand dunes, and oceanfront than Norb Psuty. He'd been studying the coast for decades and had produced a series of deeply researched reports, including a 1979 study that revealed how developers had routinely leveled protective dunes to build beach houses.

"The tradition was to throw down sand and build a structure on top," Psuty said in an interview. "I was trying to get more of the history out there—how dunes function, their role in protection. I was almost trying to raise consciousness."

Coastal politicians attacked Psuty's findings. "They said, 'You're threatening the tax base of the towns.' That's what I heard all of the time: 'You take this land out of development, you are threatening the economy.'"

As it happened, Psuty and the regulators had an ally in Governor Brendan Byrne. Like his predecessors, Byrne was hamstrung by the politics of coastal development, which favored development over regulation. But he understood that if developers kept building along the fragile sand dunes, it was going to cost state taxpayers to fix those towns after storms. Like Governor Richard Hughes two decades earlier, Byrne raised the possibility of limiting construction and creating a protective buffer along the oceanfront "to prevent further human suffering and property damage."

In September 1979, Byrne convened a conference on the future of the New Jersey shore. Decrying the privatization of beaches, the governor called for the shore to "truly be a place for everyone." He also cited the destruction of the wetlands, ocean pollution, fish kills, marine-borne red tides, sludge, garbage dumping, and medical waste. Then he proposed "strengthening our controls over construction which threatens sand dunes and beaches."

Byrne was searching for a signature issue he could highlight in his upcoming State of the State address and passed word to DEP officials that he was interested in a bill to protect the sand dunes. The timing proved fortuitous, and David Kinsey decided to go big. "I wrote it aggressively," he said. Instead of limiting state control to the primary dunes lining the oceanfront, Kinsey proposed extending the state's authority to the first paved street parallel to the beach. Depending on local geography, that could include one hundred or even two hundred feet and encompass several rows of houses. Even more provocatively, Kinsey added language that said if a house suffered damage equal to 50 percent or more of its value in a storm, the owner wouldn't be allowed to rebuild. Instead, he or she would have to tear it down and leave the space vacant.

Kinsey said the provision wasn't meant as a provocation. Nor did he see a constitutional issue. The state wasn't seizing the land without compensating the owner, he contended. It was responding to a threat to public safety. "I was trying to protect the public. There was a safety factor. It was in the public interest for that damaged property to be torn down and left vacant."

Byrne asked Robert P. Hollenbeck, a Democrat from Carlstadt, Bergen County, to sponsor the Dune and Shorefront Protection Act. Tellingly, Hollenbeck couldn't find a single cosponsor.

"We learned that it wasn't just local officials and legislators from the CAFRA [coastal] area who opposed the bill," Weingart said. "There were legislators from Bergen County and other counties with summer homes at the shore. A lot of those legislators were skeptical of this bill. One owned property on Long Beach Island."

Not surprisingly, the beach-town mayors were outraged by the dune bill. They thought the issue of control over coastal development had been settled years earlier with the CAFRA legislation. Now here it was surfacing again. Only the dune bill was far more onerous. It usurped their control over zoning and building decisions and gave environmentalists and regulators unprecedented powers over their oceanfronts. By including houses to the first street parallel to the dunes, the state bureaucrats were wildly expanding their reach, the mayors argued. For example, on Long Beach Island, the bill would give the state control to the main boulevard in some locations, covering thousands of bungalows. Many of those houses were small, low-lying cottages vulnerable to storms. In the mayors' view, the best way to deal with them was to allow the storms to weed out the weaker properties—what real estate agents called "clearing the market." Owners could then sell the land or build bigger, safer houses. Under the dune bill, owners wouldn't be able to rebuild, leaving ugly gaps on many streets, which some mayors likened to a jack-o'-lantern effect. Property values would plummet, the mayors added, and tax revenues with them.

The question was, what could the mayors do to stop Kinsey and the DEP? The dune bill was too important to leave to letters, phone calls, and community appeals. It demanded a bigger, more sophisticated plan. Jim Mancini and the Surf City mayor, Len Connors, suggested that the six beach towns on Long Beach Island hire a public relations firm to orchestrate a campaign. Long Beach Township set aside $10,000. Surf City kicked in $9,000. Ship Bottom and Beach Haven each pledged $4,800. The smaller communities of Harvey Cedars and Barnegat Light budgeted $3,300 apiece.

The mayors hired Burson-Marsteller, one of the biggest, most powerful public relations firms in the world, based in New York City. Connors stressed that they needed to move quickly. A public hearing on the bill was scheduled in a few weeks at the St. Francis Community Center in Brant Beach. Burson-Marsteller didn't have much time to put together a plan, marshal local residents, and "rehearse the island mayors," Connors noted.

The message the public relations firm settled on was simple yet inflammatory. The Dune and Shorefront Protection Act was unconstitutional, the consultants argued, usurped the authority of the mayors, and would reduce the value of oceanfront property without compensating the owners. The mayors and local homeowners were prepped; speeches were drafted. Everything was in place.

\\\

The morning of the July 21, 1980, hearing was brutally hot and humid, with the temperature forecast to soar to 102 degrees, a record. By nine o'clock, the large hall at the St. Francis Center was jammed with 1,500 agitated, sweating islanders. Those who couldn't find a folding chair huddled along the side walls, some with their hands balled into fists. Every few minutes, one would hurl a new taunt at Robert Hollenbeck, the chairman of the Senate Energy and Natural Resources Committee, which was holding the hearing. The fifty-five-year-old legislator was prepared. A hearing a week earlier in Toms River had devolved into an angry shouting match between Hollenbeck and the crowd. At one point, the crowd had booed John Weingart off the stage. This time, Hollenbeck was resolved

In July 1980, James J. Mancini, the mayor of Long Beach Township, helped stage a massive protest against the proposed Dune and Shorefront Protection Act.
(Photograph by Ray Fisk / The SandPaper Inc.)

to maintain order. To police the crowd, he'd brought along state troopers, who formed a forbidding line at the rear of the auditorium.

Hollenbeck reminded himself to be patient. But it hurt to be called a stooge and a fool—or even worse, a communist. "Ladies and gentlemen," he shouted, "are we going to proceed or not? That is not really impressing anybody. Just be quiet a moment and we will start the hearing."

But the crowd refused to quiet down.

"Have you ever been to the shore?" demanded one homeowner. "Do you even know where it is?"

"We are not going to have anyone calling out," Hollenbeck instructed.

"You guys are taking over," bellowed another property owner. "We are the taxpayers."

"Excuse me. We are trying to hold a public meeting," Hollenbeck pleaded.

"Mr. Hollenbeck, you know this is an absolute disgrace the way you are running this meeting," a homeowner cried.

Hollenbeck eventually managed to introduce the first witnesses. But he never did gain control of the crowd. A transcript of the session is littered with parenthetical notes, such as "Outburst by audience," "Boos from audience," and "Another outburst by audience."

The first two witnesses followed the prepared script, attacking the dune bill as unnecessary and unconstitutional. Hazel Gluck, a state lawmaker who would later run New Jersey's first lottery, accused the DEP of thievery "in the guise of protecting the environment."

When it was David Kinsey's turn to speak, he stressed that DEP was trying to save lives and property, directing development away from the beaches "and in a manner that is proper so that development will withstand the fury of the ocean."

"That is not true," shouted a member of the audience.

"Long Beach Island is a barrier island," replied Kinsey. "It is a narrow strip of moving sand. That is where we are today. It is a narrow strip of land between the sea and the land."

"It has been moving for 450 years," the audience member shouted back.

Kinsey pointed out that Tucker's Island, a small spit of sand with a hotel off the southern tip of the island, had vanished beneath the bay decades ago. "It is not there anymore," he said. Provocatively, Kinsey then suggested that the mayors and property owners had "missed the boat" after the Ash Wednesday Storm in 1962 by failing to build more sensibly. As a result, they were at risk.

"It is not a question of if a storm will come," he warned. "It is *when* the storm will come, because a storm will come." A prohibition on new building was the only way to break the "historic cycle of building and rebuilding publicly subsidized structures at publicly subsidized hazardous locations," he concluded.

At this point, the audience exploded in a chorus of boos.

The mayors spoke next and spared little in their attacks.

"Hello there, freedom fighters," cried Lloyd Behmke, the mayor of Barnegat Light, a gentrified fishing village on the northern end of Long Beach Island.

"We are not going to be playing to the crowd," warned Hollenbeck.

"I am going to tell you some things that you don't even know," retorted Behmke. "You people come down here with your big pocketbooks. You'd better get off your duff. Come down here and see what we are doing.

"This 'Dune Destruction Act' is a brainchild of the governor," Behmke continued. "Given the power he now possesses, he believes he is a missionary of God, put here to protect this mainland and North Jersey. The dune experts are the mayors on this island who have lived through all these tough storms.

"Are we going to leave this island, folks?" Behmke roared.

"Mayor, we are not running a rally here," Hollenbeck interjected.

"Are we going to fight for our rights?"

"Yes," the audience shouted.

The next speaker was Surf City's Leonard Connors, a large, gruff construction worker and fisherman. "Provisions of this legislation have deeply offended the sensibilities of thousands of the working men and women of this state who have moved and invested in seashore property," he began. "There you have it . . . the Department of Environmental Protection is asking your help in turning the people you see here today into America's boat people, disenfranchised and dislocated by their own elected representatives."

Rather than worrying about the dunes, the state bureaucracy should be trying "to correct these problems, not trying to devise ways of depriving honest taxpaying people of their homes and property," Connors said. "Having lived on this island and been present during every major storm in the last quarter century, I can honestly say that I would rather take my chances here during a storm than walk some of the high-crime-area streets of this state!

"I refuse to submit to the bureaucracy that wants to enlarge itself through this legislation and to the bleeding-hearts and do-gooders that seek to deprive us of our homes under the guise of protection."

Now it was Jim Mancini's turn. The mayor of Long Beach Township rose to denounce the "absolutely catastrophic effect" that the dune bill would have on beach towns. "First, the property values it will diminish or destroy," he declared. "Second, it will cut into the tax base. Third, it will hurt the local tourism economy and result in lost jobs. Fourth, it will drive people away from the island."

Mancini estimated the island's year-round population was fourteen thousand and predicted it would continue to grow as retirees flocked there and converted their bungalows into year-round residences. The dune bill threatened to turn the island into a ghost town, he said.

"Keep in mind that your act would create a dislocation of families and retirees; financial loss and, in many cases, financial ruin; and literally the extinction of an entire segment of the economy," Mancini exclaimed.

Mancini concluded by pointing out how safe the island was. "We have been through everything here," he said. "We have been through hurricanes, the 1962 storm—we have been through it all. Take a look at our beach. I would appreciate your taking a ride along our beach. We have no problems here. We have a beautiful community. We have no problem. This bill has absolutely no merit, no merit whatsoever. There is nothing factual or good about it."

\\\

After the hearing, Jim Mancini punched a hand in the air and announced, "We won, we won."

Behmke told a reporter that the hearing was like the story of David and Goliath, proclaiming that they had slain Goliath.

"I was friendly with them," Kinsey recalled. "But their attitude was, these little mayors stopped the big, bad state."

Hollenbeck retreated to a nearby restaurant with his platoon of state troopers. A few weeks later, he and Byrne abandoned the dune bill for good. Not long thereafter, Hollenbeck was voted out of office.

Ken Smith, a local real estate agent and property rights activist, warned the state not to try to take their property again: "If we ever see anything like that original bill again, the gloves are coming off," he told a reporter for *The Asbury Park Press*. "We will expose the DEP and anyone who supports them as the land-grabbing fools they are."

\\\

Four years after the hearing at St. Francis, several oceanfront homes in Brant Beach were close to toppling into the ocean. The area, only blocks from Jim

Mancini's municipal office, had a long history of losing sand. The mayor ordered the township's bulldozers to push sand up the beach to form a temporary barricade, and then he applied to the Department of Environmental Protection for a $100,000 grant to cover the costs of dumping more sand on the eroding shoreline. A team of federal hazard experts visited Mancini a few weeks later and suggested "that no further building be allowed seaward of Ocean Avenue [the road immediately behind the primary dunes] until further studies can be conducted in this area to determine the cause of erosion and steps to mitigate it." Mancini maintained that the erosion was limited and that the island's beaches were still in good shape.

Not long afterward, Tom Kean, sponsor of the ill-fated CAFRA legislation and now the governor of New Jersey, proposed creating a statewide coastal commission to guide growth at the shore. In introducing his proposal, Kean advised the mayors that it was foolish to spend millions of tax dollars on eroding beaches and damaged roads without a plan. "It's like going to the dentist to get your teeth filled, only to go home and refuse to brush and floss."

The mayors weren't amused. Once again, they went into action. Another rally was staged at the St. Francis Center attracting a standing-room-only crowd. Len Connors accused Kean of wanting to turn Long Beach Island into a public park. It was 1962 all over again, he fulminated. The state wanted to create a buffer zone and stop homeowners from rebuilding after storms. "The bill is guided by people who want to take your property away," he warned the crowd.

Initially, Jim Mancini supported the commission as a way for the beach towns to work together to address another problem: needles and other medical waste that had begun washing up on the beaches and was now hurting tourism. But after homeowners complained that a state commission would hurt their property, Mancini pivoted against Kean's proposed commission. What was needed was a different commission "to protect us against the people in the DEP who want us off the island," he declared.

Like most of the earlier proposals to govern development, the state commission proposal died before it reached the floor for a vote. Decades later, the idea of a coastal commission surfaced again after Hurricane Sandy. But Governor Chris Christie quickly rebuffed the idea. "We don't need new government, more government," he said. "No, that won't happen under me."

\\\

In 1993, reformers made one final attempt to bolster the state's control over its eroding sand dunes and beaches. That year, the New Jersey General Assembly passed a series of amendments to plug the loophole in the original CAFRA legislation decades earlier that had resulted in nearly unchecked development at the coast. The new threshold set a trigger of two units instead of the original twenty-five.

The new rule expanded the Department of Environmental Protection's authority at the coast and was a useful tool for regulating condominiums and medium-size developments. But most construction along the oceanfront dunes and the first few rows of homes behind the dunes involved single-family houses, not condominiums or motels.

There was still "a huge loophole," said Kinsey, who was out of government by this point. "Whenever there is a threshold, someone will try to do things under the threshold. If the threshold is two, most will build one. That certainly is the case along the oceanfront."

In fact, not long after the 1993 rule passed, there was a surge of building along the dunes and oceanfront, said Mark Mauriello, a planner who was in charge of DEP's land-use division at the time, and later served as the agency's commissioner. "It was huge. There was a race to get permits, and we saw this big spike. Contractors couldn't get enough pilings [for foundations] there was so much demand."

The new rule included a controversial provision that gave homeowners an absolute right to rebuild after hurricanes and nor'easters. The provision was viewed as a compromise to placate the beach-town mayors and oceanfront homeowners. But it allowed homeowners to erect new houses in the same dangerous locations after storms, and there was nothing the state could do.

"What it meant was that all of these towns on the oceanfront and bays were calling the shots on how they managed their beaches," Mauriello said. "While we had all of these great policies and plans, we didn't have the statutory authority to regulate. There was this huge disconnect between policy and plans. As a result, it was kind of the Wild West at the coast.

"The mentality of the mayors after storms is that everything goes back where it was," Mauriello continued. "They have this weird notion that the government will always be there to protect them. There will always be these spigots of money. It was the same after Sandy. It was a rush to get back as quickly as they could."

When coastal regulators suggested slowing development, the mayors' default response was always to say no. "We'd always get a lot of pushback," Mauriello said. "It didn't matter if we were providing a tremendous benefit to their communities. Towns didn't like us telling them how to develop. Our argument was, if we're giving you taxpayer money, you have an obligation. They didn't want to hear it."

The story of New Jersey's failures to manage building at the beach and along its coastal waterways mirrors the larger story of the nation's coasts. Time and again, private interests and money have trumped sound environmental policies and public interests, whether it is restricting access to the beach or limiting risky development.

To Robert Young, one of the nation's best-known coastal geologists and director of the Program for Developed Shorelines at Western Carolina University, there is no point even talking about sea-level rise and its future effects, "as long as we're still trying to draw lines in the sand and increasing construction in harm's way. Let's talk about storms. Let's talk about flooding. Let's talk about fiscal responsibility."

In a study in the journal *Ocean and Coastal Management*, the geologist William J. Neal and his colleagues concluded that the laws and regulations intended to protect the coast are riddled with so many loopholes and gaps that they can't possibly work. The result is what he calls a "tyranny of small decisions," allowing development in high-hazard coastal zones. Some of the failures are documented by researchers; "however, most occur at the local level and only get local media attention. Backroom politics, the dynamics of wealthy stakeholders' influence, and midnight calls to the governor's office to get permit denials overturned," Neal concluded.

Mauriello puts it even more starkly: "We missed the opportunity. It's done. All of these opportunities to do creative things, it's too late. We're done."

8

Tipping Point

JIM MANCINI WAS FINISHED BUILDING. While he'd managed to get out of the ill-timed Fawn Lakes development, he was struggling financially, according to his son Joe, who succeeded his father as mayor of Long Beach Township.

"It was a terrible hardship," Joe said. "For the following fifteen years, I owned every house my dad and mom lived in. I probably paid off all of his debts; probably one and a half million dollars."

Mancini focused on politics and arranging funds for his favorite causes. He helped raise funds for a hospital in Manahawkin, the local community center, and public libraries. "He saw himself as a public servant," Joe said, as well as the first line of defense in the battles with environmentalists and state regulators. Yet even as he relentlessly promoted his beloved home, Long

Beach Island and Mancini were changing. The quiet family atmosphere that Jim revered was vanishing. The island was crowded, busier, and louder. One after another, his cherished bungalows were being scuttled for five- or six-bedroom mansions. On weekends, cars now backed up for miles waiting to get across the bridge.

"Dad was a cape guy, like the Shapiros," his son explained. "He didn't like the new McMansions that were going up. He felt they were changing the character of the place, making it less affordable, less of a family resort."

Jim remained solidly pro-business and continued to fight attempts to restrict development. But he was now willing to "toss a bone" to state regulators every so often to keep them at bay. In the 1980s, he limited the amount of space on a typical forty- or fifty-foot lot that could be used for building. It wasn't a perfect solution to the problem of crowding; developers added more space on second and third stories, blocking the views of the neighbors' smaller houses. "We are in danger of losing everything we have," Mancini told the unhappy builders. "This is a bone I am throwing to the state of New Jersey."

When Joe Mancini set out on his own as a developer, in 1980, he chose to specialize in the emerging market for large, custom beach houses. It was what younger buyers were demanding, he told his father. They wanted bigger houses and all the modern amenities of their year-round homes back in the suburbs. The decision put Joe and his father at odds.

"When I opened up, I just wanted to build semi-custom houses," Joe said. "I tried very hard not to compete with my dad. But he'd come into the office and tell me not to block the view [of his smaller bungalows]. He got very angry when I built a two-thousand-square-foot house with a rooftop deck next to one of his six-hundred-square-foot capes. Dad said I ruined the neighborhood. I said, 'Pop, in a few years that's what people will want. He didn't talk to me for a few years. But then we cleaned it up and went back to being father and son."

Perhaps the changes were more pronounced on Long Beach Island. But similar shifts were occurring from Calabash, Maine, to Calabash, North Carolina; from Myrtle Beach, South Carolina, to Miami Beach, Florida; from Sanibel Island, Florida, to Surfside, Texas. The 1980s saw a rush to the beach fueled by ballooning stock prices and investment portfolios. The excess of money ushered in a New Gilded Age at the beach, with ever-larger and more lavish houses. It also changed the expectations of homeowners. A beach house was no longer viewed as a place to hang a towel before heading to the beach; it was considered an asset, with a steady, virtually guaranteed return. Of course, bigger houses and higher prices also changed the calculus of who could afford to live at the beach—or even rent a house for a week or two.

Folly Beach, once a hangout for hippies and blue-collar workers near Charleston, began bulldozing old clapboard bungalows and replacing them with duplexes and beach mansions. Rents and land values soared. Longtime residents either decided to cash out or, in some cases, were driven away by higher taxes and other costs. Recently, the town has tried to retain its dwindling year-round population by offering homeowners discounts on their taxes, but it hasn't helped much, according to the town manager. The older residents and families keep moving out.

In his important 2012 book, *The Land Was Ours*, Andrew W. Kahrl, a professor of history and African American studies at the University of Virginia, points out that money, land fever, and greed are not an entirely new phenomenon at the coast. Following the end of slavery, he notes, African Americans owned or visited beaches in Maryland, North Carolina, the Low Country of South Carolina, and the Gulf Coast. But as the modern coast developed in the 1920s, greed, racism, and political pressure forced many of these families from their modest bungalows. In 1933, the resort of Wrightsville Beach in North Carolina went so far as to pass ordinances preventing blacks from walking on the beach and boardwalk. Nearby Carolina Beach included language in deeds preventing blacks from owning beachfront property. Kahrl blames "coastal capitalism," along with the powerful forces of segregation, for driving away African American families and transforming the coasts into "whites-only summer destinations."

\\\

By the mid-1980s, the rapidly rising cost of land at the coast motivated homeowners to build bigger houses to maximize their investments. Real estate

During an epic construction boom between 1960 and 2000, Long Beach Island added nearly fifteen thousand houses and businesses, filling nearly every lot from the ocean to the bay.
(Courtesy of the U.S. Army Corps of Engineers)

records highlight the trend: In the 1960s, the average size of a Long Beach Island bungalow was about 600 square feet. The following decade, it grew to 1,000 square feet. In the 1980s, it crept up to about 1,500 square feet and then 2,000 square feet. After Hurricane Sandy wrecked the island, the average size of a new house swelled to over 3,000 square feet, which is about 500 square feet larger than the typical American house in the suburbs.

The overall value of island property surged along with the rising land values. In 1962, when the Ash Wednesday Storm leveled the oceanfront, all

the property on the 18-mile barrier island was worth about $100 million. By 1980, land and property were worth $2 billion. By mid-decade, a land bubble saw values soar to $6 billion. Today, following several more bubbles, the 19,000 houses and businesses on the island are assessed at $15 billion, with the actual market value likely a billion or two higher.

The economics at the beach inverted as well. Instead of houses costing more than the sand beneath them, the sand rapidly became more valuable than the houses. For example, a typical Shapiro bungalow might be assessed for

As property values at the beach soar, the houses along the oceanfront grow larger and larger, with the average beach house now larger than a house in the suburbs. (Photograph by the author)

$40,000, while the sand beneath it was worth $400,000, ten times higher. It was assumed the purchaser was buying the land, not the house, which would be torn down and replaced with a larger retreat. It's no wonder a town commissioner in nearby Avalon boasted that the sand along the town's oceanfront was more valuable than gold or platinum.

Joe Mancini told me it is a matter of supply and demand. There is so little open space left on Long Beach Island, the value of the existing land goes up sharply. "The number one reason for the increase is that God isn't making any more oceanfront," he said.

But oddly, the prices of the houses don't appear to account for the risk of living in a floodplain. The oceanfront along much of Long Beach Island has been eroding for decades, in some spots precipitously. Yet buyers (and tax assessors) place a premium on these riskiest, most vulnerable properties, exposed to waves and storm surge because of the views. Conversely, properties located farther inland, and presumably safer, sell for considerably less.

It took a while to sort all this out, but then it hit me in a flash. The buyers and assessors weren't factoring risk into their decisions. Many owners had federal flood insurance or were wealthy enough to build a new home if their current house got knocked down. Federal taxpayers were also spending tens of millions to widen the damaged beaches in front of these oceanfront houses. So it was the best of both worlds. The owners got to enjoy their ocean views and rising property values while the government socialized some of the risks.

It is actually possible to trace the tipping point when Long Beach Island became unaffordable for all but the rich. In 1985, property values jumped threefold. But then prices continued steadily upward, climbing in lockstep with the stock market and financial boom. Much of the new money flowing onto the island was from Wall Street. "My typical guy comes down after he sells his company, or in December when the bonuses are handed out. That's when my phone begins to ring," Joe Mancini told me. "I have hedge fund guys, guys from tech—a guy from Google just bought a house from me—Goldman Sachs. I tell them they can get a nice oceanfront home here from three million to ten million dollars. The Hamptons will cost thirty million. People realize it is the same water."

The surge of more and bigger money also brings inflated expectations. One island mayor told me the story of a wealthy renter who was unhappy with the weather. "He was paying thousands of dollars for a week at the beach and he came into the office to complain about the weather. He wanted me to do something. I looked at him and said, 'What do you want me to do? You want me to stop the rain?'"

Tellingly, as prices, taxes, and other costs soared, Long Beach Island began emptying out. In 1980, when Jim Mancini was battling the state over the right to build along the oceanfront, he told regulators the local population would double by the year 2000, to 28,000, as baby boomers reached retirement age and moved to the shore year-round. But that surge never materialized. In fact, the year-round population of Long Beach Island (and many other shore communities) has plummeted to about 7,000 as families sell or are priced out and wealthy investors gobble up more of the real estate.

In winter, Long Beach Island takes on an abandoned, ghostly feeling, with row after row of blackened houses. There are fewer year-round workers, fewer families, and far fewer schoolchildren. The island once sponsored four Little League teams. Now it doesn't have enough kids for one. A few years ago, Long Beach Township tore up its field and replaced it with pickleball courts favored by the elderly.

Even in the middle of the summer, the island sometimes feels empty. With both mom and dad working and the kids off at sports camps or polishing their college applications, those big, lavish beach houses go unused. Business owners complain that the workweek is shrinking. Business might be heavy on the weekends, "but the rest of the week we stand around and look at one another," said Joey Rulli, the owner of three popular pizza shops.

"You can get a reservation at any restaurant during the middle of the week," Joe Mancini said. "You can shoot a gun in the middle of the street and you won't hit anyone."

\\\

In a 1994 newspaper interview, Jim Mancini expressed regret over some of his earlier decisions. It had been a mistake allowing developers to gouge the environmentally fragile wetlands, he told a reporter for *The Asbury Park Press*. "No question, 25 years ago I was much more supportive of development than I would be today." If someone tried to fill a wetland today, Mancini said, he would fight them "tooth and nail. We saved the island just in time. What we want to do [now] is in the opposite direction of commercialization."

But the elder Mancini continued to downplay climate change and sea-level rise, insisting he would "just add an inch" of sand every year if the water came up. The word "retreat" remained an obscenity in his vocabulary, and he continued to poke at the geologist Orrin Pilkey, calling him a phony and a fraud. But after years of denial, Mancini now acknowledged that the beaches on Long Beach Island were shrinking, and he became a tireless advocate for large-scale, federally funded beach replenishment projects. "We have to nourish the beaches every year," he said. "We have to bring in some fill, and we have to keep doing it. It's not a waste. Money beats the ocean."

Mancini lobbied members of Congress for a multimillion-dollar project for his island, working closely with the state's delegation, including the Ocean County representative James Saxton. In the mid-1990s, Congress allocated funds for an Army Corps of Engineers study of erosion on Long Beach Island. However, money for the actual repair work took nearly a decade to secure. Finally, on November 19, 2003, Saxton announced that Congress had approved the funds to begin pumping sand. But the news arrived too late for Mancini. He passed away from cancer earlier that very day.

The mayor's funeral was held a few days later at St. Francis Roman Catholic Church, adjacent to the community center in Brant Beach, where the hearings on the dune bill had taken place decades earlier. Over a thousand people came. Many others who couldn't get in congregated outside on the steps. "It was a sign of how beloved he was," Joe Mancini said. "We could have 'waked' him all day. Another thousand people would have come."

Dozens of vehicles formed a procession along Long Beach Boulevard. There were police cars, fire trucks, and other emergency vehicles. Jim Mancini was finally leaving the island for good, but he would never call it a retreat.

\\\

Joe Mancini took over as mayor of Long Beach Township in 2008, and he has held the position ever since. He is sixty-eight but appears younger, with salt-and-pepper hair, which brushes his freshly laundered shirt collar, and a bristling mustache. In some ways, the trajectory of his career has mimicked the arc of the modern coast, from a restless assistant building modest bungalows alongside his father to a developer of lavish confections glistening along the oceanfront dunes. Like his father, Joe is unapologetically pro-business and isn't particularly fond of state environmental regulators. "It takes you six months to get a simple permit from them," he complained. "I can build a beautiful five-bedroom house in less time."

Joe is both mayor and developer, but pointed out that he closely follows the rules. "Look, I'm a developer—that's my business. I'm not going to stop being a developer because I'm mayor. Do I do things that push the limits? I don't need to. In fact, I'm very careful to make sure to avoid anything that strays toward a conflict. At my age, I don't need to wake up some morning and see my name stripped across the top of the paper."

Joe is a strong personality and doesn't always censor his comments, which rubs some of his critics the wrong way. He has had run-ins with some homeowners in Holgate who feel they have been ignored in favor of those in wealthier sections of the township. But when I mentioned this, Joe said he "would be nuts" to ignore the southern end of the island. "It is growing like crazy, especially after Sandy." In fact, Joe's real estate company has been busy in Holgate and built an entire new street with a dozen million-dollar houses. He attributed the complaints to a handful of disgruntled homeowners.

During Sandy, Joe got into a row with Governor Chris Christie over the pace of the recovery. Joe wanted to move quickly, but Christie wasn't responding fast enough for him. Some testy telephone conversations and emails followed. At one point, Christie called Joe "Peachy," as in, "Aren't you just peachy?" Joe was about to send the governor a basket of peaches, but restrained himself. During one of the governor's numerous, heavily scripted town halls after Sandy, Christie banished Joe to a back bench as punishment.

It should be pointed out that Mancini was praised by local businesses and homeowners for cutting red tape, speeding up permit approvals, and passing ordinances encouraging homeowners to build back quickly after the epic storm. Christie, on the other hand, was criticized for losing interest in the recovery and frequently traveling out of state to campaign for the 2016 presidency while more than five thousand families were still struggling to return to their homes, most in poorer communities on the bays.

In July 2016, Joe offered me a tour of one of his high-end properties on 34th Street in Long Beach Township, not far from his real estate business. It was a double lot on ninety feet of prime oceanfront. Joe bought the property for $1.99 million, tore it down, and then built a large brick-and-wood mansion on spec, listing it for $4.9 million.

"The market for two-million-plus-dollar houses is a little slow at the moment," he said as we hiked up the paved driveway. Nevertheless, Joe was optimistic. A managing director at Goldman Sachs had visited the site three times and was scheduled to call him later that day. Half a dozen workers from Joe's real estate company were there staging an open house. One was putting out cheese and grapes. Another showed me around while Joe checked the arrangements. There were five bedrooms and five full baths along with two powder rooms, gleaming quartz and marble counters, floor-to-ceiling-window views, an elevator, and a two-car garage. Joe had told me earlier that he likes to design, and elaborate houses like this one allow him to stroke his ego. "I try to do one a year," he said.

Wandering by an oceanfront window, I noticed a small pocket pool built into the second-story deck. The water mirrored the blue sky. I remembered something Joe had said earlier about the pools: "I guess it's so they can sit there and enjoy the ocean without actually going in it." But it wasn't the pool that had first captured my attention. It was the brand-new beach extending from the house to the ocean. The Army Corps of Engineers and their contractors had spent weeks pumping sand there and then had groomed the beach so it looked almost natural. This particular phase of the island-wide project was costing $130 million—all of it covered by federal taxpayers in Kansas and other far-flung states, who probably wished they had a pocket pool or an ocean to cool off in during the dog days of summer.

"Wow," I murmured as I turned aside.

"Isn't it beautiful?" my guide agreed.

I am pretty sure she meant the pool. But I was thinking about something else: how much a shiny new beach must add to the value of a house with a million-dollar view.

\\\

Unlike his dad, Joe Mancini believes the seas are rising. He lives along Barnegat Bay, which has risen by over a foot in the last century, and now routinely floods the streets with standing water, even in ordinary summer thunderstorms. But, like his father, Joe for years believed that Long Beach Island was prepared to withstand a bad storm. Building codes were stronger. More houses were elevated above flood stage. Many oceanfront houses were secured by pilings buried deep beneath the sand.

A storm like the Ash Wednesday nor'easter "would take a couple of homes, but not as many as it did then," he told reporters on the fiftieth anniversary of the historic storm, in March 2012.

But just seven months later, Hurricane Sandy inundated the island, leveling the sand dunes, undermining scores of elevated homes, filling others with sand to the eaves, ripping apart bottom floors, and gutting roads and utilities, while flooding thousands of houses along Barnegat Bay, including Joe's, which suffered about $20,000 in damage.

Early the next morning, Joe commandeered a four-wheel-drive vehicle and made his way down the beach to the southern tip of the island. "It looked like '62," he told me. "I never thought I would see anything like that again in my life. But Sandy looked just like it—worse. We were living it again."

He estimated the damage to the island at $1 billion. By my count, the damage was probably closer to $700 million, including over $200 million in federal flood payments. But that doesn't include the cost of a new $350 million bridge replacing the old causeway connecting the mainland and the island, which was in the works before the storm.

Nearly every house along the bay, from the bridge to Beach Haven, roughly seven miles altogether, took on several feet of briny water. Thousands of first floors had to be taken down to the studs, with the insulation and wiring ripped out. Walls that weren't replaced filled with mold, rotting from the inside out. Mountains of trash littered the streets for weeks. It cost federal taxpayers tens of millions to haul it away, millions more to remove the sand from the roads, run it through a giant mechanical strainer, and place it back on the beach.

One of the more apocryphal stories I heard about involved a river of pavers that flooded one of the Holgate marshes. Many homeowners along the oceanfront had paved their driveways with expensive bricks. The driveways looked nice but acted as funnels for water during Sandy. In fact, one of the reasons the island floods so often is that the water can't drain because of the hard surfaces. Afterward, I asked the township's construction officer why she allowed the pavers. She told me they were "grandfathered in," under existing ordinances. Homeowners were allowed to pave up to 75 percent of their lots. It made no sense, but there was nothing she could do, she said. Sure enough, the homeowners repaved their sloping driveways after Sandy.

Perhaps most remarkably, this was only one island. There were scores of other islands, peninsulas, estuaries, headlands, and bays in Sandy's path. Most were like Long Beach Island, crowded with pricey real estate only feet above sea level. The cost of rebuilding would be extraordinary, billions and billions. The only silver lining in the disaster—if you could call it that—was that they would get help. They always got help, lots and lots of help.

PART III

Disaster Capitalism: Catastrophes, Subsidies, and Bailouts

Blow, winds, and crack your cheeks! rage! blow!
You cataracts and hurricanes, spout
Till you have drench'd our steeples, drown'd the cocks!
—WILLIAM SHAKESPEARE, *KING LEAR*

Acts of God and Man

AS A YOUNG BOY, Kerry Emanuel grew up in the landlocked suburbs of Philadelphia, not far from Long Beach Island. But when he was ten, his family moved to Palm Beach, Florida, a few blocks from the beach. There, Emanuel became fascinated by the late-afternoon thunderstorms that formed over the Atlantic Ocean. The billowing white and gray plumes appeared with surprising regularity along the horizon; as did the furious bursts of wind and gushers of rain that briefly turned day into night, and then quickly back again into day.

Emanuel grasped that the storms must have something to do with the soaring afternoon temperatures and tropical humidity, but exactly what, he couldn't say. From the beach, it appeared as if the storms soaked up the warm surface water and sprayed it inside the clouds, like a funnel. But was that even possible? Was the ocean a form of fuel?

In time, Emanuel turned his curiosity into a heralded career as an atmospheric and climate scientist. He earned both his undergraduate and graduate degrees in earth science at MIT, and other than a brief hiatus teaching at UCLA, he has spent nearly four decades in Cambridge, Massachusetts. His office is just a Frisbee toss from the Charles River, which is rising a little every year and slowly threatening the campus. "I'm actually on a committee that is looking at what we can do about flooding," he said.

Today, the sixty-three-year-old Emanuel is widely recognized as one of the nation's leading climate researchers and foremost experts on hurricanes. He has published more than two hundred peer-reviewed papers and several books, including an engaging and richly detailed history of hurricanes, *Divine Wind*.

Hurricanes are examples of the sublimely brute physical force of nature. They are essentially furnaces, Emanuel writes, feeding off the oceans, warm at their cores but even hotter near their tops. "This great warmth is one consequence of the enormous amount of heat sucked out of the ocean by the storm. On the other hand, there is very little change in temperature as you move in toward the eye along the surface of the water."

Over the last few decades, scientists have gotten far smarter at understanding and predicting hurricanes. They now have computer models, satellite images, and algorithms to help them craft their forecasts. In 2012, one model predicted that Hurricane Sandy would make an abrupt left-hand turn at the coast of New Jersey, *eight days* before it actually made landfall near Atlantic City. And yet, despite all the sophisticated models and math, forecasts are still largely an educated guess. Hundreds of small and large variables—from ocean temperatures to the amount of friction on the water surface to whether a hurricane encounters a wall of dry air to the geological contours of the ocean bottom—can abruptly alter a hurricane's track or dampen its intensity. Is a hurricane speeding up (Michael, 2018) or slowing down (Florence, 2018) as it approaches land? Are the sea-surface temperatures in the lower Caribbean historically warm (2017) or cool (2018)? Is there wind shear in the path of a storm, or are the nearby winds calm? In the busy 2017 hurricane season, warmer ocean temperatures and favorable wind conditions helped foster a surplus of catastrophic storms. Conversely, the 2018 hurricane season started out slowly, with no storms for months because of the unusually cold water in the tropical Atlantic and Caribbean seas and an excess of wind shear. Then, in the meteorological equivalent of a New York minute, the Atlantic basin exploded with four named storms within days in the second week of September, including Hurricane Florence, which resulted in torrential rainfall and flooding in North and South Carolina. A few weeks later, in October, Hurricane Michael, a Category 5 hurricane, barreled into the Florida Panhandle at Mexico Beach, near Panama City.

Florence and Michael are examples of a new, surprising evolution in hurricanes, in which storms explode in size and power in a matter of days or even hours in the warmer, favorable conditions in the Atlantic and the Gulf of Mexico. Florence grew in size from a Category 1 storm to a Category 4 storm, with 140-mile-per-hour winds. Michael exploded from a tropical storm to a Category 5 hurricane, with 155-mile-per-hour winds. The fact that storms are intensifying so quickly worries researchers because it challenges their predicting capabilities and makes it harder to track potential impacts. Some, including the geologist Robert Young, called for scrapping the current hurricane rating system, which is based on wind speeds, in favor of a new system that takes rainfall and flooding into account.

In the early 1970s, when he was still a student, Emanuel found himself struggling with the prevailing explanation that hurricanes emerged from a clumping of thunderstorms in a given region. It made no sense to him. "There was no reason why wind should blow stronger in a clump," he said. So he looked backward and rediscovered research papers from the 1940s concluding that hurricanes were powered by the evaporation of seawater. "I kind of finished what they started," he told me.

Emanuel is boyishly handsome, with long, dark hair liberally streaked with gray. He is not averse to publicity but, unlike some of his colleagues, doesn't seek it out. He tolerates interviews, but finds many reporters ill-informed, and too quick to attribute every meteorological quirk to climate change. It is exactly the wrong way to think about the complicated nature of hurricanes and storms, he said. The smarter questions would be to ask how likely it is that climate change is contributing to a particular hurricane and what percentage of a hurricane is likely being caused by climate change.

Not that Emanuel doubts the potential for climate change to impact hurricanes and other weather events. His own computer models predict as much. For decades, he has warned that future hurricanes may increase in size and intensity by nearly half if temperatures continue to rise from humans pumping greenhouse gas into the atmosphere. We are probably already seeing the effects in storms like Hurricane Harvey, which dumped sixty inches of rain on Houston and its suburbs. "It is simple physics," Emanuel pointed out. Higher temperatures produce more water vapor, saturating the atmosphere. "If you have more water in the atmosphere, the storm will rain more."

We are likely to see more catastrophic storms as the climate warms because, theoretically, hurricanes can have more power, he added. Even if humans were to suddenly stop pumping carbon dioxide, the long-lived greenhouse gas, into the atmosphere, it will take centuries to dissipate. In the meantime, the planet will continue to heat up, producing conditions favorable for calamitous storms.

Over history, oceans warm and cool, and temperatures vary. But the current trend is clear: the planet is warming at an alarming rate, disrupting harvests, fueling wildfires, and spurring both droughts and floods. Seventeen of the eighteen warmest years since modern record-keeping began have occurred since 2001. And while many scientists are reluctant to attribute the accelerating temperatures to the recent surplus of catastrophic hurricanes, there appears to be a correlation. Consider that over two-thirds of all hurricane damage in the last century, costing $725 billion, by my count, has occurred in the last two decades, or the same period of escalating temperatures.

So what can be done? Orrin Pilkey suggests getting out of the way. Emanuel focuses on ending financial incentives and government programs that reward bad decisions. "Stop rewarding risky choices," he said.

In July 2006, Emanuel and eight other prominent climate researchers published a surprising statement on the "U.S. hurricane problem." But instead of focusing on climate change, they wrote, policymakers should address "the ever-growing concentration of population and wealth in vulnerable coastal regions."

The researchers then pivoted to the question of risk. "Rapidly escalating hurricane damage in recent decades owes much to government policies that serve to subsidize risk," not to mention "political pressures that hold down [flood insurance] premiums in risky coastal areas." While disaster aid provides humanitarian benefits, they wrote, it also serves "to promote risky behavior in the long run."

Market forces and risk signals at the coast are clearly distorted, Emanuel said. Low interest rates and myriad subsidies encourage property owners to build larger, more lavish houses close to the water, and then to demand help after storms. "Ironically, some of the strongest proponents of free markets support the demands of wealthy coastal homeowners. It results in a big income transfer from the poor to the rich."

Emanuel isn't optimistic that government spending to help coastal communities adapt to sea-level rise and climate change will alter the calculus dramatically. As long as the world is awash in carbon, rising water and more explosive hurricanes will continue to overwhelm coastal defenses. A smarter approach would be to build smaller, cheaper houses, he suggested. "That's what they do in the Philippines and Taiwan, which are battered every year by bigger typhoons. You see a handful of fortresses built for a Category 5 [typhoon]. Everything else is a shanty, plywood shacks so poor people can go out there, nothing of value. Every few years, they blow away, and so what? It's a pretty smart adaptation, actually."

It isn't likely Americans will begin building tiny houses at the beach anytime soon. Not until the land bubble bursts, anyway. In the meantime, Emanuel said, the government should eliminate or reduce subsidies that encourage reckless development and drive up disaster costs. "It's a fraught issue politically. But the whole system is highly irrational," he said.

9

Federalizing Disasters

IT IS THE PECULIAR NATURE of hurricanes that they are both uncommon and utterly predictable. Depending on an island's geography, it may have a one-in-ten chance of being hit, or a one-in-a-thousand chance. Those are only odds, of course, but they are important because hurricanes are best understood as numbers and probabilities. Some areas are simply more vulnerable than others—Southeast Florida, Puerto Rico, the Florida Panhandle, and the Gulf states of Mississippi, Louisiana, and Texas. While you may reassure yourself that you have only a one-in-a-hundred chance of being leveled by a devastating storm in a given year, it's highly likely that there will be a hurricane in one of these geographies, and someone's house will be destroyed.

Moreover, the chances appear to be increasing, though not necessarily for the reasons you might imagine. Even accounting for years with lots of hurricanes, including 2004, 2005, 2017, and 2018, the number of hurricanes has held relatively steady for centuries, dating back to the founding of the nation. What has changed is the amount of property at the coast, which amplifies the opportunities for damage and the likelihood that federal taxpayers will spend ever-larger sums to help coastal towns rebuild after hurricanes.

In July 2014, the National Academy of Sciences, a nonprofit arm of the federal government that helps fund and direct critical research in medicine, engineering, and the social sciences, reported the findings of a yearlong study of coastal risks. Damages from hurricanes and nor'easters have "increased substantially over the past century," the researchers noted, "largely due to increases in population and development in hazardous coastal areas." The chief beneficiaries of the land boom at the coast have been the beach towns and property owners who perversely shoulder little of the risk of building in harm's way yet enjoy most of the wealth, the report added.

Critically, the report, *Reducing Coastal Risk on the East and Gulf Coasts*, observed that there is "no central leadership, unified vision," or national strategy to reduce the costs associated with hurricanes. The preponderance of federal funding is paid out after storms, with scant attention to zoning or land-use issues, buyouts, or retreat from vulnerable floodplains. "Over the past century, most coastal management programs have emphasized coastal armoring, while doing little to decrease development in harm's way," the report concluded.

A 2018 study by Philip J. Klotzbach, an atmospheric scientist and hurricane expert, associated with Colorado State University, made many of these same points. "Growth in coastal population and regional wealth are the overwhelming drivers of observed increases in hurricane-related damage. As the population and wealth of the United States has increased in coastal locations, it has invariably led to growth in exposure and vulnerability of coastal property along the U.S. Gulf and East coasts," Klotzbach and several colleagues wrote.

To paraphrase the words of the Clinton-era campaign strategist James Carville, It's the property, stupid.

\\\

In the last two decades, hurricanes and coastal storms have caused over three-quarters of a trillion dollars in damage at the coast—far more than earthquakes, tornadoes, and wildfires combined. That represents a nearly sixfold increase from the prior two decades (1980–1990), as well as most of the hurricane damage in the last century ($725 billion of $1.2 trillion), after adjusting for inflation and population. Alarmingly, the pace of destruction is accelerating, with seventeen of the twenty most expensive hurricanes occurring since 2000. In 2017, Harvey, Maria, and Irma alone accounted for over $300 billion in damage, the single-most expensive hurricane season ever.

Absent a dramatic but unlikely shift in weather patterns, or Americans abandoning the coasts, this sharp spike in hurricane damage is likely to continue, experts say. This is even as the federal government is spending tens of billions on building seawalls, widening beaches, elevating houses, and undertaking an array of other costly efforts to protect coastal property.

"There is no way I know to mitigate your way out of the problem, unless you find a way to make carbon go away," said MIT's Kerry Emanuel.

That doesn't seem likely in the fossil fuel–focused Trump administration, which favors coal, oil, and gas over renewable-energy sources such as wind and solar. Greenhouse gases, including long-lasting carbon dioxide, are at historic levels, which may grow even more dramatically by century's end, current research suggests. More gas translates into higher temperatures, warmer oceans, and increased fuel for hurricanes. Combined with the explosive development at the coast, it is the perfect calculus for disasters.

Hurricanes are unquestionably doing more damage than ever: $163.8 billion for Katrina in 2005 (adjusted for inflation); $35.4 billion for Ike in 2008; $71.5 billion for Sandy in 2012; $126.3 billion for Harvey in 2017; $50.5 billion for Irma in 2017; and $90.9 billion for Maria, also in 2017. Damages are still being tabulated for 2018. But it is likely that Florence and Michael caused

A HURRICANE PROBLEM

STORM	YEAR	DAMAGE (IN BILLIONS)	TYPE OF STORM
Maria	2017	$90.9	Hurricane
Irma	2017	$50.5	Hurricane
Harvey	2017	$126.3	Hurricane
Matthew	2016	$10.5	Hurricane
Sandy	2012	$71.5	Hurricane
Isaac	2012	$3.0	Hurricane
Lee	2011	$2.8	Tropical storm
Irene	2011	$15.2	Hurricane
Ike	2008	$35.4	Hurricane
Gustav	2008	$7.1	Hurricane
Dolly	2008	$1.5	Hurricane
Wilma	2005	$24.9	Hurricane
Rita	2005	$24.2	Hurricane
Katrina	2005	$163.8	Hurricane
Dennis	2005	$3.3	Hurricane
Jeanne	2004	$10.0	Hurricane
Ivan	2004	$27.5	Hurricane
Frances	2004	$13.1	Hurricane
Charley	2004	$21.4	Hurricane
Isabel	2003	$7.5	Hurricane
Lili	2002	$1.6	Hurricane
Allison	2001	$12.1	Tropical storm
TOTAL		$724.1	

Hurricanes have caused $1.2 trillion in damage in history, with 60 percent of that damage occurring in the last two decades. Six of the most costly hurricanes have occurred since 2005. SOURCE: NOAA, NATIONAL CENTERS FOR ENVIRONMENTAL INFORMATION

at least $50 billion in damage, including devastating losses in poor rural areas, and massive damage to utilities and other public infrastructure.

Again, this isn't to suggest there haven't been massive hurricanes in the past. History is replete with examples dating back hundreds of years. Recent evidence detected in archaeological remains and carbon samples depicts ferocious paleo-hurricanes from thousands of years ago. But the key difference between then and now is that the coasts are now littered with expensive beach houses, second homes, boardwalks, and hotels. And there were no government programs or huge taxpayer payouts in the past.

A good example of the past foreshadowing the future is the Great Miami Hurricane of 1926. At the time, Miami was a relatively small, new city, unlike today, with its population in the millions and cranes towering over one new development after another. That September, a Category 3 hurricane barreled through downtown, killing about one thousand citizens, toppling houses, and wrecking businesses, while causing about $100 million in damage. Still, as devastating as the Great Miami Hurricane was, it pales in comparison with the damage a similarly powerful storm would cause today—well over $200 billion, according to Philip Klotzbach and other researchers.

"It would be massive," Klotzbach told me. "It all ties back to population and wealth. Miami is a very desirable place to live, but it's also a very dangerous place and is overdue for a massive hurricane. That entire area is."

Meteorologists thought 2017's Hurricane Irma might make a direct hit on Miami, with winds exceeding 140 miles per hour. However, while crossing Cuba, the storm encountered wind shear, weakened, and then dodged to the west, into the Gulf of Mexico, where it later threatened Tampa, another highly vulnerable city.

The last two major hurricanes to strike southeast Florida—Andrew in 1992 and Wilma in 2005—also spared Miami. Headline writers at *The Miami Herald* warned that Andrew was going to be "the Big One" that wrecked the city. But the hurricane wiped out the city of Homestead, about forty miles southeast of Miami, instead causing $25 billion in damage, or about $49 billion in today's dollars. Yet for all its power, Andrew was a relatively small, compact hurricane that cut a narrow swath of destruction. Wilma, meanwhile, surged across the Florida Keys, causing $25 billion in damage; but it, too, missed the densely developed Miami-Dade metropolitan region. Neither of the storms truly was the Big One. That will be a Category 4 or 5 hurricane that directly strikes Miami, Tampa, or Jacksonville.

It is only a matter of time. Florida is a long, narrow peninsula bordered by the Atlantic Ocean on one side and the Gulf of Mexico on the other. The geology of swamps, sinkholes, and porous limestone leaks water at every turn and is highly vulnerable to rising seas. The shallow offshore shelf in the Gulf serves as a launching pad for storms racing up to the Panhandle, such as Ivan (2004) and Michael (2018). Coupled with the massive inflow of people and an unrelenting land boom, Florida is uniquely vulnerable. More than $1 trillion worth of property straddles the coast, including more than a million properties in what FEMA euphemistically calls a "special flood hazard area." Florida, one clever writer recently observed, is a "vast harvest of risky building."

It is also a meteorologist's nightmare, a veritable shooting gallery for hurricanes. The Sunshine State has experienced five of the most powerful hurricanes in history: unnamed Category 4 hurricanes in 1947, 1948, and 1949; 1960's Hurricane Donna, a Category 4; and 1992's Hurricane Andrew, a Category 5. Now add Hurricane Michael, a Category 5 storm, which was one of the most powerful hurricanes in the Gulf's history. The state is low and vulnerable, effectively sinking in places. It is crisscrossed with lagoons, lakes, and estuaries. During king tides and full moons, some residents of Miami are trapped in their houses by rising water. Over time, state regulators have adopted stronger building codes. But those only help so much, and hurricane damage keeps rising. Nor can regulators elevate an entire state or build a wall high or long enough to barricade a coastline more than a thousand miles long. Even if they did, water would likely seep beneath the walls. Widening beaches helps in the short run, but at an increasing cost. Some areas of Florida are running out of sand, and at least one city has explored importing sand from the Bahamas. In 2017, the research arm of the real estate company Zillow estimated that rising seas could swallow upward of a million Florida homes. The houses—and not just the mortgages—would literally be underwater.

Of course, the risks extend well beyond Florida. Some of the fastest-growing areas in the nation are located along the hurricane-prone Gulf and Atlantic Coasts, where the combined population has vaulted from about 16 million in 1940 to nearly 70 million today, with fresh new suburban communities dotting the shorelines and marshes.

"There was a period of time when it was relatively quiet for hurricanes (1960–1990), and a lot of this building happened," Klotzbach said in an interview with me. "They haven't lived through a bad hurricane, and have no idea what it's like."

\\\

In 2015, FEMA published a list of all the natural disasters in the last two decades that had cost federal taxpayers $500 million or more in emergency aid and recovery efforts. Fourteen of the fifteen disasters were hurricanes (93 percent), underlining the vulnerability of property at the coast and the nation's escalating hurricane problem. The lone exception was the Midwest floods in 2008.

Another revealing data point was that major hurricanes—those listed as Category 3 to Category 5—accounted for three-fourths of the $90 billion that the federal agency spent on aid in that period. Bigger, punishing storms like Sandy and Katrina are gouging the heavily developed coastline and consuming larger shares of the agency's budget.

The FEMA report didn't include all the federal costs from hurricanes, only emergency aid. Nor did it cover the 2017–2018 hurricanes, which, combined, will cost the agency additional billions. Including Harvey, Irma, and Maria, hurricanes account for 100 percent of the agency's most expensive disasters since 2000.

It needs to be acknowledged that government spending is full of kinks, making it hard to know the exact price tag for some disasters. Historical data aren't always available or reported consistently, with disaster recovery programs scattered across numerous federal agencies. Nevertheless, based on figures that FEMA and other agencies have published, it is safe to say that federal taxpayers have spent at least $500 billion since 1950 responding to hurricanes and coastal storms, including over $350 billion in the last decade alone, a phenomenon that some researchers have likened to a "stealth entitlement" that primarily benefits the wealthy.

In his revealing 1999 study of federal disaster spending, the University of Massachusetts geographer Rutherford H. Platt coined a nice phrase, "the federalization of disasters," to capture the growing inclination of politicians and bureaucrats to declare every disaster a *federal* disaster, followed by a gusher of government funds to help pay for the recovery.

"The law since 1950 was always that federal assistance should be secondary to local assistance. It should be a residual level of protection, not the major level of protection," Platt told me in an interview in 1998. "But clearly the politics have changed."

But it wasn't only the politics that shifted; it was the public's attitudes as well. There was a growing expectation among coastal property owners, mayors, and governors that federal dollars would flow their way after hurricanes to help underwrite their recovery. In the 1970s, FEMA administrators pointed out the distorting effects of this shift in attitudes, noting that "first-dollar coverage" by the government (versus private insurance or homeowners paying for their own repairs) subsidized risky building in floodplains and encouraged owners of coastal property to forego private insurance. In effect, the government was creating a moral hazard by rewarding reckless behavior and then serving as the primary insurer when catastrophe struck.

David A. Moss, a professor at the Harvard Business School, has linked the increased federal role in disaster spending to passage of the Disaster Relief Act of 1950, which created a permanent disaster-relief fund and gave the president broad discretionary power to decide when a disaster is eligible for federal dollars. Afterward, Congress and various administrations dramatically expanded disaster aid "in most cases with little debate or controversy," Moss wrote in his 1999 study, "Courting Disaster." As a consequence, "Americans increasingly expected protection against an ever-widening array of hazards."

Indeed, federal payouts for hurricane damage have increased virtually in lockstep with coastal development. In the 1950s, when the modern coast was just beginning to develop, the federal government covered about 5 percent of the cost of rebuilding after hurricanes. By 2012, the federal share had ballooned to 70 percent on average, and even higher for some storms. That year, after Hurricane Sandy inundated the New Jersey shore, Congress agreed to pay for 100 percent of some damage, including repairing the beaches in front of millionaires' beach houses. Viewed by decades, the federal share climbed from 3.3 percent in 1927 to 12.8 percent in 1964, to 48 percent in 1972, to 52.5 percent in 1993, according to Moss. And now, 70 percent in the 2000s.

"We shouldn't be doing first-dollar coverage," Craig Fugate, the head of FEMA during the Obama administration, told me in an interview. "We need to have incentives for states to take more ownership."

But the politics of federal disaster aid are fraught, making it difficult, if not impossible, for federal officials to question spending decisions or to link funding to zoning and land-use decisions. There is a powerful incentive among coastal politicians to get as much money as possible for their constituents. And, for the most part, the generous approach of Congress is bipartisan, with lawmakers on both sides of the aisle watching out for one another.

There are some exceptions, especially in today's toxic political environment. In the wake of Hurricane Sandy, in 2012, conservative Republicans from Texas, South Carolina, and several other red states voted against emergency disaster funding for New Jersey and New York, both blue states. Both Texas senators, John Cornyn and Ted Cruz, voted against the initial aid package. Cornyn's spokesman tweeted that the senator believed the multimillion package included "extraneous money for items unrelated to disaster relief." Cruz declared that "two-thirds of that bill had nothing to do with Sandy." Congress eventually passed a $50.5 million Sandy disaster bill. But in 2017, both Cornyn and Cruz lobbied for tax deductions and massive federal aid for Texas after Hurricane Harvey flooded thousands of homes in their districts.

"A colleague of mine once said there are no conservatives in disasters," Fugate told me. "You know who the only politician is who never asked me for help? It was Rand Paul's father, Ron"—the former Texas congressman and libertarian candidate for president. "One thing a politician doesn't want to do is tell their constituents no. No one wins votes by voting against disaster packages."

Near the end of his tenure, in 2016, Fugate proposed adding a deductible to the disaster-aid process. Essentially, it would have worked the same way an insurance deductible works. Before a beach town or coastal state could tap into federal disaster dollars, it would have to spend a fixed amount of its own funds, thus ensuring it had "some skin in the game," Fugate said.

The proposal was backed by fiscal conservatives and environmentalists alike, "which kind of led me to think it might be a good idea," Fugate
explained. "But it took me too long to get through the gates of the Obama
administration. And then Trump came in and he didn't spike it, but it hasn't
been something they've gotten to."

\\\

Congress occasionally tinkers with the rules for disaster aid in an effort to
constrain spending. Yet lawmakers have added a startling assortment of programs to rebuild houses; repair roads, bridges, and water treatment plants;
clear roads and haul away storm debris; pump sand onto eroding beaches; fix
damaged jetties, groins, and seawalls; provide low-interest home and business
loans; and distribute checks of up to $33,000 to families to cover short-term
rentals, food, clothing, and living expenses; not to mention an array of tax
breaks for property losses, depreciation, and mortgage interest for second
homes—all of which help inflate the value of coastal real estate and encourage
rebuilding in the wake of damaging storms.

New Jersey officials used about $2 billion of the federal aid they got after
Sandy to fund a massive rebuilding effort at the shore. The goal was to get the
state back in business as quickly as possible. Virtually overnight, the Christie administration transformed the state's Department of Consumer Affairs
into a housing agency, awarding grants of up to $150,000 to owners of flood-
damaged homes. The program was hampered by staff turnover, delays, and
fraud. Eligibility rules seemed to shift every few weeks, leading some homeowners to complain that they needed an MBA to wade through the mountains
of paperwork. Local construction and zoning offices were also overwhelmed
and often provided contradictory advice.

For months, no one seemed to know how many feet that homeowners
should elevate their houses to get above the flood risk. The federal flood maps
were outdated, and different agencies gave different advice. "I'd walk into
one office and they'd tell me one thing, and I'd walk into the office next door
and they would tell me something completely different," said Chuck Grif-

fin, a seventy-year-old retiree. His modest Mystic Island bungalow in Ocean County was flooded with six feet of water. Griffin gutted it and started repairs himself but ran out of money and hope. He waited years for help, camping out in his cold, dark, empty bungalow for several weeks. Finally, with the help of a nonprofit, he qualified for state help. And in fall 2017, he moved into a new modular house on the same lot, elevated ten feet above sea level. It was a slog, but at least he was finally home, he said.

Governor Christie talked about building back smarter and stronger. But it was never clear what that meant, because other than generalities, the administration never explained what it wanted the state's coast to look like in an age of rising water and more ferocious storms. Most decisions involving land use and zoning were still left to the beach towns.

"I think Governor Christie saw planning as a delay to building back," said John A. Miller, an engineer and floodplain manager who testified and wrote about the state's recovery plan. "There was never any plan or a vision. It was a very, very short-term vision, and pretty much just called for putting things back so the beach resorts could be up and running again. We're not going to recognize sea level. God forbid we do any long-term planning. The farther out the recovery got, the less interested the governor seemed."

By 2015–2016, the state's newspapers were reporting that Christie was out of the state campaigning more than he was in it. By then, the governor was running for president, and among many claims, he touted how he had saved the state from Hurricane Sandy. "When the worst natural disaster in your state's history hits you, they expect you to rebuild the state, which is what I've done," he told fans along the campaign trail.

One thing Christie was good at was tapping federal disaster dollars to fund a resettlement program in which homeowners received $10,000 cash grants to return to their damaged homes. The only requirement was that they had to promise to remain there for three years. There were no income guidelines; rich and poor alike were eligible. At least some of those who collected checks lived out of state. Remarkably, no one in the federal government questioned the governor's approach, let alone asked why the state was effectively bribing its citizens to build back in harm's way.

\\\

There is a kind of permissive elegance to disaster relief that filters through government agencies, programs, and rules. Requests for federal aid begin at the state level and then are forwarded to FEMA, which makes a recommendation to the president. In theory, a disaster is supposed to exceed a state's financial ability to respond. But the threshold used to define financial ability is, to put it mildly, generous. For decades, FEMA used a figure of $1 per capita for each of a state's citizens. So, if New Jersey had seven million residents, the state had to document just $7 million worth of damage to trigger a federal disaster declaration and access recovery dollars. Surprisingly, the $1 trigger wasn't adjusted for inflation for years. As a result, even modest coastal storms qualified for federal aid. FEMA was effectively marking on a curve, so everyone got an A or a B. Meanwhile, final decisions in the Oval Office were "often influenced by congressional and media attention," Rutherford Platt said, further undermining the process.

With such a low bar, the number of federal disaster declarations climbed steadily, with 1,300 federal disasters declared in the last three decades alone. The loosening of eligibility standards prompted the normally cautious Congressional Research Service to declare the aid packages an entitlement. "As long as victims (public or individuals) meet eligibility requirements, they are entitled to disaster relief assistance. While this ensures that relief is provided to all victims (regardless of economic need) it may be a potentially expensive arrangement," the researchers noted in a 1998 study.

There are "way too many federal declarations, and way too many of them are not really beyond the capability of state and local government to handle," said Larry Larson, the former director of the national Association of State Floodplain Managers, and one of the nation's more thoughtful observers of government-disaster policies.

To make sure that copious funds are available for their states, members of Congress have resorted to a form of budgetary chicanery, using emergency supplemental appropriations to fund disasters instead of setting an annual budget for disaster spending. As a result, the unchecked spending directly adds to the nation's cascading deficit, now about $1 trillion annually, according to the Congressional Budget Office.

By my count, Congress has approved seventeen separate supplemental appropriations from 2003 to 2018, totaling $210 billion. That includes $120 billion for the 2017 hurricanes in Texas, Puerto Rico, and Florida. The growing reliance on off-budget maneuvers raises a variety of issues, the Congressional Research Service observed in a 2010 study. For one, lawmakers are able to move funding streams through Congress on an expedited basis with minimal debate. For another, they can exceed discretionary spending limits designed to reduce the federal deficit. The supplemental allocations are also hard to track, allowing states to use funds for projects that appear far removed from the disaster. Following Hurricane Sandy, New Jersey officials were criticized for using disaster dollars to build low-income housing and fund repairs at an apartment complex over fifty miles from the coast.

\\\

By law, if not always in practice, beach towns and coastal communities are supposed to contribute toward their own recoveries. The amounts vary by program but can be substantial. For example, in 1988, Congress stipulated that local governments should pay a quarter of the cost of repairing government buildings, parks, roads, bridges, and other public infrastructure damaged in storms, with FEMA covering the other 75 percent.

But coastal lawmakers often step in after disasters to help lower or eliminate the required local payments. A 2010 study by the Congressional Research Service found 222 instances since 1986 in which Congress, FEMA, or the president either reduced the local share or expanded the time period in which coastal communities were eligible to collect federal disaster aid, resulting in higher federal spending. Federal waivers eliminating any local contribution at all have also become more common, the researchers reported, especially after large storms such as Katrina and Sandy.

The most popular target for waivers is FEMA's Public Assistance program, by far the largest and most expensive in the government's cupboard of disaster-relief programs. Since 2000, FEMA has awarded more than $45 billion in grants to beach towns and coastal states to scoop sand off highways, repair damaged water lines, rebuild town halls, and pay overtime for police, among an array of eligible expenses, federal records show. Local shore towns were supposed to pay a quarter of the costs. But in dozens of cases involving Texas, Louisiana, and New Jersey, FEMA agreed to cover 100 percent of the repairs.

In another wrinkle, FEMA allows states to use federal dollars to cover their required "local" contributions, thus defeating the purpose of the cost-share. New Jersey used $54.5 million from FEMA to cover its required share while rebuilding a damaged highway in Ocean County. It used another $25 million to cover its share for three other projects, records show.

Altogether, New Jersey received $1.2 billion to cart away debris following Hurricane Sandy. It got $1.6 billion for police and emergency workers, $1.8 billion to repair public buildings, and $2.5 billion to fix broken utilities. In 2012, Governor Christie asked FEMA to cover 100 percent of the cost.

I reviewed more than four thousand Sandy Public Assistance grants and found more than a few surprises. For example, FEMA spent $75 million to repair boardwalks for beach resorts in Belmar, Atlantic City, and elsewhere; $32 million to fix a seawall damaged by the storm; and over $100 million for broken lifeguard stands, gazebos, lampposts, garbage cans, restrooms, and marinas. It paid tens of millions to buy new cars and replace vehicles damaged by saltwater, and to patch sand dunes and replace wooden crossovers and dune fences. It also replaced docks and bulkheads, traffic signals, benches, and cameras. FEMA allocated $204,000 to repair a hockey rink in Monmouth County and $194,000 for a baseball field in Bergen County, a hundred miles from the coast; it awarded $168,000 for an ice house in Monmouth County. It also paid to fix tennis courts, streetlights, rowing clubs, and restaurants. It even paid for spoiled food.

Applying for Public Assistance money has become an industry unto itself, requiring full-time attention and specialized help. "The paperwork is unbelievable," groused the Long Beach Township mayor Joe Mancini. "You have to make sure you hit every box. If you don't, they'll say you don't qualify."

For that reason, Mancini and many other coastal mayors hire consultants to wade through the paperwork and maximize FEMA payments. Some prominent consultants are former FEMA managers and administrators. And if for some reason FEMA still says no, the towns can always turn to their congressional representatives to lobby agency officials.

It must work. Long Beach Township has received over $13 million in Sandy Public Assistance grants to date, with millions more expected. It received $2.5 million for police and emergency workers, $80,000 for a modular trailer, $110,290 to replace damaged dune fencing, $5,000 for benches, $390,000 to repair streets, $165,000 for a comfort station, $67,000 for street signs, and $3 million to remove debris. It still has open claims for trash containers, fire hydrants, a tennis court, a gazebo, and restrooms. In most cases, federal taxpayers are paying 100 percent of the cost, township records show.

"The program exists. We'd be fools not to take advantage of it," the mayor told me.

Brock Long, Fugate's replacement as FEMA director in the Trump administration, suggested in 2017 that a disaster deductible or some other approach was needed to reduce federal disaster spending. "I don't think the taxpayer should reward risk going forward," he told *Insurance Journal*. "We have to find ways to comprehensively become more resilient."

But as of this writing, the deductible remains an idea, not a reality, and federal spending keeps rising. Long, who became mired in an ethical quandary involving his use of government automobiles for personal use, announced in February 2019 that he was leaving his federal post.

Meanwhile, the Congressional Budget Office warned in a 2016 working paper, "Damage from hurricanes is expected to increase significantly in the coming decades because of the effects of climate change and coastal development. In turn, potential requests for federal relief and recovery efforts will increase as well."

10

A Flood of Trouble

Floods are a normal, not an abnormal, part of the laws of nature. Man's brief lifespan compared with nature's eons tends to cause man to overlook this fact.

—SENATE COMMITTEE ON BANKING AND CURRENCY, 1956

IN AUGUST 1966, Gil White, a tall, thin man with brush-cut white hair and cornflower-blue eyes, traveled to Washington to deliver a report on the nation's flood risks to President Lyndon B. Johnson. The administration had ordered the report a year earlier, after Hurricane Betsy swept across the Gulf of Mexico at Grand Isle, Louisiana, and then flooded New Orleans with ten feet of water, the worst inundation of the city in decades. Researchers nicknamed the hurricane "Billion-Dollar Betsy" because it was the first hurricane to cause $1 billion in damage (nearly $10 billion in today's dollars). Johnson personally reassured victims that he would take care of them and tasked the Army Corps of Engineers with constructing a larger and stronger system of interlocking levees to protect the city.

The levees were welcome. But the damaging hurricane spotlighted an even larger gap in the nation's safety net at the coast. Thousands of Betsy victims had no insurance and were now facing financial ruin. Charity and donations helped only so much. Where would the money come from to rebuild? And even if homeowners did manage, how would they protect themselves against the next hurricane?

Private insurers had once covered storms like Betsy. But after the Great Mississippi Flood of 1927, they fled the perilous market. There was no good way to insure against a flood, executives informed members of Congress, for the simple reason that there was no good way to calculate the risk. Hurricanes and floods were acts of God. You never knew when one would roar up the coast. But you knew they were inevitable—as were the massive losses that followed the storms. History was littered with examples: the deadly Galveston hurricane in 1900 and the Miami hurricanes in 1926 and 1928, among others. Insurers would have to raise their rates to unaffordable levels if they continued writing flood policies. And so, instead, they walked away.

Proposals to fill the gap with a government-backed flood insurance plan had kicked around Washington for decades. Each time the mighty Mississippi overflowed its banks or a hurricane wrecked some coastal resort, lawmakers would rise to declare it was finally time to protect their beleaguered citizens. But after the experts pointed out the costs, the idea would just as quickly fade into the background.

In 1952, President Harry Truman proposed a federal flood program after record flooding in Kansas and Missouri. His successor, Dwight Eisenhower, pushed his own version of a flood bill following destructive back-to-back hurricane seasons in 1954 and 1955. The bill made it through Congress but was never funded. After the ruinous Ash Wednesday nor'easter in 1962, Senator Harrison Williams of New Jersey introduced flood legislation in each of the next two congressional sessions and then again after Betsy in 1965. The political stars finally appeared to be aligning. The idea had the backing of a trio of presidents: Democrats John F. Kennedy and his successor, Lyndon Johnson, and then, perhaps most surprising of all, Republican Richard M. Nixon. Critically, government-backed flood insurance also had "the wholehearted support of the home-building industry," a representative informed Congress.

Two government-funded studies added to the momentum. The first was under the guidance of Marion Clawson, a noted geographer working with the Department of Housing and Urban Development. The other, known as the U.S. Task Force on Federal Flood Control Policy, was chaired by Gilbert Fowler White, a brilliant, iconoclastic researcher.

White was a Quaker pacifist and conscientious objector who had served with the American Friends Service Committee in World War II and been interned a year in Germany. He actively opposed the Vietnam War and didn't hesitate to signal his opposition to Johnson and Nixon. He was a prodigiously original thinker, yet fiercely disciplined when it came to drawing scientific conclusions. His doctoral dissertation on floods was considered the capstone in the field; his work as a geographer, both evolutionary and revolutionary.

The report that White delivered to the Johnson administration in 1966 was ambitious yet cautionary. Yes, a government-backed flood insurance program was feasible, his task force concluded, but only under a number of strict conditions. First, insurance had to be closely linked to rigorous land-use policies limiting future development in floodplains. Second, the government had to price its premiums at levels reflecting the actual risk of flooding; anything less would be fiscally reckless. Third, the government shouldn't offer subsidies to policyholders, because they would distort the market and incite even more risky development. And fourth, the government should test its program in one or two markets to see whether it worked before offering flood insurance nationwide.

A sound flood insurance program should balance private and public risk, White believed. Individuals who built in low-lying areas known to flood regularly should shoulder the financial risks associated with their choices. Taxpayer-backed insurance shouldn't underwrite those choices; at most, it should serve as a modest backstop.

"Floods are an act of God; flood damages result from the acts of man," White wrote in the task force report. "Those who occupy the floodplain should be responsible for the results of their actions."

White envisioned what he termed an "occupancy charge" for owners who build in floodplains. The charge would serve as a "price signal" reflecting the risk, with two main purposes: discouraging future development and shifting the full cost "to the prospective occupants themselves." Subsidies would "needlessly" increase damages, followed by more building, then additional subsidies, he wrote. In effect, White was foreshadowing the reiterative loop of subsidized building, storms, and more subsidies that characterizes coastal disasters today.

"For the federal government to subsidize low-premium disaster insurance or provide insurance in which premiums are not proportionate to risk would be to invite economic waste of great magnitude," White concluded.

President Johnson accepted most of the task force's precepts. But with the nation's annual flood bill already topping $1 billion, "excessive, even in a growing economy," he was eager to quickly move forward. "The key to resolving the problem lies, above all else, in the intelligent planning for and State and Local regulation of use of lands exposed to flood hazard," he wrote in a letter of transmittal to Congress.

The reaction of lawmakers can best be described as confounding. For more than a year, they emphasized the importance of steering development away from floodplains and charging property owners risk-based premiums. However, as the legislation neared its final form, they inexplicably rejected the task force's key recommendations, including White's warning about subsidizing premiums. Instead, they opted to offer discounts to what lawmakers and their staffs called "a comparatively small number of present occupants of high flood-risk areas."

Without those concessions, proponents feared the flood bill wouldn't pass—or work. The flood program needed a large pool of policyholders to spread the risks (known as the risk pool) and cover future losses; otherwise, rates would be so high no one would purchase insurance. The legislators also were concerned that owners of older, flood-prone properties wouldn't buy insurance without government help, relying on disaster relief instead. Debate continued for months. Finally, in 1968, backers won approval by attaching their flood plan to another unusual piece of legislation, a federal plan to reinsure business losses in the nation's then riot-plagued cities.

"In my experience, the flood insurance program would never have been enacted without riot reinsurance," George K. Bernstein, the first administrator of the federal flood insurance program, told me. "After Martin Luther King was killed, it stoked a demand for insurance in the inner city. Ironically, it turned out to be one of the few federal moneymaking programs." It remained on the government's books until the 1980s.

\\\

It is always possible to design a program that fails. Sometimes, it happens by accident or bad luck. Other times, it is the result of poor planning and bad choices. In the case of federal flood insurance, it took all three of these elements—poor planning, reckless choices, and bad luck.

Over its troubled fifty-year history, the National Flood Insurance Program (NFIP) has lost $40 billion, including claims from Harvey, Irma, and Maria in 2017. In this instance, the term "loss" refers to the huge gap between what the flood program collected in premiums and what it paid out in claims. Crucially, most of the losses stemmed from hurricanes and other coastal storms, not river flooding—a common misperception among Americans.

If federal flood insurance were a private program, and not a government-backed program with the U.S. Treasury serving as a backstop, regulators would have declared it insolvent years ago. But because it is operated by the government and backed by federal taxpayers, the NFIP operates with a level of immunity unavailable to private insurers, and gets to pass its mistakes on to taxpayers.

Many of the program's shortcomings can be traced to a series of decisions made at the program's inception. Government officials bypassed Gilbert White's advice and awarded steep subsidies to entice owners of risky properties to purchase insurance. Perversely, the biggest discounts went to older, low-lying houses at or below sea level that flooded over and over. Those owners paid premiums equal to as little as 10 percent of their actual risk of flooding—and when they inevitably did flood, taxpayers covered the losses.

Members of Congress and their aides estimated that the number of these high-risk properties was limited, and predicted that they would be weeded out of the new flood insurance program after a few years. But that was only a guess.

BILLION-DOLLAR FLOODS

STORM	YEAR	AMOUNT
Allison	2001	$1,105,003,344
Ivan	2004	$1,607,456,621
Katrina	2005	$16,257,661,592
Ike	2008	$2,699,982,523
Irene	2011	$1,345,530,083
Sandy	2012	$8,702,594,207
Louisiana	2016	$2,451,760,141
Harvey	2017	$8,366,653,032
TOTAL		$42,536,641,543
COAST		$40,084,881,402 (94%)

Eight floods have cost the federal flood insurance program more than $1 billion. Seven of the eight were coastal floods. Note: The Louisiana flood was a torrential rainstorm, also called a rain bomb. It occurred near Baton Rouge, about sixty miles from the coast. SOURCE: NFIP SIGNIFICANT EVENT DATABASE, AUTHOR'S ANALYSIS

They didn't have actual data. In fact, tens of thousands of risky properties were in low-lying floodplains, including second homes at the coast. And rather than declining, the number grew sharply as hurricanes, erosion, and rising seas exposed ever more property to flood damage.

In a surprising number of cases, the government's payments exceeded the actual value of the houses by hundreds of thousands of dollars. But after each flood, the owners would take the government's check and rebuild in the same place, until the next flood, and then repeat the process. Today, half a century later, these so-called repetitive loss properties account for about a fifth of the program's losses—or $12 billion, according to the NFIP, which is operated by FEMA, as well as a recent analysis by the nonprofit National Resources Defense Council.

At this point, it might seem reasonable to ask why federal officials didn't kick the high-risk properties out of the program the way an auto insurer would drop a risky driver who's had too many accidents. The simplest answer is that they couldn't. By law, the flood program had to accept all comers; it couldn't pick and choose the way a private insurer might. Nor was it allowed to raise its rates to reflect the excessive risks of individual properties. Premiums were based on national blended averages that overstated the risks for some inland houses and understated the risks for others at the coast. But even if they wanted to raise their rates, flood-program officials faced another vexing issue: the higher the premiums, the more likely it became that homeowners would drop their policies and rely on federal disaster aid to cover their losses.

"No one wanted to pay a real rate," Bernstein said. "Every time I testified before Congress, I would remind them this was a social program, not an insurance program. If this can break even, there would be no need for the federal government. The reason the federal government got into it was because no one was going to write it. It was a clear loss."

Homeowners also appear to have short memories. After hurricanes, the number of policies in the affected states typically surges by thousands as the owners scramble to cover themselves. But then, a year or two later, the number of policies begins to drop off again. This is exactly what happened in New Jersey after Hurricane Sandy in 2012. The number of policies ballooned by tens of thousands initially but then fell by 7 percent by 2017.

In 1968, Bernstein was picked by Nixon's Housing and Urban Development secretary, George Romney, to run the flood program. At the time, he was serving as the general counsel to the New York State Insurance Department, and had a long background in the industry. The flood program operated out of the Department of Housing and Urban Development and, in Bernstein's view, "it was the most effective program [in HUD]. We were getting kudos from all over the world."

Bernstein headed the flood program for five and a half years. During that time, it struggled to sign up policyholders. But after devastating floods in Hurricane Agnes in Wilkes-Barre, Pennsylvania, in 1972, Bernstein convinced the Nixon administration to include a flood insurance mandate as part of every federally backed mortgage issued in a flood zone. "After that, it took off," he said.

Bernstein suggested that the flood program's problems began after it was moved from HUD to FEMA in the late 1970s: "That was a mistake. It lost its identity." After the 9/11 terrorist attacks, the Bush administration moved the flood program again. This time, it became part of the newly created Department of Homeland Security, where it has been overshadowed by the administration's antiterror and border-security programs.

In a surprising historical twist, Gilbert White worked to derail his own flood program before it even started. White was dismayed by the changes that lawmakers and government officials made to his plan and objected to Bernstein's decision to roll the program out nationally before first testing it in a handful of small markets.

"I found myself working very hard to prevent it from ever going into effect because as the first administrator had planned to carry it out it would have had the opposite effect" of discouraging floodplain development, White told an interviewer in 1985. "In my opinion, they might have done much better to carry on a more modest program."

Bernstein said he was under pressure to get the program up and running as quickly as possible. "There had been a lot of losses. People wanted to see if this could work," he said.

\\\

After the flood program was introduced, federal officials quickly began hiring engineers and consultants to map the nation's floodplains and identify risks. There were very few detailed maps at the time, and thousands of miles of rivers and coasts to study. The maps that did exist were often out-of-date and understated the risk of flooding, still true today. However, producing detailed flood maps was slow, expensive work. Some years Congress appropriated large sums for mapping, but other years lawmakers gave the program little or nothing. It was nearly impossible to keep up, especially at the coasts, where shorelines were continually shifting because of erosion, storms, and rising seas. Many of the flood maps for New Jersey and New York were twenty-five years out-of-date at the time Sandy swamped their coasts in 2012. Even today, with digital maps, satellites, and other improvements, over a fifth of the federal flood program's losses are in areas that mapmakers have deemed to be safe from flooding, known as X Zones on the maps.

Another decision that doomed the flood insurance program to epic losses was the lack of reserves. To keep rates low and attract customers, program administrators didn't build a cushion into the premiums to cover catastrophic events—a standard industry practice. This seems especially reckless in hindsight, but it is important to recall Bernstein's earlier explanation that lawmakers saw flood insurance as a social program as much as an insurance program. Members of Congress also pressured managers to keep premiums affordable, even as they complained that the flood insurance program was losing huge amounts of money. It is likely that many members didn't understand the financial mechanics of the program, or simply chose to ignore them to respond to the demands of their constituents.

Instead of including a reserve for catastrophes, NFIP administrators charged just enough to cover what the program's actuaries called an "average historical loss year." That is, they added up all the losses to a given point in time and produced an average. Then the actuaries set the premiums to cover that average. The problem was that the rates didn't account for large, unexpected losses, or what statisticians call fat-tail events with outsize impacts. As a result, when a huge, unexpectedly damaging storm like Katrina, Sandy, or Harvey hit, the flood program didn't have anywhere near what it needed to pay the claims, and managers were forced to pivot to the U.S. Treasury for a bailout.

That, too, was by design. Each time the NFIP required a cash infusion, it asked Congress for permission to borrow more money from the taxpayers. In theory, there was supposed to be a cap on how much it could borrow. But in extreme storms with heavy losses, Congress simply raised the bar. For example, after Katrina, the flood program borrowed $17 billion from the Treasury to pay claims in Louisiana and Mississippi. That figure swelled to nearly $25 billion overall after Sandy. The three hurricanes in 2017 would have pushed the program's debt to over $35 billion, except the Trump administration quietly forgave $16 billion that the NFIP owed the taxpayers, adding to the nation's ballooning debt. Today, the flood program's debt stands at about $24 billion.

No one expects the flood insurance program to pay back all the billions it still owes the Treasury. That would require federal officials to raise premiums to unaffordable levels, or for there to be no devastating hurricanes for a decade or two, an unlikely prospect in an era of rising seas and catastrophic storms. In the meantime, Congress has added a small fee to premiums to build a modest reserve, and has begun to purchase reinsurance from the private market to cover some losses. Those are a help. Yet, as quickly as the flood program seems to build a small cushion of cash, another big hurricane like Harvey washes ashore and wipes out the reserves.

\\\

One of the key tenets of federal flood insurance was that future losses would be reduced by requiring innovative land-use provisions and building restrictions in river and coastal floodplains. In exchange for insurance, participating communities were required to adopt stronger zoning and steer new development away from high-risk areas, including barrier islands and rivers.

"It was supposed to be a trade-off for better land use. If you don't have that, then you're just throwing away your money," Bernstein said. "You're subsidizing construction."

Bernstein characterized flood insurance as "the first federal zoning program." Except it was always something far less than that. Federal officials couldn't stop builders from putting houses in coastal floodplains; they had no control over zoning or building decisions. All beach towns were required to do was meet the government's minimal standards for elevation and construction. Local communities still had final say where houses went and how many could be built. And, history shows, they continued to fill their floodplains with risky development.

According to property records and federal data, more than 7 million houses and businesses are in the nation's floodplains, including some 3.1 million houses in high-risk coastal floodplains. Many of the coastal properties are insured by the NFIP, including more than a million houses in Florida alone and over $200 billion worth of coastal property in New Jersey and New York. Altogether, the NFIP insures over $800 billion of property at the coast, including thousands of heavily subsidized houses, according to my research.

Improbably, federal flood officials have insisted for decades that their insurance program doesn't underwrite development in floodplains. In the late 1990s, they even hired consultants to study the issue. The consultants reviewed the existing literature and concluded that there wasn't enough evidence one way or the other. The flood program's own data, meanwhile, showed that 2.3 million houses were built in floodplains in the first few decades of the NFIP. Recently, the nonprofit American Institutes for Research observed that "although the NFIP is widely perceived to encourage safer floodplain construction, it is seldom perceived to inhibit floodplain development, particularly in coastal areas and high-growth communities."

In the 1980s, state environmental officials in New Jersey concluded that rampant development on flood-prone barrier islands was due at least in part to federal flood insurance and other government subsidies. Flood insurance helped create a moral hazard at the beach, they wrote, by lowering the incentive to guard against the risk of flooding. The expectation was that government assistance "will be available at public expense," they noted.

In the late 1980s, government investigators found that communities were ignoring the NFIP's minimal land-use requirements. They even kicked a community or two out of the flood program. But then officials added a new wrinkle, introducing the Community Rating System (CRS) to reward communities that exceeded their standards. Under the CRS, towns could earn premium discounts of up to 25 percent for their homeowners by educating them about flooding and taking other modest steps. Some analysts have likened the CRS program to discounts for good drivers. By including a financial nudge, towns have an incentive to lessen flood risks, they say. Others contend that the discounts perversely encourage even more development in floodplains. Several New Jersey beach towns that suffered hundreds of millions in flood losses in Hurricane Sandy enjoyed the highest CRS discounts in the state.

Even with these recent efforts to reduce flood risks, the government's losses are only likely to grow. A 2013 study for FEMA estimated that high-risk coastal floodplains may expand by up to half by the end of this century because of rising sea levels. That will expose more property to damage and result in more claims, with losses possibly doubling, the researchers concluded.

In 2016, Sean Becketti, the chief economist for the housing giant Freddie Mac, wrote that the economic losses resulting from rising seas and wider floodplains are likely to be "greater in total than those experienced in the [2008] housing crisis and Great Recession." To lower its exposure, the flood program would have to raise its premiums and reduce its subsidies, but so far those proposals have met with stiff resistance, he said.

\\\

One of the enduring mysteries of the federal flood insurance program is how the federal government came to insure vacation houses and investment property at the coast. After all, it is one thing to insure a primary residence where someone lives and works. It is quite another for the federal taxpayers to insure second homes.

Congressional hearings and flood-program histories provide few insights. Bernstein told me that the flood program "was always intended to include the coast." However, the question of insuring second homes, he said, "never surfaced in any of the authorizing documents I saw, and I think I read them all."

One of Bernstein's top assistants at the time, Richard Krimm, expressed surprise when informed that the flood program was insuring beach houses. "That was never the intention," he said in an interview. "The original intention was only primary homes."

Krimm speculated that private insurance agents may have sold flood insurance to owners of beach houses without the government's knowledge to boost the overall number of flood policies. Since the 1980s, the flood program has paid approximately seventy-five private companies to market its policies and settle claims. These so-called Write Your Own insurers receive hundreds of millions in fees and bonuses annually, and have been criticized for siphoning funds needed to pay claims.

"That could have been how it came about," Krimm said. "Insurance agents were selling directly, and it was difficult sometimes for the government to know. I don't think it was intentional on the government's part. I don't think . . . we issued memos or anything to the insurance industry. Certainly the intent was just the primary homes."

Some flood experts suggested to me that it doesn't matter if an insured property is a primary residence or a second home. "A house is a house," said Larry Larson, the former executive director of the Association of State Floodplain Managers. "Water is water."

But the issue raises questions about apportioning risk and encouraging risky development. Most second homes FEMA insures are in low-lying, high-risk areas at the coast that have been pummeled by hurricanes in recent years, resulting in a dramatic surge in claims—up by nearly a third since 2011, to $68 billion altogether. The owners generally are wealthy enough to pay hundreds of thousands or even millions of dollars for their houses. Why should the federal government be their insurer?

Curiously, FEMA officials told me they don't know how many second homes they insure. In 2015, a spokeswoman informed me that they don't track the data that way and that it would be expensive to run a computer search to identify the beach houses. The agency also turned down my Freedom of Information Act (FOIA) request for data, saying it couldn't identify claims by house addresses or even by street names because of privacy concerns.

All this struck me as a strange response for an agency that appears to have no shortage of data. So I did a little back-of-the-envelope math using the agency's own records. I quickly came up with an answer. As of 2016, the federal flood program insured approximately 1.2 million beach houses and second homes—or what the NFIP calls "non-primary residences." Most of them appear to be at the coast. Assuming I am right, that means one of every four properties—1.2 million out of 5 million houses—that the federal government insures is a beach house, an investment property, or a second home. Apparently, I was conservative in my estimate. A 2013 study by the U.S. Government Accountability Office estimated that the NFIP insured nearly 1.7 million second homes, or one of every three insured houses.

\\\

During the first few decades of its existence, the federal flood program more or less broke even. The main reason was that the program was struggling to sign up customers, and fewer policyholders resulted in fewer claims. Another reason had to do with the weather. With one or two exceptions, there weren't many catastrophic storms in the first two decades of the program (1970–1990) to drain its coffers.

That began to change in the mid-1990s. By then, the coastal floodplains were crowded with vacation houses. Many of those owners were required to purchase flood insurance as part of their federally backed mortgages. The simple math of more property in harm's way translated into higher program exposure. During this period, the flood program also raised the ceiling for what it covered, to $250,000 per house and $100,000 for contents. The number of policies also climbed to about five million nationwide, with the average policy in a coastal floodplain costing less than $1,000 annually. Many newer beach houses worth $500,000 or more are charged as little as $600 or $700 for an annual premium. Presumably, that's because they are elevated and at lower risk of flooding.

Property owners filed 110,000 more flood claims in the 1990s than they did in the 1980s, federal data show. Losses increased threefold, to over $6.5 billion, as more homeowners filed larger claims. Just two storms in 1995 (Hurricane Opal and a Louisiana coastal flood) cost $1.3 billion. Still, this was only the beginning.

The following decade got off to an ominous start when Tropical Storm Allison stalled over Houston in 2001, flooding thousands of homes. The federal flood program paid out over $1.2 billion in claims. Three years later, Hurricane Ivan inundated Pensacola Beach on the Florida Panhandle, costing the NFIP $1.6 billion. Then Katrina broke through the levees in New Orleans, resulting in a startling $16 billion in payments, swamping the flood program's balance sheets. In 2008, Hurricane Ike flooded Galveston, costing $2.7 billion. Four years later, Sandy flooded the New Jersey and New York coasts, resulting in $8.7 billion in claims. And in 2017, Harvey led to $8.4 billion in flood claims.

Clearly, something big was happening. Huge, costly storms were striking heavily developed coastal areas (Galveston, Houston, New Orleans, New Jersey, and New York, among others), and losses were mounting alarmingly. The flood program was now deep in debt, with few options. It couldn't raise premiums enough to cover its debts without losing customers, and by law it couldn't stop writing risky policies. With each hurricane, more of the program's faults were exposed—an inadequate risk pool, below-market premiums, few if any reserves, large numbers of properties that flooded repeatedly, and a significant and growing problem along the ocean and bays.

The federal program has paid out nearly ten times as much for hurricanes and coastal storms as it has for all other flood events combined, including flooding from rivers. Since 2000, it has paid more than $45 billion in claims for coastal floods, but just $5 billion for all other types of floods.

Seven of the eight most expensive flood events have been hurricanes or tropical storms. The lone exception was a torrential rainstorm in 2016 in Baton Rouge, Louisiana. Strikingly, all have occurred since 2000: Allison (2001), Ivan (2004), Katrina (2005), Ike (2008), Irene (2011), Sandy (2012), and Harvey (2017).

Many coastal states have received far more in flood payments than policyholders paid in premiums. For example, policyholders in Alabama have paid $481 million in premiums since 1978 but have collected $1.018 billion in flood payments—a net loss to the government of $537 million. Louisianans, meanwhile, have received over $19 billion in flood payouts while paying just over $4 billion in premiums. The only coastal state that has paid significantly more than it has received is Florida. That's because most of the hurricane damage in Florida is caused by wind, not storm surge, a trend that is likely to shift as rising seas push water closer to the state's densely developed shorelines.

A single storm can also emphatically alter the flood profile of a state. Take New Jersey. For decades, policyholders poured millions into the federal flood insurance program while collecting relatively little in return. But then Hurricane Sandy inundated the coast in 2012, flooding tens of thousands of homes on barrier islands and along back-bay communities. Virtually overnight, New Jersey went from being a moneymaker for the flood program to a deadbeat, as claims swelled from $1.6 billion to nearly $6 billion.

The impact was especially dramatic in Ocean County, ground zero for flooding in Hurricane Sandy. In the thirty-four years prior to Sandy, homeowners in Ocean County collected $115 million in flood payments. Following Sandy, they received nearly $2.5 billion, a nearly twenty-two-fold increase. Ocean County, with a population of fewer than 600,000, has now received more flood payouts than forty-three states, including North Carolina, Virginia, South Carolina, and California.

\\\

Joe Rulli, the owner of a popular pizza shop in the Beach Haven Crest section of Long Beach Township, knew that his restaurant would probably flood during Sandy. It didn't take much anymore. Even summer thunderstorms sometimes left half a foot of water at his doorstep.

Rulli owns three pizza shops, including one in Manahawkin and two on Long Beach Island. He purchased the one in Beach Haven Crest with a partner, also named Joe, which explains the name, Joeys' Pizza and Pasta, even though his partner left the business years ago.

The Beach Haven Crest shop is probably as good a window into the issues of floods and flood insurance as any. It is located less than one hundred yards from Barnegat Bay in one of the narrowest and lowest sections of the barrier island, where there is only a few feet of elevation. Barnegat Bay now regularly tops the wooden bulkheads at the end of the street, and water pours down the street to form what is effectively a bowl. To make matters worse, the county has raised Long Beach Boulevard four or five inches because of the constant flooding, and stormwater runs off the crown toward Rulli's squat concrete restaurant.

At least Rulli has a sense of humor. Years back, after a heavy flood, he added a sign outside of his shop: OCCASIONAL WATERFRONT DINING. Everyone gets the joke. Joeys' is their signpost for flooding. If a nor'easter blows in or, God forbid, a hurricane, the first thing they do is put out an e-mail or Facebook post: "How's Joeys' doing? Are the roads flooded? Can we get past?"

Rulli recalled that it was in the early 1990s "when the water started to come up. There was the Perfect Storm in 1991 and then the bad nor'easter in December 1992." He said, "After that, it seemed like it just kept coming, and we started to get more and more. Some people say it's climate change and warming. I don't know. There's also more building than ever. The storm drains can't handle all of the water . . . and everything is paved. The water has nowhere to go when it rains."

Rulli has done what he can to flood-proof the restaurant: replacing wood walls with tile, elevating the pizza ovens and other appliances, running the electric through the ceiling panels. But without federal flood insurance, he said, he would be out of business.

"I'm very fortunate I've had flood insurance. I've probably filed seven or as many as ten claims over the years. In the old days, if I had a loss of, say, thirteen thousand dollars, I'd file a claim. Now I don't even bother unless I get three feet of water in there. I just go in there with a broom."

Sandy pushed six feet of water and mud into Joeys' in Beach Haven Crest. Rulli filed two claims: one for damage to the eighty-year-old building, which isn't worth much, he said, and one for the contents. "An adjuster was here for, like, three days. He was very thorough. He wanted me to get what I deserved. I was very pleased with the outcome." So was Joe's insurance broker, which featured him in a national advertisement for flood insurance.

Rulli declined to say how much he has received altogether. He did say he received $50,000 for his damaged ovens after Sandy. Flood-program officials initially rejected the claim. But then Joe's adjuster told him to file an appeal, "and I got a check," he said.

A few years ago, Rulli said, he was approached by state officials about elevating his ground-level restaurant. The request was part of a program funded with federal dollars. He said he never got a grant. "I looked into elevating it myself after that, but it was too expensive. The only other thing I could do is tear it down, but it would cost me one million to build something new."

In the meantime, he keeps a broom and a pump handy. "If I have to pump water a couple times a year, no big deal," he said. (In spring 2019, Long Beach Township agreed to purchase the Beach Haven Crest location for $365,000, with plans to install a small pump station to drain floodwaters into Barnegat Bay.)

\\\

About the time that water was pouring into Joe Rulli's pizza shop during Sandy, lawmakers in Washington were debating ways to fix the troubled flood program. It wasn't the first time they had held hearings. In fact, Congress has been trying to repair the program almost since its inception, but without much success.

But this time, a surprising thing happened. The lawmakers actually managed to push through reforms. Led by Judy Biggert, a Republican from Illinois, and Maxine Waters, a Democrat from Southern California, they shepherded an unprecedented overhaul of the flood program through the House of Representatives. The changes called for risk-based premiums, higher rates for second homes, and the elimination of subsidies for houses that flooded repeatedly, among other fixes. Under the changes, some property owners at the coast would have to pay thousands of dollars or more annually for flood insurance that had cost them just a few hundred dollars in the past. The idea was to restore the program to solvency and to have homeowners pay rates that reflected their actual risk of flooding.

The Biggert-Waters Flood Insurance Reform Act sailed through the House in summer 2012 by a vote of 373 to 52. The Senate then approved it by a vote of 74 to 19.

Howard Kunreuther and Erwann Michel-Kerjan, experts on risk and insurance based at the Wharton School at the University of Pennsylvania, called the Biggert-Waters reforms a bold step forward. "At a time when Congress was criticized for inaction, [the legislation] offered a counter example," they wrote, and "would ultimately help America become more resilient to future floods."

But a few months after the reforms passed, Judy Biggert lost her bid for reelection, and Maxine Waters became the face of flood reform. Waters represented a diverse swath of geography that corkscrews from the scrubby neighborhoods around LAX to upscale Westchester. She is perhaps best known for her work on issues affecting consumers and minorities. But she also held a ranking position on the House Financial Services Committee, which includes oversight of the federal flood insurance program.

Waters's interest in the subject appeared to center on two issues: guaranteeing that flood insurance was available to her constituents and ensuring that they could rebuild quickly after floods. Less clear was how familiar she was with her own legislation. For example, Waters praised the law for delaying rate increases and slowly phasing in higher premiums for risky properties, even while the Government Accountability Office forecast that nearly half a million property owners would see immediate rate hikes as a result of the new law.

The real estate industry attacked the legislation, predicting that rising premiums would lead to coastal chaos. "This is a prime example of why voters are sick and tired of Washington ineptness," one California agent wrote on a blog. "The new real estate crisis will cause coastal real estate owners to default on loans by the hundreds of thousands."

Senator Mary Landrieu of Louisiana was also alarmed. She led a furious assault against Biggert-Waters, introducing a proposal to delay the bill. She was joined by the Mississippi Department of Insurance, which sued FEMA to block the premium increases. Meanwhile, Representative Rush Holt of New Jersey argued that policyholders would likely drop their insurance and rely on federal disaster aid instead. "I am concerned that they will decide flood insurance is something they can do without," he said.

Maxine Waters appeared taken aback by the outcry and quickly began to backpedal from her legislation, advising the media, "Neither Democrats nor Republicans envisioned it would reap the kind of harm and heartache that may result from this law going into effect." She then joined Landrieu in calling for a delay. "Relief is on the way," Waters promised.

While all this was going on, Craig Fugate and his FEMA colleagues were busily working to incorporate the Biggert-Waters changes into new flood rules. "I actually was yelled at by Maxine Waters," he recalled in an interview. "She said, 'What the hell are you doing?' I said, 'I'm implementing your law . . . that's what I'm supposed to do.'"

Fugate added, "I always find it fascinating—here is a delegation against deficits, for cutting government, for less bureaucracy, but don't you dare raise the rates for the federal flood insurance program. It's almost like they turn into socialists," he said.

About this time, a group called Stop FEMA Now bubbled up in New Jersey. It was led by a real estate agent named George Kasimos from Toms River, Ocean County. Kasimos was alarmed that the higher premiums of Biggert-

Waters would drive retirees from their coastal homes and hurt property values. "If flood insurance increases are not slowed, it will have a devastating effect on the housing market across the country," he wrote in one Facebook post. "It will 'stigmatize' flood zone properties and will accelerate the demise in property values in flood zone communities."

Of course increases or decreases in flood insurance premiums are supposed to signal risk, not prop up the housing market. But many homeowners in coastal floodplains don't see it that way. When the flood-program officials moved to implement the higher rates, they staged protests and mounted campaigns to preserve lower premiums. Kasimos's group won the attention of New Jersey's congressional delegation, which took the lead in walking back the Biggert-Waters reforms. Two years later, the Homeowners Insurance Affordability Act of 2014 reinstated subsidized rates, delayed higher full-risk premiums, and placed caps on other increases. It also allowed property owners who sold their houses to pass along their subsidized rates to the new buyers.

"This critical law . . . is a tremendous victory for thousands of New Jersey homeowners who were facing skyrocketing flood insurance costs as they continued to recover from the worst natural disaster in the state's history," the bill's cosponsor, New Jersey senator Robert Menendez, said in a press release.

Tax-advocacy groups complained that, once again, Congress was kicking the program's problems down the road. "While politically expedient today, this abdication of responsibility by Congress is going to come back and bite them and taxpayers when the next disaster strikes," said Steve Ellis, vice president of Taxpayers for Common Sense, a Washington-based nonprofit. And that is exactly what happened in 2017 when Hurricane Harvey flooded the insurance program with nearly $9 billion in claims, dramatically adding to the program's debt.

\\\

In 2017, members of Congress again began debating the future of the federal flood insurance program, holding hearings and introducing legislation. The proposed reforms appeared to be of two stripes. Conservative lawmakers wanted to turn more profitable portions of the program over to private insurers, arguing it would lead to a more efficient and rational market. Liberal law-makers, meanwhile, wanted to forgive the NFIP's colossal debt and trim government payments to the private insurance companies that process claims, while also ensuring that premiums remained affordable.

None of these proposals dealt with the flood program's core problems, its unsustainable and unaffordable risks, or the growing threat posed by increasing numbers of homes—especially second homes—in coastal floodplains. Allowing private companies to cherry-pick profitable, less-risky properties will leave the government insuring the riskiest and costliest houses. And while trimming fees for private insurers is likely to save the government millions, it won't be nearly enough to cover the program's mounting losses. The much tougher solutions—eliminating subsidies, raising premiums to reflect the actual risks of flooding, adopting strict land-use requirements that limit rebuilding after hurricanes, and even getting out of the business of insuring beach houses—have largely been unaddressed.

In the end, Congress punted on any major reforms, temporarily extending the current flood program into 2019.

Even after the Trump administration's decision to forgive $16 billion in losses, the flood program still owes the U.S. Treasury $24 billion. Some groups have called for a massive taxpayer-funded effort to elevate houses in coastal floodplains. But it is unclear what such an effort would cost or how effective it would be in an age of rising seas. This much is clear. The bill would easily be in the billions, if not the tens of billions. New Jersey alone has asked FEMA for $1 billion to raise 12,500 houses.

Meanwhile, government efforts to buy flood-prone property at the coast have largely failed. After Sandy wrecked the small, tightly knit neighborhood of Breezy Point on Rockaway Peninsula, Queens, flooding half of the 4,000 bungalows, FEMA officials suggested retreating to higher ground.

But "no one was interested," said Michael Moriarty, a regional mitigation expert for FEMA who's based in New York City. "We can't get anybody to mention the words 'strategic retreat.' It's not in the vocabulary" of municipal officials.

Instead, homeowners used insurance payments and grants to rebuild along the same narrow alleyways and streets. By the first anniversary of the hurricane, new houses were rising, and newspapers were cheering the can-do attitude of the four thousand residents, which includes scores of New York City firefighters and cops. Other than FEMA, no one appeared to question the wisdom of rebuilding along a slender spit of sand that researchers predict will be underwater by the end of the century, with or without another massive hurricane.

Federal taxpayers are now poised to spend millions more to armor Breezy Point against future storms. Plans are still being developed. But one calls for a massive hurricane barrier stretching from Sandy Hook, New Jersey, across the New York Harbor to Breezy Point. It could cost $20 billion or more and take a decade to complete.

Craig Fugate suggested to me that it may be time for the federal government to get out of the flood business. "Why not just stop writing [premiums] for new construction?" he asked. "Take an arbitrary date, say, January 1 of 2019. If you build brand-new in a flood zone, you can't buy insurance from the federal government. The private sector is going to write it. If you can't get private coverage, sorry. But don't subsidize growing the program. If you build in the flood zone, why should we keep underwriting the risks? It would be a line in the sand. We're not telling you 'you can't build.' But it has to be the private sector."

Fugate told me he floated this idea to Obama administration officials before he left the government in 2016. "You know who our biggest opponent was who got this killed? It was the National Association of Realtors. What the hell? Are you that wedded to selling property in the flood zone? They said it would be detrimental to home sales. Property values would plummet."

11

The Secret History of Sand

THE UNWRITTEN RULE FOR PRESS CONFERENCES was to wear something with a logo, if for no other reason than you might end up on television or in the background of a newspaper photograph. The logo was how you picked out the engineers. They were the ones with the dark-blue polo shirts and nylon jackets with the medieval castle stenciled proudly on the front. The castle represented the muscular architecture of the U.S. Army Corps of Engineers, which for over two centuries had helped to design and fortify the nation's defenses, building Fort McHenry in the Baltimore Harbor, bridges during the Spanish-American War, airfields in World War II, and housing for troops in the Iraq War. Nowadays, the engineers had another, if unlikely, mission: defending the nation's eroding shorelines and widening beaches in front of expensive vacation homes.

It was the reason they were gathering on this warm, hazy morning in early May 2015. The engineers were about to begin the latest phase of a massive, multiyear project to widen the beaches on Long Beach Island, the biggest and richest barrier island in New Jersey. The resort had been losing sand for decades and was now so narrow in places that vacationers had to huddle in the dunes at high tide. The Corps of Engineers and its contractor, Great Lakes Dredge & Dock, planned to pump six million cubic yards of sand—enough to fill a sixty-five-thousand-seat football stadium—onto the beaches. They would then extend the beaches seaward by one hundred feet and build a gradually sloping twenty-two-foot-high sand dune, or what the engineers call a berm. If everything went according to plan, the work would take a year and serve as the first line of defense in the next big storm.

The cost of the latest work was $128 million. However, the total price tag for the project was dramatically higher, an astonishing $505 million to widen and maintain 16.5 miles of eroding shoreline over the next fifty years, or nearly $32 million for each mile of beach. That figure was buried in one of the Corps' thick project summaries and not often publicized.

Needless to say, it was an enormous sum. Yet the owners of the exclusive beach mansions overlooking the sand dunes probably weren't too concerned. Thanks to some deft maneuvers by the congressional delegation in New Jersey, federal taxpayers in Kansas, Colorado, and other landlocked states were paying for 100 percent of the latest work, as well as the majority of the overall project.

That likely explained the extra bounce in the steps of the engineers this morning. Keith Watson, a boyishly handsome engineer in his early fifties, with floppy dark hair and a bemused smile, bounded across the soft sand, shaking hands and mixing easily with the local mayors and politicians. "Great day," he said, greeting the guests. "We're back in business building beaches. It doesn't get any better than this."

Keith was in his third decade at the Corps. He'd earned undergraduate and master's degrees in coastal engineering from the University of Delaware. Other than a brief stop at the Corps' North Atlantic Division in New York City, he'd spent his entire career in the Philadelphia District Office, which includes

In May 2015, the U.S. Army Corps of Engineers began the second phase of a multiyear, $500 million project to rebuild eroding beaches on Long Beach Island. (Courtesy of the U.S. Army Corps of Engineers)

much of the New Jersey coast, working his way from designing beaches to managing hundreds of millions of dollars' worth of coastal projects. Like most of his colleagues, he was a civilian employee, with no military rank. Keith was pragmatic about his mission and saw no irony using federal tax dollars to repair resort beaches. The property was already there, he told me. It was his job to protect it.

"Whether it should be there in the first place is a different question," he said during one of many interviews we shared. "That's a question above my pay grade. My job is to protect the community. It may be a summer community, but it's still a community."

Keith and his wife, an orthopedic surgeon, owned a five-bedroom beach house in Barnegat Light, on the northern end of Long Beach Island. They had purchased the house more than a decade earlier for about $400,000. Like nearly all the real estate on the island, it had appreciated sharply as land values soared. But Keith liked to point out that Barnegat Light had the widest beaches on the island and didn't require any extra sand. "I may be a lot of things," he said, "but I'm not stupid."

It was warm for early May, already 80 degrees Fahrenheit and windless. A thick, wet mist hovered over the much cooler Atlantic Ocean, obscuring a large hopper dredge positioned a hundred yards off the beach. The belly of the dredge bulged with twelve thousand yards of sand that it had siphoned earlier that morning from the ocean bottom three miles offshore. Now, workers were preparing to attach a large nozzle to a pipe extending onto the beach and begin pumping the sand ashore, where bulldozers and graders waited to groom it into a new, wider beach. The dredges—there were three—worked around the clock, seven days a week. The only time they didn't work was when the conditions were too rough—during a hurricane or a nor'easter, for example. Then the pilots steered the dredges north and parked them safely in a harbor until the storm exhausted itself.

"That noise I hear is sweet music to my ears," the Ocean County freeholder Joseph H. Vicari exclaimed as sand surged ashore. He was standing at a wooden podium that someone had dragged down to the beach for the press conference. "That is the sound of progress, the sound of this island recovering from one of the worst storms [Sandy] in history."

Vicari continued for several minutes, touting the importance of the repaired beaches to the local tourism economy. He was followed by several other politicians. Then Keith Watson agreed to take a few questions from the reporters. Although Watson wasn't the engineer on-site, he was one of the people overseeing the project and a familiar face on Long Beach Island.

A writer wanted to know whether the wider beach would protect the $15 billion worth of property on the island from another massive storm like Hurricane Sandy.

"I'm glad you asked that question," Watson said. "The name is a little misleading. It is called a fifty-year-storm protection project, but that doesn't mean there is a certain level of storm it will protect against. What we are saying is that it will help reduce damage over the lifetime of the project, and the lifetime of the project is fifty years."

The distinction was subtle enough to confuse the writer.

"We don't make guarantees," Watson added.

"But it will last for fifty years?"

"That's different," Watson said. The writers wanted him to make it easy; to say the sand would remain in place and protect the houses against a certain level of storm. But he couldn't say that. Too many variables were outside his control—powerful storms being just one. The last thing he wanted to do was oversell the project. The engineers had done that in the past and had been embarrassed when their projects didn't perform up to expectations. These days, some of the engineers even referred to their sand as "sacrificial," meaning it was a temporary solution to a long-term problem.

"Let me try again," Watson said. "When we sign a contract like this, it is for fifty years. That doesn't mean we are guaranteeing that it will protect against a fifty-year storm or a hundred-year storm. What we are saying is that we are making a fifty-year commitment to help maintain a certain level of design, assuming Congress continues to provide us the money. That's an important distinction, okay? I know it's hard to understand. But we are not in the storm-prevention business. We are in the damage-reduction business. It's different."

\\\

The Corps of Engineers claims to be agnostic about beach-building. They are simply carrying out the wishes of Congress, the engineers say. Congress orders them to study eroding coasts and appropriates the money to repair damaged beaches. "The Corps can't do anything on its own," Keith Watson told me more than a few times.

Even so, repairing beaches is the engineers' livelihood. They depend on beach-town mayors to invite them to mend their beaches. And they depend on members of Congress from coastal states to arrange the funds for their studies and projects. Without those funds, the engineers would be out of jobs, or doing something different. Unsurprisingly, they spend a large amount of time holding the hands of politicians to make sure they are happy and on board. This creates an awkward kind of codependency in which the engineers often defer to the mayors and politicians, referring to them as their "business partners."

"If you don't have a federal project, we want to talk to you," the head of coastal projects for the Corps' Jacksonville, Florida, district advised a gathering a few years ago. "We are pulling out all the stops to get funding for you."

The late Dery Bennett, director of the nonprofit American Littoral Society, once likened the engineers to "Fuller Brush men," a humorous reference to the door-to-door salesmen who called on American homes in the 1950s with suitcases full of cleaning products. "They're selling a product, and that product is sand, millions and millions of yards of sand," he said.

At 141 miles, New Jersey's coast is far from the largest. It is about one-third the size of the North Carolina and Texas coasts, and one-tenth the size of Florida's. Yet the state has received significantly more sand than all states except Florida. Since 1962, the Corps of Engineers has pumped over one hundred million cubic yards of sand on New Jersey beaches, with repair jobs extending from Sea Bright in the northern part of the state to Cape May in the south. It is hard to find a beach that hasn't gotten at least some sand courtesy of federal taxpayers. Some towns, such as Ocean City, have received multiple repairs. If you took all the sand the engineers have placed on New Jersey's beaches, it would fill MetLife Stadium, home of the New York Giants football team, over fifteen times.

"Any way you cut it, it's a shitload of sand for practically nothing," said Stewart Farrell, a well-known coastal geologist based at New Jersey's Stockton University who monitors New Jersey beaches for the state's Department of Environmental Protection. "It's a hell of a deal."

Farrell recently estimated that various agencies have spent about $1.2 billion widening the state's eroding beaches over the last sixty years, with the federal government accounting for the largest share. That figure is likely to grow after the engineers finish Sandy repairs on Long Beach Island and other sites, and it could top $2 billion, including future costs associated with maintaining the beaches. Along with disaster aid and flood insurance, beach-building is now one of the most coveted and controversial federal entitlements propping up coasts and property values.

Why are New Jersey politicians so good at procuring federal sand dollars? Part of the answer is history. The state congressional delegation began lobbying for federal assistance earlier than anyone else, and has more experience. New Jersey lawmakers from coastal counties view beach-building as an important component of their constituent service and work closely with beach-town mayors and their Washington lobbyists to secure federal funds.

"I want to hear from the mayors. It's important. They depend on the beaches for their livelihood," said Frank LoBiondo, a Republican congressman representing several New Jersey coastal counties. LoBiondo, who owns a house in Ventnor, a beach community near Atlantic City, helped arrange for taxpayers to cover 100 percent of the latest Long Beach Island project. He retired from Congress at the end of 2018.

"From my perspective, the congressional delegation does an outstanding job," Keith Watson told me. "They have worked extremely hard to get their projects funded. Maybe other delegations don't work as hard."

There is certainly an art to getting federal taxpayers to build you a beach. A handful of beach towns on the northern Outer Banks of North Carolina have been trying for years to grab federal sand dollars, without success. They are currently spending millions of their own money to widen eroding beaches from Duck to Nags Head. "We desperately want a Corps project," John Ratzenberger, a Nags Head commissioner, told me. "But I guess our delegation doesn't have the pull like you do in New Jersey."

Nationally, the Corps of Engineers has pumped over five hundred million cubic yards of sand onto resort beaches since the late 1950s, at a cost of nearly $5 billion, according to federal records and a database kept by the geologist Andy Coburn at Western Carolina University. The numbers have to be interpreted with caution because Corps record-keeping in the early years was sloppy at best, and even now, the engineers are skittish about discussing costs. Still, records show that the engineers have repaired beaches from Winthrop, Massachusetts, to Boca Raton, Florida, including Virginia Beach,

Virginia, and Bay St. Louis, Mississippi. After Hurricane Katrina, the Corps received hundreds of millions of dollars to restore barrier islands in Louisiana and Mississippi. That legislation also called for the Corps to buy up to two thousand flood-prone houses and leave the space vacant. But over a decade later, Congress still hasn't funded those buyouts.

The 2013 Sandy Disaster Relief Appropriations Act of 2013 included $5 billion for the engineers to rebuild beaches, fix seawalls, and conduct coastal studies. At least $1 billion is being used to widen and repair resort beaches, including the latest work on Long Beach Island, the second phase of a project expected to last fifty years, including touch-ups.

\\\

The Army Corps of Engineers didn't set out to be in the beach-building business. For years, the engineers fought efforts to add beach repairs to their mission statement. But eventually, coastal interests won the engineers over, thanks in part to the efforts of an engaging and persistent lobbyist from New Jersey who convinced them that beach erosion wasn't only a local issue; it was a national threat.

Like many men of his era, J. Spencer Smith was street-smart, self-made, and ambitious. Although born in Canada, Smith grew up in Brooklyn. His family scrambled for work and money. In 1894, at fourteen, he ended his formal schooling to go to work. Smith was appealing and even-tempered, with an instinctive knack for politics, people, and big ideas. At the age of twenty-two, he was elected to the Tenafly Borough Council in Bergen County, New Jersey, where he'd moved. A few years later, he joined the local school board, where he would serve for fifty-two years, until his death in 1953. Somehow, even with all his commitments, he managed to find the time to teach himself law and engineering.

In 1911, Smith caught the eye of Woodrow Wilson, then the New Jersey governor, who appointed him to a commission investigating conditions at the state's ports. Three years later, Smith was named to the Harbor Commission, and later still to the powerful State Board of Commerce and Navigation, which included oversight of the state's beaches. Smith served on the board for over three decades, using it to solidify his power and establish a national reputation as an expert on ports and waterways.

As early as the turn of the century, newspapers in New Jersey had begun to highlight the precarious state of beaches in Asbury Park, Atlantic City, Cape May, and other popular resorts. The beaches were washing away at alarming rates, the reporters observed. Several hotels and amusement piers were said to be at risk of toppling into the Atlantic surf. A 1922 study by Smith's Navigation Board warned that continuing erosion would result in "further loss of physical property" and "discourage investment in capital in seashore property."

As with later studies, the Navigation Board's report didn't consider the possibility of limiting development at the coast, or retreating inland to higher ground. The state's appealing shoreline was too valuable an asset to ignore, Smith wrote. It would be foolish not to take advantage of it.

Smith was well aware that building close to the shoreline only accelerated erosion, leaving property exposed to storms and waves. Indeed, the more developers built along the ocean, the greater the risks. One of the Navigation Board's early studies even observed that "development almost inevitably resulted in the necessity of protecting beach communities from attack by the ocean." But Smith still favored development. At this point, the question shifted to who should pay to defend the coast? It turned out that J. Spencer Smith had an answer for that as well.

In the 1920s, Smith galvanized coastal mayors and beach-town politicians from New England to Florida. Erosion and "ravages from the sea" posed an existential threat to all their towns and economies, he stressed. The solution was to "unite in some cooperative scheme to bring about a continuous program of beachfront protection."

Smith arranged meetings in Asbury Park and Atlantic City, New Jersey; Coney Island, New York; Norfolk, Virginia; and Washington, D.C. It was time to bring "powerful pressure to bear on both Congress and state legislatures to get financial aid for seashore protection," he told the attendees. Shortly thereafter, Smith helped create the American Shore and Beach

Preservation Association (ASBPA), with the express purpose of marshaling a national campaign to save the beaches and millions of dollars' worth of property. Smith was elected its first president, and held the position until his death.

The ASBPA, which is still active today, quickly turned to politics. It stressed that erosion was a national issue requiring a national solution. The Army Corps of Engineers, with its vast experience working on the nation's waterways, was the ideal agency to take up the work of rebuilding damaged beaches, the group contended.

Initially, the engineers didn't see an engineering problem at the coast; they saw a *human* problem. By building in harm's way, humans had created a "self-inflicted problem," an internal Corps history notes. The nation's shorelines were now viewed "as a recreational resource and a producer of profit. Increasingly, the ocean generally, and the waves in particular, became depicted as 'enemies'—threats, which had to be controlled to the greatest extent possible."

According to the Corps history, Smith and the ASBPA were maneuvering to get the engineers involved in beach repairs. "Rather than seeing coastal erosion as a natural phenomenon and taking full cognizance of this fact when developing shore sites, some other explanation was sought . . . to account for this force which was now destroying valuable property."

Colonel Earl Ivan Brown complained that private interests were looking to the federal government as a "source of easy money . . . to force the federal government to assume the burden of shore protection."

In 1935, George H. Dorn, the secretary of war, observed: "This Department is unable to find a justification . . . looking to the expenditure of federal funds in the construction of shore protection works along the coast. The property to be protected is in general privately owned, and its improvement and protection at public expense appears to be unwarranted."

\\\

Not all the engineers opposed taking on a new mission. Several top Corps officials were closely following the beach association's efforts and were eager to begin studying the erosion problem, according to the agency's internal history. In

January 1929, the chief of engineers agreed to set up the Beach Erosion Board to study sand movement. He defended the step as a legitimate area of scientific inquiry, as there was little data available at the time on how coastal processes worked. The engineers set up two field studies on the Jersey Shore, one in Long Branch and the other in Seaside Heights. Much of the sampling was done by summer interns bravely wading into the surf. "They were young, fearless, and motivated," the Corps history recalls.

In 1936, Congress passed the U.S. Beach Improvement and Protection Act, establishing federal assistance for the Corps' studies and formally placing the Beach Erosion Board within the engineers' control. The federal government still didn't pay for actual beach repairs. For the time being, that remained the responsibility of beach towns and coastal states, which usually trucked in sand for emergency repairs.

But a decade later, Congress authorized the federal government to begin paying up to one-third of the cost of repairing public beaches owned by municipal and state governments. Then, in the mid-1950s, lawmakers agreed to include private beaches, arguing that widening them would benefit nearby public beaches as well. Today, the majority of beaches that receive taxpayer-funded sand are stacked with expensive beach houses and mansions, not publicly owned beaches. The Corps requires beach towns to include public accesses every half mile. But many of these right-of-ways are public in name only: hard to find and with limited parking and no public restrooms or changing facilities.

Initially, the engineers justified their beach-building efforts as critical to saving lives. But with fewer people living year-round on many barrier islands, it is difficult to use that rationale today. Instead, the engineers stress that widening beaches helps reduce storm damage and provides economic benefits, presumably meaning the tourism economy.

These arguments appear to suffer from the same fundamental flaw as the rationale behind federal flood insurance: If widening beaches and elevating sand dunes reduce damage, why are hurricanes and nor'easters causing more destruction than ever? The Corps has pumped more sand in the last two decades than in the rest of its history. Yet storm-damage costs continued to soar, to nearly $800 billion, in the same period. Essentially, the engineers appear to be saying, "Yes, but imagine how much worse it would have been without our sand?"

The economic benefits associated with beach-building are also limited. Coastal states and lobbying groups pay for studies that invariably show wide impacts on jobs and income. However, as with many such studies, the data appear to be cherry-picked and liberally overstate the role of the coastal economy. Nationally, only 4 percent of all jobs are "dependent on coastal and ocean resources," according to NOAA. In New Jersey, less than 3 percent of the jobs are at the immediate coast.

There is a beach economy. But it is different from the one depicted in the studies. Most of the money is associated with real estate and construction. The tourism jobs touted in the studies—retail clerks, cooks, dishwashers, life-guards, waiters—are seasonal and low-wage. Meanwhile, many beach towns are losing year-round jobs as populations tumble and barrier-island resorts transition from places where people live and work to seasonal communities of second homes and investment properties. On Long Beach Island, about half of the year-round residents have to travel off the island for work, federal records show.

The biggest beneficiaries of beach-building are the property owners with the largest, most expensive houses—those in the first two rows along the oceanfront. On Long Beach Island, the average value of an oceanfront house is about $2 million, though many are worth millions more. Nine of ten are seasonal vacation homes.

The engineers insist that they aren't repairing beaches for millionaires; they are protecting property from storm damage. They also contend their projects don't increase the value of oceanfront houses. These are subtle, even confounding claims. For example, a 2015 study by Dylan McNamara, a professor of physics and physical oceanography at the University of North Carolina Wilmington, found that federal beach projects had inflated oceanfront properties in New Jersey by up to 34 percent. If those subsidies vanished, he told the Associated Press, there "would be a pretty severe loss of value up and down the coast."

"Our projects benefit lots of people," Keith Watson told me, "though it's true people along the oceanfront probably receive the most benefits. They are garnering a special benefit."

\\\

As with disaster relief, most of the money for the Corps beach-building comes from the huge supplemental appropriation bills that Congress relies on to fund hurricane-recovery efforts. If there are no storms, funding lags. On the other hand, if a huge storm, such as Katrina or Sandy, washes ashore, the engineers often receive billions for their projects.

Beach resorts are supposed to contribute 35 percent of the cost of repairing their beaches. However, as with disaster relief, politics often comes into play and the required local contributions frequently are shifted to federal taxpayers. Prior to 1962, when the Ash Wednesday Storm gutted Long Beach Island, beach towns were required to pay for two-thirds of beach projects. Congress first reduced that share to 50 percent, and later to just 35 percent, effectively reversing the original formula. In New Jersey, the state pays for most of the local share, with beach towns usually paying just 8.75 percent.

Critics contend that the minimal contribution encourages oceanfront building and shifts the risk from private homeowners to federal taxpayers. Lawmakers from inland states have tried to restore the original funding formula, but their efforts have failed. Meanwhile, presidents from Jimmy Carter to Barack Obama have attempted to eliminate beach-building from Corps budgets—without success.

In 1986, members of Congress made another costly change to federally funded beach projects, extending the amount of time the Corps is responsible for maintaining its beach repairs—from fifteen years to fifty. As a result, the engineers typically have to return to touch up their work every three to five years—a taxpayer-funded form of Botox for the beach.

\\\

The initial phase of the Long Beach Island project began in February 2007. That year, the Corps' contractor pumped 800,000 cubic yards of sand onto a mile-long stretch of beach in Surf City, a town on the northern half of the island. The plan called for the engineers to move their dredges up and down the beaches as additional funding became available, until all of the island's eroding beaches were widened. Barnegat Light was excluded.

The cost of the Surf City work was $8.6 million, according to federal records. But that proved to be just the beginning. The following summer, vacationers were startled to discover unexploded ammunition while digging on the beach—not exactly the kind of shells they hoped to find. The leftover ordnance was from World War II training exercises conducted off the beach. The dredges swept up the shells from the ocean floor while siphoning sand. Great Lakes later added sieves to prevent ammunition and other large objects from entering its pipes. No one was injured. But Surf City had to close its beaches at the peak of the summer while workers combed the sand for shells. It was a black eye for the Corps and cost federal taxpayers an additional $13 million to clean up.

In November 2009, a powerful nor'easter named Ida washed away 220,000 cubic yards of the widened Surf City beach. The engineers estimated the cost of repairing their repairs at $6.9 million—or nearly as much as the original work. The funds came from a little-known account, the Flood Control and Coastal Emergencies (FCCE) program, which Congress established in the 1980s for the Corps and pays for 100 percent of lost sand with federal tax dollars.

A year later, the dredges moved up the island to Harvey Cedars, where the narrow shoreline is especially vulnerable to erosion, and in 1962 the ocean broke through to merge with Barnegat Bay. This time, Great Lakes pumped 3 million cubic yards of sand—but no leftover ammunition—onto the beach, at a cost of $26 million.

The dredges then headed south to an area of heavily scarred beaches in Brant Beach, Long Beach Township, where developers had built houses close to the fragile sand dunes. The area is known as a "hot spot" because it routinely loses sand in nor'easters. The contractor pumped 1.2 million cubic yards of sand at a cost of $17 million.

This meant that, so far, the first phase of the Long Beach Island project had cost $71.5 million, including the expense of removing the ammunition but not factoring in the future cost of touch-ups. But, once again, it was only the beginning. Just weeks after completing the Brant Beach repairs in 2012, Hurricane Sandy hurled ten-foot waves onto the Corps' rebuilt beaches, sweeping away much of the new sand and scouring the refurbished dunes.

"The good news is, it worked. The sand did what it was supposed to do. There was far less damage where we pumped sand than areas that didn't have replenishment. The bad news is, we lost half of the sand," Keith Watson said.

\\\

Hurricane Sandy swept away more than two million cubic yards of sand from the original three work sites. Once again, the engineers tapped their emergency account, using about $40 million for additional sand, according to Corps reports I obtained under the Freedom of Information Act. That brought the running total for the three beaches to $111.5 million, with federal taxpayers picking up most of the cost.

The 2013 Hurricane Sandy Disaster Relief package was flush with money for beach repairs, including $128 million for the second phase of the Long Beach Island project, covering the remaining twelve miles of beaches. Great Lakes decided to begin in Ship Bottom, the site of the May 2015 press conference, in the middle of the island. The decision proved to be controversial. Ship Bottom had fairly wide, stable beaches, while the beaches along the southern end of the island, especially in Holgate, were narrow and sand-starved.

Even before Sandy, Holgate looked like a moonscape, with holes, divots, channels, and exposed concrete, wood, and rocks. The dunes were low and vulnerable. Property owners were understandably distraught and worried that the dredges wouldn't reach them before the inevitable winter storms. "We're like sitting ducks," complained Tom Beaty, a Holgate resident and community leader who was renting an apartment after Sandy flooded his family's trailer.

Beaty and the other Holgate homeowners were still waiting for sand when the new year arrived eight months later. Adding to their anger and frustration, Great Lakes announced that it was shutting down for the winter and hauling its dredges south, to Georgia, to work in calmer waters. The Atlantic Ocean was too rough in January and February, a spokesman explained.

Sure enough, only weeks later, a nor'easter spiraled up the coast toward Long Beach Island. As winter storms go, the January 2016 nor'easter was one of the worst in years. Towering waves and storm surge battered the beaches for days. A state engineer estimated the storm swept away 70 percent of the Corps' sand. Keith Watson initially put the loss at 40 percent but later lowered that to 25 percent. In any case, it was a huge amount of sand, and once again spotlighted the precarious nature of beach-building.

But Mother Nature wasn't done. Two weeks later, a second nor'easter crashed ashore, sweeping away even more sand. It was beginning to feel like the story of Sisyphus, wherein the gods condemn Sisyphus to roll a large rock up a hill only for the rock to roll back down, over and over. But in this story, the part of Sisyphus was being played by the Corps of Engineers. Each time they pumped more sand onto the island's damaged beaches, a new storm would roll in and wash it out to sea.

At this point, the engineers had lost between three and four million cubic yards of sand, by my estimate. The cost of replacing all that sand was mounting sharply, with the two 2016 nor'easters alone costing $30 million for additional sand. "It has been a run of bad luck," said Jeff Gebert, chief of coastal planning for the Philadelphia District. "I'm not sure we have ever experienced anything like this."

Meanwhile, the Long Beach Township mayor Joseph Mancini faced a pressing problem. Holgate had no beaches, and the property owners were up in arms. He needed to do something—and quickly. Mancini turned to Bob Martin, commissioner of the New Jersey Department of Environmental Protection. The state wrote a check for $300,000 worth of emergency sand, trucked over from a quarry on the mainland. It took 1,252 trips—with each truck containing twenty tons of sand, local newspapers reported.

"It's a Band-Aid," the mayor told me at the time. "But the people are screaming for help, and you have to do something. But as soon as the next storm hits, it will wash it all away."

And that was what happened a few weeks later. Now a dangerous

A series of nor'easters and coastal storms washed away much of the sand from the Corps of Engineers' beach repairs on Long Beach Island, resulting in millions of dollars in losses. (Photograph by the author)

twenty-foot cliff formed near the public parking lot in Holgate. Township police cordoned off the area with yellow emergency tape, as if it were a crime scene, and warned visitors to steer clear.

The following summer, the Great Lakes dredges finally arrived in Holgate and began to pump sand. For a few months, everyone was happy. But then the new sand began to drift through and around an old wooden groin and onto a nearby federal wildlife reserve, which wasn't part of the Corps project. It was great for the piping plovers, though the locals weren't amused. The following fall and winter, a new wave of nor'easters hollowed out the rest of the recently rebuilt beaches and formed even steeper cliffs. Once again, yellow tape went up.

Curiously, while all this was going on, Holgate, the last bohemian enclave on Long Beach Island, was undergoing an extensive facelift. Instead of retreating after Sandy, the area was undergoing a remarkable transformation. Scores of small old bungalows and 1970s-era duplexes were torn down and replaced with five- and six-bedroom suburban-style homes. Joe Mancini, the mayor and developer, built an entire new block of million-dollar vacation homes on spec and sold most of them within a year or two. Meanwhile, new houses along the oceanfront were selling for as high as $4 million.

By my count, the number of homes in Holgate valued at $1 million or more soared from fewer than a dozen in 2000 to 183 by 2015, just three years after the hurricane. Altogether, the number of million-dollar homes on Long Beach Island increased from 50 to 3,116 in the same period. This latest building boom was a powerful reminder of how urban renewal works at the beach, and yet was alarming at the same time, given how vulnerable the island is.

The Holgate trailer park where Tom Beaty had lived for nearly a quarter century was cleared after Sandy and later sold to a local developer for $12 million. For decades, the 4.2-acre park had stood as a symbol of a simpler, cheaper lifestyle, with an eclectic mix of surfers, beach bums, doctors, lawyers, even a nun, who arrived each April and remained until the owners shut off the water in October. After promising to reopen, the owners decided it would cost too much and informed their renters by email that they had a month to remove their damaged trailers. In 2018, a new owner announced plans for forty-two houses starting at $1 million. Roof decks were optional.

\\\

In 2017, the dredges returned to Holgate and pumped an additional 300,000 cubic yards of sand at a cost of $5.7 million. Another $20 million went to repair nearby beaches in Beach Haven. And $30 million more was set aside for yet another emergency touch-up at the original three beaches in Surf City, Harvey Cedars, and Brant Beach.

ANATOMY OF A BEACH PROJECT: LONG BEACH ISLAND

YEAR	TOWN	WORK DETAILS	COST (IN MILLIONS)
2007	Surf City	800,000 cubic yards of sand	$8.6
2008–2009	Surf City	Remove ammo	$13.0
2009	Surf City	Ida Beach repairs	$6.9
2010	Harvey Cedars	3,000,000 cubic yards of sand	$26.0
2012	Brant Beach	1,200,000 cubic yards of sand	$17.0
2012	Sandy Repairs	2,000,000 cubic yards of sand	$40.0
2015	Phase Ii Sb, Lbt	6,000,000 cubic yards of sand	$128.0
2016	Winter Storm Repairs		$30.0
2016	Holgate	Emergency	[$300,000]
2017	Beach Haven, Holgate	Sand	$25.7
2017–2018	Surf City, Harvey Cedars, Brant Beach	Repairs	$30.0
2018	Holgate Beach Haven	State repairs	$18.4
TOTAL			$343.9

SOURCE: CORPS OF ENGINEERS. FINAL COST ESTIMATED AT $505 MILLION, BUT IS SUBJECT TO CHANGE. AS OF JUNE 2018.

As best as I could tell, the Corps had pumped over thirteen million cubic yards of sand onto the island's beaches, including the many emergency repairs. That was equal to nearly seven hundred cubic yards of sand for each of the island's nineteen thousand houses and businesses—an extraordinary amount by any measure.

In 2018, the New Jersey Department of Environmental Protection spent $18.4 million of its own money to replenish the beaches in Holgate and Beach Haven, only to watch it wash away in a storm a few days later. Now, as I write, there is a new plan to build a huge steel sheet covered by giant boulders at the end of Holgate, adjacent to the federal wildlife reserve. The hope is that the wall will act like a catcher's mitt and trap the sand before it washes down the coast. No one knows how well it will work. But the cliffs have moved even closer to the oceanfront homes, and the owners are desperate. Most of the estimated cost of $7.5 million will be covered by the state.

I suppose the lesson is this: The nature of sand is that it doesn't want to remain in one place. It moves constantly. Currents transport it down the shoreline. Storms wash it out to sea, where it forms sandbars and shoals. Winds blow it across barrier islands, which is how the islands gain elevation and protect themselves against rising seas. Whether you favor federally funded sand projects or don't, there are no easy fixes to what is a nonlinear problem.

Another lesson: If you can get federal taxpayers to build you a new beach, why wouldn't you? Altogether, the Long Beach Island project has cost more than $340 million. But that will keep rising when the dredges return every few years—for forty more years. If you believe the most recent reports, all this will cost $505 million. Then again, maybe it will cost $600 million, or more. At this point, it's impossible to say.

12

The Unluckiest Island
in America

ON THE NIGHT OF SEPTEMBER 12, 1979, a bruising Category 3 hurricane named Frederic roared up the Gulf of Mexico and across Dauphin Island before surging into Mobile Bay. The 120-mile-per-hour winds and 12-foot storm surge toppled the only bridge to the island and destroyed 140 houses. For several years, the only way for workers to commute to nearby Mobile was by ferry.

Travel guides from the era described Dauphin Island as one of the Gulf's hidden gems, a quaint, unpretentious oasis of pastel bungalows, white sugar-sand beaches, and spectacular sunsets. They didn't mention hurricanes or the fact that the fourteen-mile island was slowly sinking into the Gulf of Mexico.

Dauphin, named for French royalty, is shaped like a drumstick, widest on its east end, where there is a lush maritime forest, a historic Civil War–era fort, and a nationally celebrated bird sanctuary; and pinched on its west end, where it has lost over one hundred feet of shoreline to erosion and storms in the last few decades, and vacation houses now perch like birdhouses above the water. It is one of a score of low-lying islands, some no more than sand spits, which dangle like a necklace along the Gulf Coast from Alabama to Louisiana. Once a formidable barrier between the Gulf and the mainland, the islands are now tattered and uneven, some dense with sedge and trees, others ripped asunder by storms and all but vanished beneath the water.

Frederic wasn't the first hurricane to pummel the Alabama resort, nor would it be the last. For as long as anyone has kept records, Dauphin Island has been a magnet for violent storms. In 1699, when the French first landed there, they discovered a field of skeletons, possibly hurricane victims, and for a time called the place Massacre Island. In the early 1900s, five powerful hurricanes lashed the then mostly empty barrier. More recently, a dozen hurricanes and tropical storms have battered the resort, including Camille in 1969, Frederic in 1979, Georges in 1998, Ivan in 2004, and Katrina in 2005. In 2017, Nate, a weak storm with 65-mile-per-hour winds, pushed several feet of water into dozens of homes.

"Dauphin is like a bowling alley," said Hank Caddell, an attorney and the head of a local nonprofit environmental group. "It keeps getting hit with all of this heedless destruction."

It isn't hard to see why. The razor-thin section of coast where Dauphin Island lies is a veritable runway for late-season hurricanes sprinting up the Gulf of Mexico. The offshore bathymetry is long and shallow, an ideal launching pad. The island itself is a complex geometry, bordered on the east end by the busy Mobile Bay Ship Channel, with towering sand dunes in the middle and virtually no shoreline or dunes on the pancake-flat west end. The Mobile Bay and Mississippi Sound border the island's backside.

It might seem surprising, then, that the largest and most expensive homes are located along the vulnerable west end, where Katrina gutted hundreds of second homes, sweeping some off their fifteen-foot-high stilts into the Mississippi Sound. Yet that's where owners and investors want to build. "It's flat and has the best views," said Mayor Jeff Collier.

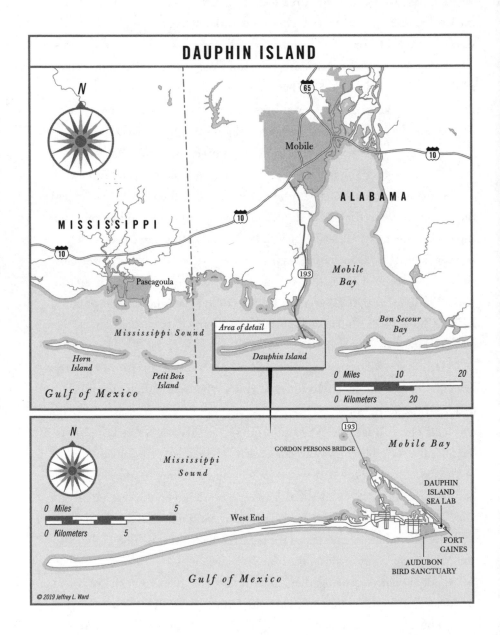

DAUPHIN ISLAND

N

Mobile

65

10

MISSISSIPPI

ALABAMA

10

10

Pascagoula

193

Mobile
Bay

Mississippi Sound

Area of detail

Bon Secour
Bay

Horn
Island

Dauphin Island

Petit Bois
Island

Gulf of Mexico

0 Miles 10 20

0 Kilometers 20

N

193

Mobile Bay

Mississippi
Sound

GORDON PERSONS BRIDGE

DAUPHIN
ISLAND
SEA LAB

0 Miles 5

0 Kilometers 5

West End

FORT
GAINES

AUDUBON
BIRD SANCTUARY

Gulf of Mexico

© 2019 Jeffrey L. Ward

Under Alabama law, there's little Collier can do, assuming he even wanted to stop them. The state has no requirements for setbacks. Property owners can—and do—build right to the water's edge. In theory, there is a state construction line limiting building beyond it. However, the line was adopted in 1973 and now sits about a hundred yards offshore, under the Gulf of Mexico.

"The state has never gone back and reset the line to take into account erosion, storms, or sea-level rise," said George F. Crozier, the former head of a marine research center on the east end. "It's kind of a joke. It fell into the water."

"We've had a run of bad luck," Collier allowed. "We've had a run like every year with a hurricane. The west end is especially vulnerable. It washes over in every storm. Like I say, the west end goes under in a heavy dew."

\\\

Most of Dauphin Island's income comes from the five hundred or so houses on the two-mile-long west end. Nearly all are rental properties and vacation homes owned by absentee landlords. Some rent for up to $5,000 a week. Critically, the owners pay a special fee to the town. "Without those funds, Dauphin Island would be broke," Collier told me. "Our budget is only about three million dollars, and we need every penny we get."

And so, following each storm, Collier and Dauphin Island homeowners follow a familiar script. First, they plead for disaster aid from the federal government. Then they file claims with the federal flood insurance program. Finally, with tax dollars and insurance payouts in hand, they rebuild in the same dangerous location, assuming it isn't underwater. That's what happened after Frederic, and after Georges, Ivan, and Katrina, and is now happening again after Nate.

It is unclear how much federal aid Dauphin Island has received over time. The records are incomplete and don't go back far enough. But it is at least $100 million and some put the figure as high as $200 million. Crozier told me it could be higher yet. But even the lower estimate works out to about $170,000 for each of the island's 1,200 year-round residents.

"Dauphin Island, and especially the west end, is a poster child for all of our failed public policies, local, state, and federal," Crozier said. "Really, it is a case study of schizophrenia. The property owners want to be left alone, except when there is a storm. Then they want the taxpayers to pay for new roads and bridges and sand and [to] help them rebuild."

\\\

Paradoxically, Hurricane Frederic couldn't have made landfall at a more convenient time for residents of the resort. Four months earlier, in April 1979, President Jimmy Carter had shifted most of the nation's disaster-response functions into a newly created department, the Federal Emergency Management Agency. The idea was to consolidate the work of a dozen disparate agencies into one superagency so the government could respond more efficiently to disasters. With widespread damage along the central Gulf Coast, Hurricane Frederic presented FEMA's first test.

Two days after the September storm, Carter flew over the coast to see the damage firsthand and to reassure Alabamans that the federal government had their back. It was part of a standing tradition among presidents. In 1965, Lyndon Johnson famously visited a darkened New Orleans shelter after Hurricane Betsy inundated the city. Shining a flashlight onto his heavily wrinkled face, he announced: "My name is Lyndon Baines Johnson. I am your president. I am here to make sure you have the help you need."

Carter wasn't quite that dramatic. But according to press releases, at the time of his visit he did promise to restore Dauphin Island and the rest of the Gulf Coast. "Carter walked on the sand and told us to build everything back just like it was and send him the bill," an aide to the Alabama governor Fob James recalled in an interview a few years later.

FEMA set aside $200 million for Alabama's recovery. Millions went to Dauphin Island to repair roads, cart away debris, and help year-round homeowners pay bills while they rebuilt their homes.

The Frederic aid package included $33 million to rebuild Dauphin Island's only bridge. After the storm, islanders were forced to use a ferry to get to and from their mainland jobs in nearby Mobile, adding hours to their workdays. Curiously, Alabama representatives balked at the offer, believing it might be more economical to keep the ferry. Frustrated federal officials responded with a pointed message: if Alabama didn't want the money, they would find someone who did. Local politicians quickly decided to take the funds and built a new elevated concrete span linking the mainland and the island. Federal taxpayers picked up 100 percent of the cost, which eventually swelled to $40 million.

The Carter presidential archives include correspondence suggesting the president's aides worried that a new bridge would encourage a wave of development on the vulnerable barrier island, leaving even more homes exposed to future hurricanes. Nevertheless, they issued the check, and the new bridge opened in 1982. That same year, the Reagan administration awarded Dauphin Island a $9 million grant for a sewer plant to serve the west end, where growing numbers of vacation homes were being built.

\\\

In September 1998, Georges, a Category 2 hurricane, swept forty-one bungalows from their concrete pads along the Gulf of Mexico and hurled them across Bienville Boulevard into houses near the Mississippi Sound. I was in Mobile at the time and drove over to see the damage. While there, I encountered Gail Leacy taking pictures of her damaged home on the sound side on the west end.

"It just flew at us," she said, pointing to the crumpled roof of a bungalow sandwiched beneath her elevated house. Leacy and her husband, John, a builder, lived in Mobile but visited their Dauphin Island home frequently. Thankfully, she said, they had federal flood insurance and would be able to recoup some of their loss.

Dauphin Island received over $2 million in federal disaster aid, including $1,125 to replace the town's welcome sign, which reads THE SUNSET CAPITAL OF ALABAMA. FEMA also agreed to pay for a temporary sand dune to protect the remaining beach houses along the sand-starved west end. Environmental groups protested that the dune would encourage owners to rebuild in harm's way. Nevertheless, FEMA paid over $1 million for a five-foot wall of sand designed to last five years.

In August 2005, Hurricane Katrina swept scores of vacation houses from their pilings on Dauphin Island into the nearby Mississippi Sound. (Photograph by the author)

The temporary dune washed away in less than two years. FEMA officials then wrote a second check for $4 million for another temporary sand dune. It, too, washed away. After the Deepwater Horizon oil spill in 2010 fouled its beaches, Dauphin got a third dune, costing $10 million. The money came from a legal settlement, not FEMA, and the dune was placed along Bienville Boulevard, the main access road on the island, not the beach. Remnants of that dune are still visible, though the road continually floods, even in thunderstorms.

After Hurricane Georges, property owners on the west end elevated their houses on pilings. The hope was that surge from future storms would pass harmlessly beneath their homes. Many were raised ten to fifteen feet in the air.

It was a good idea as such ideas go. But then Hurricane Katrina pushed

a nineteen-foot wall of water across the west end in 2005, destroying or damaging 450 of the 500 houses there. It was staggering to see. Entire rows of
vacation homes were swept from their lofty perches and pitched into the Mississippi Sound. All that remained were empty pilings, debris, and the efflu-
vial stench of rotting seaweed.

Katrina twisted and undermined the pilings of the Leacys' home.
"We're still standing, but we're pretty severely damaged," John told me at
the time. He was getting ready to file another claim with the federal flood
insurance program, though he stressed the payout wouldn't cover his losses.
"A lot comes out of our own pockets," he said. When I asked how many
claims he had filed over the years, John said, "To be honest, they probably
lost money on me."

He wasn't alone. The flood program has lost a bundle insuring Dauphin
Island property. After Katrina, payouts surged nearly fourfold, from about
$15 million in 2005 to over $75 million in 2017, records show. Remarkably,
one hundred houses account for over half the losses. One owner has filed a
dozen claims and received over $300,000, double the value of his house, ac-
cording to data provided by the National Resources Defense Council. Another filed ten claims for almost $400,000. His house was worth $180,000.

Brad Cox lost thirty-seven of the ninety rental properties his company,
Boardwalk Realty, managed at the time. "Well, thirty-eight if you include the
one that burned," he elaborated.

Cox runs the real estate company with his wife, Beth, but also works
as a fireman in Mobile. He was standing next to his crumpled office days
after Katrina when I found him. His cell phone was already ringing with
owners inquiring what it would take to rebuild. Home values dropped for
a time after the storm. But then owners began building bigger, more lavish
beach houses along the west end, "some with six bedrooms," Brad said,
marveling at their size. A local newspaper announced that Dauphin Island
was back.

About the same time, the Western Carolina University geologist Rob
Young was testifying on Capitol Hill about coastal disasters. "I can tell you
with near certainty that we will be rebuilding the west end of Dauphin

In 2005, Hurricane Katrina damaged or destroyed nearly every house on the west end of Dauphin Island, Alabama. Those that weren't washed away were bent and broken. (Photograph by the author)

Island again at some point in the next 10 years. Probably sooner, rather than later."

\\\

In October 2017, I met George Crozier in the parking lot of his old employer, the Dauphin Island Sea Lab, a nonprofit educational and research institute on the east end of the island, near Fort Gaines, best known for its role in the Civil War's Battle of Mobile Bay. The plan was for Crozier to lead me on a tour. But a week earlier, Hurricane Nate, a Category 1 storm, had washed over the island and the west end was still flooded.

We concentrated on the rest of the island, which includes a forest of towering pine trees, the 126-acre Audubon Bird Sanctuary, and, surprisingly, an eighteen-hole golf course, where Jeff Collier served as the golf pro until recently.

For years, the east end had been growing. But lately it had begun losing sand in front of Fort Gaines and the Sea Lab. Locals blamed the nearby Mobile Ship Channel, which they contend is disrupting the flow of sand along the island, robbing sand from the east end and depositing it in the middle of the island, where huge sand dunes are migrating landward and threatening to bury several houses on the otherwise sand-starved island.

The locals call this area Pelican Bay, though technically it isn't a bay but more of a spit with impounded water behind it. In the distant past, the water was deep enough for pirate ships to hide in the coves. Today, local shrimpers work the waters. For reasons no one can quite explain, the sand migrating along the island abruptly stops near a town pier here. The beaches below that point, including the heavily developed west end, are sand-starved and vanishing.

The loss has been dramatic. The far end of the island has lost about one hundred feet of shoreline over three decades. Dozens of pilings that once held houses are now buried beneath the water. Much to the chagrin of environmentalists, Alabama coastal regulators have allowed property owners to erect seawalls and bulkheads around their sinking properties, which the environmentalists say exacerbates the sand loss.

Following each storm, Jeff Collier sends out trucks and bulldozers to collect the sand that washes onto the west-end roads and place it back on the shore. "We try to put the beach back on the beach," he said.

Collier has pleaded with the Corps of Engineers to pump sand from the ship channel in front of the vulnerable west-end homes. "But we haven't gotten anywhere with them," he told me. Apparently, it is cheaper for the engineers to deposit the sand offshore than it would be to pump it down the island. Replenishing the west-end beaches would cost up to $60 million. But it may be the only thing standing between Dauphin Island surviving or vanishing entirely beneath the Gulf, according to the mayor.

"A significant restoration is the one thing that will essentially roll back the clock, if you will, and make the island a little more resilient. Instead of $8 million in damage after a storm, we might only have $2 million," Collier said.

A few years back, Dauphin Island received $7 million from the Deepwater Horizon settlement fund to widen the newly eroding beaches in front of Fort Gaines and the Sea Lab. The locals were especially proud of their new, wider beach, and the town even received an award as one of the nation's "Best Restored Beaches." But the patch didn't last long. Hurricane Nate swallowed 20 percent of the sand, and now Collier hopes FEMA will reimburse the town for the thirty-five truckloads of sand it plans to cart over from the mainland.

"We have many challenges," Collier said. "But solutions are few and not cheap."

\\\

At fifty-six years old, Collier is tall and lean, with thin blond hair and a golfer's tan. He grew up on the island and has been its mayor for over two decades. "He works hard, and it isn't easy, what he is dealing with," George Crozier told me.

Collier said he has "gone to hundreds of meetings and written hundreds of letters" in an attempt to find an answer to the island's erosion problem. "But at the end of the day, it is frustrating that we still don't have a solution. It's almost like we are expendable."

The mayor said Dauphin Island property owners can't afford to pay for sand themselves. "You're talking about tens of millions. We're going to need some outside intervention," he said.

That leaves Dauphin dependent on a steady stream of federal dollars for its beaches and recovery efforts. Maybe it was time to consider abandoning the unlucky barrier island and move to higher ground? I suggested.

Collier quickly rejected the idea. "The analogy I use, it is like losing an arm or a leg. Do we give up and die, or find another way to keep going? I look at the island the same way. I am a fighter. I don't give up."

After Katrina, a few dozen homeowners were ready to sell their homes to FEMA and leave the space vacant. Dauphin Island officials even helped with the paperwork.

"I was confident it was going to work," Collier told me. "We finally had people coming to the table waving the white flag."

But the mayor didn't hear anything for two years. "At the end of the day, we got notification they weren't going to fund us," he said. "They didn't say why, except they didn't have the money. I was disappointed and surprised. My take was that they figured those houses would be under six feet of water, so why bother?"

PART IV

The Coming Storm:
Fat Tails, Rising Water,
and the Nature of Risk

There is a new geography to the coast now, and Sandy clearly showed us the most vulnerable spots.

—TIM DILLINGHAM, EXECUTIVE DIRECTOR, AMERICAN LITTORAL SOCIETY

13

Building a Better Hurricane

AS AN UNDERGRADUATE ENGINEERING STUDENT in China, Ning Lin was fascinated with the way wind interacted with the skyscrapers near her university in Hubei province. The wind was like an invisible river, bulging in the open spaces and flattening as it pressed around the corners of glass and steel. When it was strong enough, the buildings wobbled, raising interesting questions about how much flexibility you could incorporate into a design. Lin's fascination became an obsession. In 2003, she enrolled in graduate studies at one of the seemingly more unlikely places a bright, ambitious student from China might land—Texas Tech University in Lubbock.

If you aren't from Texas, you probably don't know a lot about Texas Tech except for its gunslinging football team, the Red Raiders. The university is located on the High Plains in the northwest corner of the state, "in the middle of nowhere," Lin explained through a faint smile. But for the young researcher, Lubbock did have one thing in its favor: an abundance of wind. "It was very good for measuring wind, very flat, and we had a very big lab with a wind tunnel."

One thing led to another, including a Ph.D. from Princeton University, where Lin now teaches in the civil engineering department and leads a group that studies hurricanes and risk. Lin became interested in two simple yet profound questions: Why did some hurricanes do more damage than others? And how could the government, insurers, and risk managers do a better job of predicting and adapting to storms?

Before she could answer these questions, Lin needed a tutorial in hurricanes. So in 2010 she took a postdoc under Kerry Emanuel at MIT. Together, they wrestled with designing better models to predict the hurricanes of the future. Emanuel had already shown through simple physics that global warming could fuel far more intense storms, with up to 45 percent more destructive power, in the decades ahead. He'd also created a computer model for studying potentially monster storms. Lin hoped to apply the model to flood insurance, risk, and probability—the calculus of catastrophe.

Emanuel also wanted to test whether the superstorms of the future might occur more frequently. The idea is still being debated. Some researchers believe that the warming planet and oceans are already fueling more and bigger storms; temperatures have risen 1.8 degrees Fahrenheit since the industrial revolution and may warm even more by the middle of this century, with catastrophic results, according to a 2018 study by the United Nations' Intergovernmental Panel on Climate Change (IPCC). Others maintain that there have always been catastrophic storms. What is different now is that far more property is in harm's way. Still others contend that the 24-7 coverage of hurricanes by the Weather Channel, along with social media, feeds the perception that there are more violent hurricanes today than there were in the past. For now, the idea of more frequent superstorms remains theoretical, but it is worth exploring, Emanuel said.

Needless to say, an increase in the number of catastrophic hurricanes would be devastating, with over three trillion dollars' worth of property stacked along the Atlantic and Gulf Coasts. The three hurricanes of 2017—Harvey, Irma, and Maria—alone caused over $300 billion in damage, a record. Imagine if you double or triple that figure? Who pays for the recovery? Will the federal government finally reach a point when it runs out of money for repairs? Will the financially strapped federal flood insurance program collapse?

Lin and Emanuel aren't talking about next week, next year, or even the next decade. Climate change usually occurs slowly, over decades, hundreds, or even thousands of years, which is why many people don't necessarily see it, and cynical politicians dismiss it as a rounding error in geologic time. However, a near consensus has coalesced around the scientific concepts and the role of humans in accelerating damaging change. The planet is clearly warming, climate experts note, and it will continue to heat for decades, largely because of human-produced greenhouse gases. Most of the additional heat is being transferred to the oceans, researchers add, which, in turn, are warming at alarming rates. The availability of heat and added water vapor form a positive-feedback loop, resulting in yet more heat and more energy, the fuel hurricanes feed on.

Even so, modeling future hurricanes is an exercise in probability and must account for the fundamentally chaotic nature of weather. For instance, some areas of the world may be cooling even as the rest of the planet is warming, or in the case of Australia, burning up. The nature and trajectory of individual hurricanes are also unique. A hurricane in the lower Caribbean may rapidly blow up to Category 5 status in the overheated tropical waters only to weaken as it encounters dry air, shear, or land. Or it may harmlessly curve into the northern Atlantic Ocean if its path is blocked by a bulge of high pressure.

To account for the inherent chaos, Lin and Emanuel massaged their models, adding inputs and variables, using longer time frames and, most important, incorporating climate effects into both actual and hypothetical storms. Instead of looking at, say, one hundred hurricanes, they looked at one hundred thousand; instead of studying one hundred years of historical data, they expanded the horizon to one thousand years or even more—in effect, inventing the hurricanes of the future.

Here, you might ask: Why bother if the probability of such destructive storms is so low—say, one in ten thousand, or even higher? Isn't that just an elaborate form of game playing? some researchers have suggested. But what if the odds of such hurricanes increase as the planet and oceans warm? Wouldn't you want to know that such a catastrophic storm is possible if you are planning for the new future at the coast?

Truly damaging hurricanes tend to be statistical outliers that aren't predicted very well in the relatively short historical record of hurricanes, which extends about one hundred years. For example, Hurricane Sandy was an unusual storm that pushed a massive wall of water into and over Lower Manhattan and nearby Long Island, causing billions in damage. But it was by no means the worst hurricane that could strike New York City. In September 1821, a massive storm with estimated winds of 135 miles per hour (Sandy's winds barely topped 75 miles per hour) slammed into the city, pushing fourteen feet of water up to Canal Street. What would happen if an equally intense storm hit the city today? In 2014, the giant reinsurer Swiss Re wanted to know. So it ran its own simulation of the 1821 hurricane, adjusting for population and property. It found that an 1821-type storm hitting New York City now would cause nearly $110 billion in damage—roughly double the damage from Hurricane Sandy. Given that the federal government would probably pay for most of the recovery, that seems like useful knowledge to have.

Hurricane modeling is a lot like baseball analytics. Researchers are searching for the sweet spot between randomness and certainty. They study historical trends. But they also understand that storms have no memory. Just because one hurricane behaved a certain way doesn't mean the next hurricane will behave similarly. It is here that the concept of fat tails comes into play. Simplified, fat tails are statistical events that occur far from the mean (average) and have outsize results. In the case of hurricanes, they are the exaggerated storms at the end of the statistical curve that account for the majority of damage. Recall that just seven hurricanes have caused nearly 80 percent of all damage since 2000—$566 billion out of a total $724 billion. These storms represent the low-probability, high-impact hurricanes that keep meteorologists up at night and are infuriatingly hard to predict.

Historical data are an imprecise guide, observes the Wharton economist and flood insurance expert Carolyn Kousky, because each catastrophic storm is likely to be even larger and more violent than the last. For example, Hurricane Katrina caused $125 billion in damage ($160 billion in today's dollars)— three times as much damage as the next-largest storm on record at the time, Hurricane Andrew. Clearly, Andrew didn't predict Katrina. Nor can Katrina predict the $250 billion hurricane that is likely to roar ashore in the not-too-distant future, hitting Miami, Tampa, or another large coastal city. The only way to accurately predict such a storm is by extrapolating it from thousands of possibilities, the way Lin and Emanuel did in 2012 in an important study.

The researchers collaborated on a study of black swan events—in this case, hurricanes so massive and anomalous they couldn't be predicted from the historical record. Black swans are essentially contradictions, events so atypical they are unknowable. After reviewing thousands of storms, Lin and Emanuel concluded that there had never been a true black swan, because all the previous hurricanes could be either predicted from the data or inferred by their computer model, including Hurricane Sandy, which some meteorologists mistakenly called a black swan.

"Sandy was not a black swan," Lin told me when I visited her in 2015 at her Princeton office. "It wasn't even close. We wrote a paper a half year before Hurricane Sandy predicting the surge in the Battery [in Lower Manhattan]. There was no surprise."

The unusually timely study was published in the journal *Nature Climate Change* in June 2012, four months before Sandy inundated the coasts of New Jersey and New York. It was based on models simulating potential surges in New York City, which Lin, Emanuel, and Michael Oppenheimer, a professor of geosciences at Princeton, determined is highly vulnerable because of its shallow bottom and unique bathymetry. Lower Manhattan is susceptible to a surge upward of sixteen feet, the authors wrote, or two feet higher than the actual fourteen-foot surge at the Battery in Sandy. Even more troubling, New York City is likely to experience more record flooding in the future, they concluded, because of climate change and sea-level rise.

"Instead of a Sandy every one hundred years, it could be once every ten years, or even less," Lin said.

New York, Charleston, Miami, and other coastal cities are now spending billions of dollars to armor themselves against future storms. Some of these efforts are inspired. Others are largely symbolic, or intended to buy time. However, if the seas continue to rise, and the hurricanes of the future prove to be as damaging as models suggest, "there is no way that coastal cities can adapt to that level of change; they will simply have to relocate," Emanuel has written in other reports.

John A. Miller, the floodplain expert and a critic of New Jersey's rebuilding plan following Hurricane Sandy, put the risks even more starkly. "I've started to call it the Big Hurt," he told me. "There is a lot of pain coming."

Nevertheless, many homeowners and beach-town mayors appear to be betting that the future will look more like the past than the future portrayed by Lin and Emanuel. Some are merely uninformed. Others believe that another catastrophic hurricane won't lash their communities tomorrow, next year, or anytime soon. They are wrong, of course, but the politics of climate change and storms is fraught with misinformation and denial.

In 2015, Lin and Emanuel collaborated on another study, focusing on gray swans, rare monster hurricanes with a low but real chance of happening. Unlike a black swan, a gray swan can be teased from computer models, assuming the samples are large enough. The researchers said they were trying to draw attention to low-probability, high-impact storms that account for most of the damage. However, rather than highlighting a flood-prone nation like Bangladesh, which is hit with devastating regularity, they sorted through thousands of examples for someplace a little more surprising, landing on the city of Tampa, part of a rapidly growing metropolitan area of three million on the west coast of Florida.

Tampa is the proverbial disaster waiting to happen, Lin and Emanuel wrote. It has a heavily developed coast checkered with hotels, condominiums, and houses. That means a great deal of wealth is at risk. It is also highly vulnerable, with many low-lying communities that already flood routinely. Critically, it is a veritable water park, surrounded by bays and rivers, with a shallow offshore shelf and a long, narrow bay that will funnel billions of gallons of water into the city in a major hurricane.

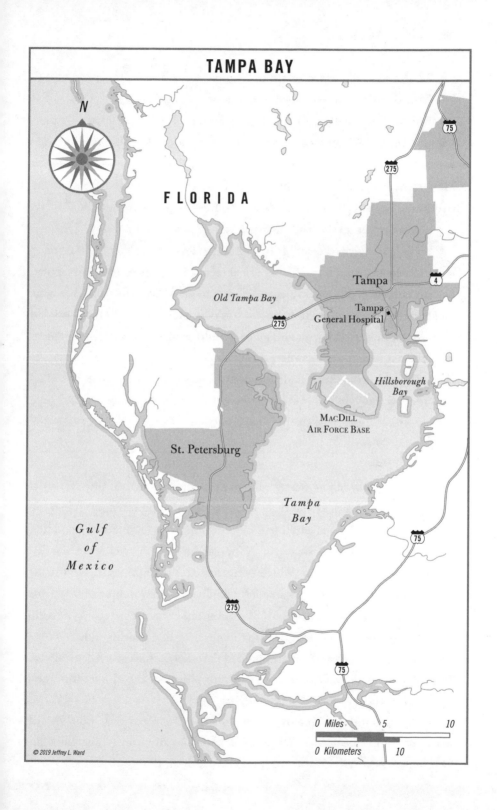

TAMPA BAY

FLORIDA

Old Tampa Bay

Tampa

Tampa
General Hospital

*Hillsborough
Bay*

MacDill
Air Force Base

St. Petersburg

*Tampa
Bay*

*Gulf
of
Mexico*

© 2019 Jeffrey L. Ward

0 Miles   5   10

0 Kilometers   10

The researchers were aware of Tampa, Lin told me, but they "didn't know the damage could be so large. It was surprising."

Lin and Emanuel calculated that a Category 3 or larger hurricane roaring up Tampa Bay could cause $175 billion in damage—billions more than Katrina, the most expensive hurricane in history. About the same time, Jeff Masters, another hurricane expert and cofounder of the popular Weather Underground website, wrote that a rare but devastating storm could push forty-three feet of water up the bay and cause $250 billion in damage.

So here was a good example of a fat tail, a storm so large and damaging it couldn't be predicted from the historical record alone. It had to be imagined from thousands of computer runs and climate models. Even then, it was so large and horrific many refused to believe it could happen. I decided that I needed to go see for myself. What made Tampa so vulnerable? And what, if anything, were the politicians and planners doing about it? I made arrangements to fly there. But as I was getting ready, a massive new storm suddenly appeared on the radar, as if to confirm everything Ning Lin and Kerry Emanuel had been saying. And it appeared to be heading straight for Tampa.

\\\

Hurricane Irma began modestly enough as a tropical wave off the west coast of Africa. Over the next few days, it gained shape and strength. Then, on September 1, 2017, Irma exploded, nearly doubling in strength in just forty-eight hours. Meteorologists at the National Weather Service were startled by the rapid intensification. Most hurricanes gain strength as they cross the warm waters of the lower Atlantic and Caribbean, but not this quickly. Irma added 70 knots (81 miles per hour) of wind speed in two days. Only a handful of hurricanes in history had done that, and most had quickly faded. Three days later, approaching the small island of Barbuda, in the eastern Caribbean, Irma blew up to 185 miles per hour, a catastrophic Category 5 hurricane, and then improbably continued to hold its strength.

It was around that time Bob Buckhorn began to pay attention. As the mayor of Tampa, he needed to keep close watch on any storm threatening his city. Irma was still days away from making landfall. But it wasn't too soon to ask for updates from his staff or think about evacuation plans. After all, it wasn't a simple thing to get millions of people out of harm's way. It could take days, even under ideal conditions. The worst thing you could do was to wait too long and then watch the highways turn into parking lots full of panicky people. Or even worse, have one of the bridges shut down, trapping residents in their homes as the storm bore down on them. All it took was 40-mile-per-hour winds to shut a bridge. It was hardly anything.

Like many of the three million residents of the Tampa–St. Petersburg metro area, the fifty-nine-year-old Buckhorn wasn't a native. After graduating from Penn State in 1980, he'd made his way south, initially working in marketing for a consumer-products company, then moving over to the powerful Tampa Bay Builders Association as director of government affairs. After two unsuccessful tries, Buckhorn was elected mayor in 2011. Here he was, a Democrat in a conservative state, but importantly pro-business and pro-growth. One of his key initiatives was a waterfront development covering sixteen downtown blocks along Tampa Bay. The forty-two-acre project, scheduled for completion around 2027, was backed by the Microsoft founder Bill Gates and Jeffrey Vinik, the owner of the Tampa Bay Lightning pro hockey team. With two hotels, voluminous retail space and restaurants, and 3,500 apartments and condominiums, the $3 billion project promised to reshape the city's waterfront and add to its growing sense of self-confidence.

The Tampa–St. Petersburg metro area was growing by the day and had added over a million residents in the past decade. The city of Tampa now had a billion-dollar municipal budget and 4,500 employees. A parapet of property lined the bay, only blocks from city hall. It was surprising, given the risks. The highest point of elevation in downtown Tampa was just five feet.

"If we had a Cat 3 coming through, this office would be fifteen feet underwater," Buckhorn explained matter-of-factly as we spoke one afternoon at city hall. "All of the areas around the bay tend to be wealthier areas. They would all be exposed."

The mayor's family lived in a historic neighborhood on nearby Davis Island, a short drive from Buckhorn's office. It was a highly desirable location, with stately Victorians and modern architectural gems. The New York

Yankees legend Derek Jeter owned a mansion "as big as a Best Buy" a few houses up the street. Still, it was a coastal floodplain, facing one of the largest estuaries in the world. And if a major hurricane rolled in, "Davis Island would probably be totally destroyed," Buckhorn said.

Buckhorn was boxed between his dual roles as a development proponent and protector. People would continue to move to Tampa for the water and the casual lifestyle, he said. "Believe me, I understand the risks," he told me. "But even if I wanted to, I don't know how I could stop it. There are property rights associated with demand for waterfront in Florida. It's unabated. I get the argument. I don't want to be rebuilding over and over. But I don't think you are going to be slowing development at the coast anytime soon."

The city government wasn't exactly a passive participant in its growth spurt. Local officials planned to spend $100 million on road, sewer, and other infrastructure improvements associated with the Gates-Vinik waterfront development. The payback, they argued, would be thousands of visitors to the cafés, restaurants, and shops. "I've been dreaming of this for a long time," Buckhorn told a *New York Times* reporter.

Part of Buckhorn's challenge was that Tampa hadn't been hit by a major hurricane since 1921, nearly a century ago. "Many of our new residents have never been through a hurricane. Or if they have, they tend to suffer from hurricane amnesia," Buckhorn said.

Many residents believe Tampa is protected by its unique geometry. It is cut deeply into the coast. To hit the city, a hurricane would have to hug the west coast of Florida and then veer sharply up Old Tampa Bay. Most hurricanes never get that close. After they enter the Gulf of Mexico, they sprint past the city toward the Panhandle, hundreds of miles to the north. "They think we are sheltered," Buckhorn said.

The probability of a catastrophic storm is low. Since the 1880s, Tampa has only been struck twice by major storms, including the Category 3 hurricane in 1921. But that doesn't mean Tampa is immune. The city has experienced several near misses in the last decade. In 2004, a Category 4 hurricane named Charley, one of four hurricanes that struck Florida that year, appeared headed for Tampa with 155-mile-per-hour winds. There were dire predictions and painful evacuations. But at the proverbial last minute, Charley took a sharp right-hand turn into a less-developed area 100 miles south of Tampa, and the city escaped relatively unscathed.

"Charley was a warning. If it hadn't made that turn, it could have come right up the bay," Buckhorn said.

And so in the days leading up to Irma, the mayor began to issue stronger, direr warnings. "Our day has come," he told residents on September 10, one day before Irma made landfall. "I have no doubt we will get hit. We're not protected. We're no less vulnerable than anyone else in the state of Florida. We've just had the good fortune of not having been hit, but there's nothing we do or don't do that's going to stop that."

There was a surprising fatalism to the mayor's comments. In another widely reported interview, Buckhorn noted that the city had been "duct-taping" its infrastructure for years. What did he mean? I asked. The mayor explained that federal funding to help cities such as Tampa repair its bridges, sewers, and water systems had dried up decades ago. The infrastructure was in disrepair, metaphorically held together by tape. The water and sewer pipes in particular were clogged with barnacles and debris. Water couldn't get out quickly enough and flooded the streets. It was so bad that residents in some neighborhoods had put up NO WAKE ZONE signs. Some of the roads and bridges were crumbling or sinking. A seawall along the bay was pocked with holes. A year earlier, sewers in nearby St. Petersburg had overflowed in a rain burst and dumped millions of gallons of partially treated waste into the bay, which already suffered from runoff, toxic red tides, and fish kills. In 2018, the worst red tide in a decade left beaches from Sanibel Island to Clearwater littered with dead fish.

"The very best we can do is patch things," Buckhorn said. "We average four or five water-main breaks a day. We didn't even have a dedicated revenue source to fix things until two years ago. Last year, we removed fifty thousand tons of debris from the sewer pipes. The pipes couldn't push the water out. Plus, we had standing water there. So we went in there and basically Roto-Rootered many of the pipes to get the water flowing. And we re-dug some of the retention ponds and canals."

It was a good start. But it wouldn't save the growing city in a major hurricane. Most of the downtown was in a high-risk flood zone. Tampa General Hospital and MacDill Air Force Base were located next to the bay. They had taken steps to elevate generators and strengthen windows, but a massive surge would cut them off from the city for days or longer. Meanwhile, "the downtown would have trouble getting back on its feet," Buckhorn acknowledged. "There would be hundreds of millions in damages."

Until recently, the nearby counties, cities, and towns didn't talk with one another, let alone jointly plan for a major hurricane. Unlike South Florida, where Miami and the surrounding communities have formed a regional coalition to address sea-level rise and climate change, Tampa and the surrounding areas were still largely working alone. The Tampa Bay Regional Planning Council did produce a report on the potential economic impact of a catastrophic storm on the metro area, but the group is seriously underfunded and struggling to find its footing. "We're nowhere as far along as South Florida," one of the organization's planners, Brady Smith, told me.

"The Tampa Bay Regional Planning Council isn't looked upon as a body anyone cares what they say," Buckhorn bluntly observed. "I think they just turned to this issue because they had nothing else to do."

\\\

The coastal geologist Al Hine smiled when I mentioned the mayor's comment. He has been arguing for years that local government in Florida is an oxymoron. "It doesn't work, or at least it doesn't work very well," he told me. "There are sixty-seven counties in Florida, and they are all always tripping over each other."

Meanwhile, state lawmakers are walking back a decades-old law that regulates building along the immediate coast, creating a veritable free-for-all for developers. Governor Rick Scott, a Republican with a net worth estimated at $250 million, owns a $14.1 million beachfront mansion in Naples, on the Gulf. According to news reports, he has refused to allow state employees to even mention the words "climate change." "Everyone in Florida is on their own sheet music, as they say," Hine said.

The genial seventy-three-year-old is tall and lean, with sun-streaked hair and a professorial beard flecked with gray. For years, Hine worked out of the geology department at the University of South Florida, in Tampa. He is semiretired now, though still deeply engaged in coastal research, and is the author of several well-received books on sea-level rise and the unique geology of Florida.

The 1,200-mile-long peninsula, now crowded with twenty million people and countless sun-starved visitors, is more or less an afterthought, geologically speaking. It formed hundreds of millions of years ago from the remnants of other landmasses. It was a time of great physical chaos and luminal, shifting boundaries. The supercontinent known as Pangaea was drifting apart, and the Gulf Trough was filling with silt and sand. What is today the Florida platform slowly took shape from carbonates, limestone, and quartz veneer, Hine explained, and is overlaid on a sheet of bedrock: "The rocks are sort of like Swiss cheese. There is water everywhere."

I met Hine in Belleair Bluffs, a small, suburban-style city on the western shore of Pinellas County, to tour some of the nearby beaches and talk about the challenges ahead. He spread a series of topographic maps across the trunk of his 2011 Ford Focus and began educating me. The talk lasted half an hour, and by the end my head was spinning. But I was also excited because I knew at least some of the information would seep in, like water bubbles percolating through the limestone cracks of the Florida substrate.

We began on the barrier islands in Clearwater Beach and Honeymoon Island and worked our way south toward Indian Rocks and Treasure Island. Towering hotels and condos crowded the shoreline. Hine pointed out one condo that draped over an inlet. The owners had pumped in sand and built a seawall to save their investment. But the water kept rising. It was unclear how long the seawall would last. In the meantime, the nearby beaches were being starved of sand because of the breakwater.

"Human beings are lousy planners," Hine said. "They're not bad people. But they are sloppy."

Houses and bungalows filled the interior of the barrier islands. Some were old and modest—what the locals fondly call "cracker boxes"; others, big and new. Many sat at ground level and would no doubt be sacrificed to rising water in the future. It could take until the middle of this century or possibly longer. So much depends on the warming climate and the ice sheets in the north. Thousands of years ago, during the last ice age, the shoreline here extended seventy to one hundred miles from where it is today, Hine pointed out. Then the ice sheets and glaciers retreated, and the seas rose. Now the old barrier islands are buried under the Gulf of Mexico. It was the third or fourth time the Florida landmass has drowned. No doubt it will happen again.

Hine described one barrier island we drove along as "a three-thousand-year-old bulge of sand wrapped around a limestone ridge." Cranes and bulldozers dotted the eroding beach. The Corps of Engineers was busy pumping sand. Hine wasn't opposed to replenishing beaches, he said, even though it is "a stopgap measure." There were other things that could be done, he said, but first the politicians and developers had to stop thinking in "political time" and start thinking in geologic time—and stop attacking the scientists for delivering bad news.

"People have to understand science isn't perfect; it is an infinite work in progress," he said. "People don't understand uncertainty. That's a problem. But at the same time, we know a lot. Don't be dismissive. We can help."

Hine suggested that a time will come when the hotels and condos on these barrier islands will have to be abandoned. "You can't jack up a thirty-story tower. There's not enough sand," he said. It may take a few more decades, "but at a certain point, cheap flood insurance is going to end. Banks are not going to write thirty-year mortgages. Maybe by 2050, a condo that you bought for a million dollars will sell for half that. It's going to be chaos."

Tampa will be in the middle of that chaos. It lies at the end of one of the largest estuaries in the world, covering four hundred square miles and encompassing eleven smaller named bays. Tampa Bay is also uniquely shallow—averaging twelve feet in most places—and shaped like a funnel. A large hurricane running parallel to the coast at the right angle will drive billions of gallons of water up the funnel toward Tampa, Davis Island, Apollo Beach, and other nearby communities.

"Downtown Tampa is low and flat," Hine pointed out. "Tampa General Hospital is one of the region's primary trauma centers, and it's right on Tampa Bay. It is virtually at sea level and connected to the mainland by a single bridge. In an ideal world, it shouldn't be where it is. But it's there. And you can't relocate it."

Some of the local officials were finally beginning to talk about the threats. But there was no sense of urgency, as far as Hine could see. "The leadership isn't there," he said. "The problem comes back to politics. Decisions are made in terms of election cycles, and that discourages politicians from taking steps to reduce long-term vulnerability. What gets done is short-term, so it has some political value. When you combine that with the fact that many people in Florida still don't believe in climate change and sea-level rise, it creates a culture of denial and cheap fixes become the norm, instead of real adaptation."

\\\

After Hurricane Irma crashed across Cuba and the Florida Keys, it encountered strong winds and drier air and weakened as it entered the Gulf of Mexico. Like Charley, in 2004, it veered landward, near Marco Island, nearly two hundred miles south of Tampa. It then began moving up and across the Florida peninsula in a north by northwest direction, losing more strength, though it was still large enough to cover much of the state.

As Irma spun north, the winds turned offshore. Instead of experiencing a thick, driving surge, Tampa Bay drained, revealing mud and shells. Some of the tourists who hadn't evacuated foolishly began walking out to sea to have an adventure. It was a different story along the Florida-Georgia border, where Irma was still strong enough to push water and waves up the rivers in Jacksonville, flooding streets and houses, and to tear up beaches and houses in the resorts of St. Augustine and South Ponte Vedra.

Altogether, Irma caused $50 billion in damage. The hard-hit citrus groves in central Florida saw their smallest harvest since 1941. Most of the damage near Tampa was caused by wind, not water. Thousands of homes lost power for days, and trees and debris littered the streets. However, for most residents, the aftereffects were more inconvenient than tragic. Mayor Buckhorn was relieved. "If we had taken a direct hit, I wouldn't be talking to you," he told me. "We'd be devastated right now."

"Tampa dodged a bullet in Irma," Kerry Emanuel told me a few weeks later when I visited him at MIT. At the time, he was preparing to give a campus talk about the busy 2017 hurricane season. Coincidentally, only hours before his talk, another massive hurricane stormed across Puerto Rico. Maria wiped out the nation's power grid, leaving millions in the dark, and caused nearly $100 billion in damage, especially in poor mountainous areas. It was a "tragic irony," Emanuel told the crowd, but there would be more catastrophic hurricanes "as far as the eye can see."

14

A Finger in the Dike

SHORTLY AFTER HURRICANE IKE pushed eight feet of water into an apartment building Bill Merrell owned in the historic Strand District of Galveston, in September 2008, he began to sketch a way to defend the city. Galveston already had its famous seawall, built after a hurricane in 1900 claimed the lives of six thousand residents. But Ike revealed that the crumbling, seventeen-foot-high dike was no longer enough. Water from the hurricane poured into the bays behind the barrier island, swamping thousands of unprotected homes and businesses and causing over $35 billion in damage.

Ike was the most destructive hurricane to strike the Texas coast since Carla in 1961, nearly half a century earlier. But in many ways, it was a very different kind of storm. Carla had slammed the coast with 160-mile-per-hour gusts. Ike was a big, slow water-maker, with winds barely reaching 100 miles per hour.

Water stacked on top of water, swelling toward Trinity Bay, one of several smaller bays that make up Galveston Bay, and then recoiling back. A twelve-foot surge sluiced over Galveston. "It was almost biblical," Merrell, a university administrator, said.

Merrell rode out Ike on the second floor of his downtown apartment. It was a strategic decision. "I escaped vertically," he said, instead of trying to escape up Interstate 45 to Houston, fifty miles inland.

The way Merrell figured, he didn't have another choice. A few years earlier, in 2005, thousands of Galveston evacuees had fled the barrier island ahead of another hurricane, Rita, which was forecast to make landfall near the city of forty-eight thousand. The highway had quickly clogged with traffic. Evacuees ran out of gas and food, with dozens dying in the heat and from auto accidents. Then, as hurricanes often do, Rita changed direction and missed Galveston. Merrell listened to the bitter recriminations afterward and decided that if there were ever another hurricane, he would stay put. "I uncorked a damn good bottle of Bordeaux," he told me, "and settled in to watch the storm. It was even fun, until the power went off and the water flooded the first floor," causing tens of thousands of dollars in damage.

Later, Merrell thought, "Enough is enough." He took out a pen and began to draw. It wasn't much more than a few lines, yet in Merrell's mind it was perfectly clear. What was needed was a way to keep the surge out of Galveston Bay. And the simplest way to do that was to build a massive wall with giant steel gates that could be closed when storms approached the Houston Ship Channel and two other openings to the bay. Merrell even came up with a catchy name for his project. He called it the Ike Dike.

\\\

The name was inspired by the Dutch. Merrell, an oceanographer by training, had spent most of his professional career in academic administration, including serving as president of the local branch of Texas A&M University. But he had traveled to the Netherlands and seen their massive coastal defenses, the most admired in the world. At a certain point while sketching, he turned to his wife, June, and blurted, "The Dutch would never put up with this."

It was a pivotal observation, and set in motion a long and at times controversial plan to armor the Texas coast. But the Dutch analogue wasn't necessarily exact. Galveston wasn't Rotterdam, and the United States wasn't the Netherlands. The entire coastline of the Netherlands was smaller than Florida's. At least half the nation was at or below sea level. The Dutch couldn't retreat to higher ground because, well, there was no higher ground. Rising water and powerful storms posed an existential threat. So they planned accordingly, spending billions each year keeping water out of their cities. There was even a national tax to pay for water defenses, though no government flood insurance. If a community decided to build in a floodplain, it had to pay for its own defense, unlike Americans, who richly subsidize risky development and then lurch from disaster to disaster. Dutch engineers also continually reassess their approach. Lately, they have begun to shift away from building barriers, levees, and surge protectors in favor of using green spaces, parks, and other public land to harbor floodwater until it recedes.

Bill Merrell rejected greener solutions. Galveston was already filled with houses, businesses, and amusement piers. Building wetlands and setting aside land wouldn't provide the level of protection the city needed. You could argue that the problem was self-inflicted, he told me: people should never have built on a shifting barrier island in the first place. "But history shows people always move toward the coast and now the seas are rising to meet them. And like the rest of the world, we need to look to proven engineered solutions for our protection."

Galveston already had a long history of engineering solutions. After the 1900 hurricane, the city built a ten-mile-long, seventeen-foot-high seawall and then imported millions of yards of sand to elevate the business district in the center of the island. A century later, in 2001, the American Society of Civil Engineers declared the Galveston seawall a National Civil Engineering Landmark. There was no going back at this point, Merrell suggested.

Merrell didn't have standing: he wasn't an elected official and didn't work for the city. His was a self-appointed mission driven by his love for the city and decades spent in research and administration. In addition to his role at Texas A&M, Merrell had worked in Washington at the National Science Foundation and the Heinz Center, a nonprofit environmental organization named after the late U.S. senator John Heinz. With a little luck, he hoped to work his connections and get the powers that be to look at his idea.

Shortly after Ike, Merrell reached out to the Dutch engineers. Even though they were shifting away from fortifying their own coasts, the Dutch were more than happy to export their expertise. It was a boutique industry. Dutch engineers frequently appeared in the United States following major hurricanes, looking for consulting work. They even had a liaison in their Washington embassy tasked with routing business their way. They, too, had a catchphrase. They referred to their outreach efforts as "Dutch dialogues."

In late 2008, Merrell met with the Dutch engineers at the Galveston branch of Texas A&M. The Dutch helped him flesh out his thinking, especially regarding building a huge steel gate across the mouth of the Houston Ship Channel at the east end of Galveston Island. The channel was as wide as a football field, deep and unruly, and would be expensive to control.

Initial estimates for the Ike Dike came in at between $1 billion and $2 billion. But they would go up dramatically in coming years. The plan called for a fifty-five-mile levee built out of clay and sand and three separate steel barriers, or surge gates, one at the mouth of the Houston Ship Channel, one across the High Pass on the nearby Bolivar Peninsula, and one at the San Luis Pass on the western end of Galveston Island, which is checkered with pricey, suburban-style second homes. In theory, the barriers would prevent surge from flooding the bays—and houses.

Merrell imagined that most of the funding would come from federal taxpayers. The Houston Ship Channel was a federal waterway. Therefore, it made sense to him that the federal government should pick up a large share of the cost. The channel served the Port of Houston, one of the largest and busiest in the nation, and was lined with oil and gas refineries and petrochemical storage facilities. A storm surge rushing up the channel toward Houston would create an environmental nightmare dramatically larger than the Deepwater Horizon blowout, which had spewed more than 200,000,000 gallons of oil into the Gulf of Mexico and caused billions in environmental damage.

Surely, it was in the nation's interest to make certain something like that didn't happen, Merrell reasoned.

Merrell began to circulate his Ike Dike proposal for comment. But instead of embracing it, local officials ridiculed it as impractical, environmentally unsound, and prohibitively expensive. "I think someone even wrote a piece suggesting I must be smoking grass," he recalled. The county commissioners dismissed the plan out of hand, noting that it was impossible to prevent hurricanes. "That really pissed me off," Merrell said. "So I kept after it. I put out the idea. I must have given two hundred talks. I can't prevent hurricanes, I told them. I *can* prevent surge."

Merrell faced a bigger challenge than captious politicians. Two days after Ike crashed ashore in 2008, flooding 80 percent of the island's properties, the investment house Lehman Brothers filed for bankruptcy, precipitating the Great Recession. The nation's attention quickly shifted from Galveston to Wall Street. Here was an epistemological question then: If a bruising hurricane wipes out an island, but there are no news helicopters hovering overhead, did it really happen? "We were miserable here, too, but no one seemed to notice," Merrell said.

The usual script after a major hurricane is for the national media to pour in, followed by an intense burst of attention. State and local officials then leverage the attention to win federal promises, money, and grants. Occasionally, rock stars hold a benefit concert. But with the financial and housing markets in collapse, Merrell couldn't get the attention of the Texas legislature, let alone his state's congressional delegation. "It was like we didn't exist," he said.

\\\

I landed in Galveston in late August 2017, nearly a decade after Bill Merrell first scratched out his plan for saving the historic, hurricane-prone island. Much had changed since then. The resort had largely recovered and real estate prices were once again stable. Several new hotels even loomed behind the seawall, gleaming in the midday sun as if they'd just been power-washed. There was also a new, wider beach, courtesy of federal taxpayers.

One thing that hadn't changed was Bill Merrell's deep conviction that the Ike Dike was the best way to save Galveston from drowning in the next big storm. "We've had a dry spell for hurricanes," he told me. "We haven't had one in a few years. But that could change tomorrow. All it takes is one big one at the right angle."

Merrell was seventy-seven years old. He slumped in a chair in his corner office at the university, putting his shoeless feet up on a desk as we spoke. A large tinted window looked down at the Houston Ship Channel wending through the industrial scrub and marsh. Merrell was still relentlessly working his contacts, advocating for the dike. But he now had an associate, Len Waterworth, a former colonel with the Corps of Engineers, to help with the load. Recently, they seemed to be gaining political traction, with a number of prominent Texas politicians lining up behind plans to armor the state's coast. Separately, the Corps was also studying the best way to defend the beaches.

On one level, I was curious why Bill Merrell was still at it instead of settling back with a glass of Bordeaux in his restored apartment. But I was also trying to get a handle on a larger, messier question that had to do with fixing the coasts. In the wake of the recent hurricanes, there was a lot of talk about making the coasts more resilient. There were papers and books and many conferences. But it was unclear what the proponents meant by "resilience" and "sustainable coasts," another popular phrase, and even fewer good examples. What did a resilient coast look like? And what would it cost? Critically, who would pay? These weren't small or frivolous questions. With thousands of miles of shoreline to protect, the challenges were huge, and there were trillions of dollars at stake. I was hoping Bill Merrell could provide some insight.

Merrell was still committed to hurricane barriers and a fifty-five-mile-long levee, or what some were now calling a coastal spine. But the focus appeared to have shifted to emphasize protecting the Port of Houston, with its oil refineries and thousands of jobs. It is said that a third of the nation's oil supply passes through the Houston Ship Channel, and with a boom in oil shale production in the Texas Panhandle, that figure only seems likely to grow. Galveston wasn't exactly an afterthought at this point, but it seemed clear that the Ike Dike proponents needed Houston and the ship channel to sell the plan.

The Ike Dike, or coastal spine, was unique to Texas, Merrell told me. Other approaches might be more appropriate elsewhere, but not here. Indeed, the term "resiliency" seemed to mean many different things to many different people. It included everything from building wider beaches and higher sand dunes; to restoring wetlands, marshes, and barrier islands; to elevating houses and roads; and to purchasing open space, assuming there was some left. One Florida developer was even marketing concrete condominiums elevated thirteen feet above sea level as stormproof structures. The starting price was $5 million. Meanwhile, some architects were suggesting building floating cities and houses that would rise and fall with the tides.

Some of these ideas would help in the short term. They might even buy barrier islands and lagoon communities a few extra decades before the seas buried them. The problem was that no one could say for sure. If the rate of sea-level rise accelerated or the ice sheets collapsed into the oceans, adding several more feet of water, no amount of extra sand or seawalls would save Galveston or other barrier islands.

There was also the vexing issue of cost. No one seemed to want to discuss what a resilient coast would cost—or who should pay. How much would be private; how much public? It may in fact be worth investing a trillion dollars to save the coasts. But no one—let alone Congress—has made a compelling case. Armoring the coasts also must compete with other needs. After all, a trillion dollars represents a lot of moral capital. It would go a long way toward fixing the nation's crumbling roads, bridges, and schools, or covering several years' worth of medical expenses for the elderly and disabled.

The point is that it's easy to toss around buzzwords, write grant proposals, and hold what now feels like an endless series of conferences on resilient coasts featuring the usual suspects. The actual challenges are huge and expensive. You can float a few dozen houses along a canal without too much trouble. But are you going to float six or seven million houses in the coastal floodplains? Are you going to float Atlantic City, Norfolk, and Miami? Build walls around New York City? Continue to pump sand in front of the vacation homes of millionaires? This at a time when the national debt is expected to grow by $1.5 trillion as a result of the Trump administration's tax cuts for corporations and wealthy Americans?

In the decade since Bill Merrell had crafted his original plan, the estimated cost of the Ike Dike had ballooned to between $12 billion and $15 billion, depending on the source. Merrell himself used a lower estimate of $6 billion to $8 billion. The wide range suggested that no one really knew. At this point, they were guessing.

But even by Texans' inflated notions of money, $15 billion is a gusher. To cover the cost, state lawmakers and the congressional delegation appeared to be counting on federal taxpayers. George P. Bush, son of Jeb Bush and head of the politically important Texas General Land Office, was now an ardent proponent. In 2017, he wrote a letter to President Trump endorsing the Ike Dike concept and requested that Trump include it in the administration's still-unfulfilled proposal to rebuild the nation's creaky infrastructure. The Texas senators Ted Cruz and John Cornyn also got on board. Cruz endorsed a plan to use $3.9 billion in federal taxes to build three smaller barriers to protect the oil refineries, calling it a "tremendous step forward."

Environmentalists pointedly noted that Cruz was a climate change denier. But here he was proposing to use federal dollars to protect oil refineries and petrochemical suppliers against rising seas and hurricane surge. "It's ridiculous," said Brandt Mannchen, a Sierra Club member who has closely tracked the Ike Dike plan. "Why are taxpayers bailing out the oil industry, which is a big part of the problem?"

Merrell acknowledged that his plan would be costly. "It's a lot. I will grant you that," he said. "But it's in the federal interest to ensure a twenty-five-foot surge doesn't run up there to Houston. The Netherlands can afford it. We can afford it. Houston can afford it. Texas can afford it. We're a wealthy place."

That was Merrell's bottom line. It wasn't going to be easy or cheap fixing the nation's coasts. Galveston was one example. There were scores of others, with billions at stake. "The water is rising and it isn't going to stop," he said.

The next day, I was on my way to Houston to meet with a researcher at Rice University who had proposed a far less expensive alternative to the Ike Dike. Jim Blackburn and his colleagues wanted to build a barrier farther up

Galveston Bay, closer to Houston and its busy port. It did not include the Ike Dike's surge gates or a fifty-five-mile levee. Nevertheless, they believed it would provide nearly as much protection and, critically, would save Houston from a potential environmental disaster. Quicker and cheaper in this case was better, Blackburn believed, because it was only a matter of time before a hurricane roared up the ship channel.

As I approached the sprawling maze of elevated highways that encircles Houston, I noticed flashing digital signs along the overpasses. The signs warned residents that there was now a hurricane in the Gulf of Mexico and to begin making preparations. I had known there was a storm brewing out there, but after several hot, sunny days on Galveston Island, I'd lost track of time. Now, purely by coincidence, it appeared Hurricane Harvey was going to become an important part of the story.

\\\

Rice University likes to think of itself as Texas's equivalent of the Ivy League. The students are bright and ambitious, and competition for slots is fierce. The school itself is shaded by live oaks and features archways, quadrangles, and Mediterranean brick faces. It is the kind of dreamy setting where one, while pondering an esoteric calculation or resonant line of poetry, might easily lose track of time and wind up in some leafy, hidden corner of campus.

Jim Blackburn, wanting to make sure I didn't get lost, had sent along detailed directions to the Severe Storm Prediction, Education, and Evacuation from Disasters (SSPEED) Center, which serves as a laboratory for studying hurricanes and floods in real time. Blackburn, a seventy-year-old environmental attorney, professor, and researcher, liked to think of himself as the "spiritual protector of Galveston Bay." He is tall and lean, with shaggy gray hair and a droopy mustache—a Texas cowboy by appearance, though a more liberal cowboy than usual for these parts.

We quickly began talking about one of his favorite subjects: water. About a decade earlier, Blackburn explained, Houston had suffered one of those colossal rainstorms that now seem to routinely plague the city. One of his colleagues thought it might be a good idea to study the storm. When they assembled the data, they discerned a worrisome pattern: Houston had a long and troubling history of flooding. It had flooded epically in the 1930s, and it flooded even more now. Rainstorms previously considered one-in-a-hundred-year events were now occurring every twenty-five years. The storms also appeared to be bigger and last longer, resulting in more rain and damage. In the last three years alone, Houston had twice experienced five-hundred-year rainfalls. Something was awry, and Blackburn strongly suspected it was the climate. It was becoming hotter, boggier, and more saturated—an ideal prescription for otherwise ordinary storms to go ballistic.

No part of the sprawling, unruly Houston metropolis appeared to be immune, though certain neighborhoods and suburban tracts were more vulnerable than others. In some cases, homeowners lived alongside a reservoir, channel, or lake prone to flooding. In others, houses had little if any elevation, or were built on top of old swamps, rice fields, or prairies. Thousands of square miles were hardened with concrete, highways, parking lots, and other impermeable surfaces. Instead of draining, the way nature intended, the now-developed rice fields flooded in storms and heavy downpours. Harris County, which includes Houston and its suburbs, was choked with channels meant to funnel water safely away. But many were old, crumbling, or clogged. And there weren't nearly enough stormwater basins or drains in many neighborhoods. In the end, water was left with nowhere to go except inside the houses.

More than four million people now resided in the metropolitan Houston area, with thousands more arriving each week. The surge of population had begun in earnest in the 1950s and had continued ever since. Houston was booming. It was the epicenter of the nation's oil and gas industry and home to major employers such as ConocoPhillips and Halliburton. In recent decades, the city's medical centers had expanded dramatically and now included some of the nation's largest and best hospitals, including Houston Methodist Hospital and Memorial Hermann–Texas Medical Center.

All those workers needed someplace to live, and developers were only too happy to accommodate them. This being Texas, there was no such thing as zoning and, for decades, very few rules governing building. Crucially, there were also no federal flood maps until the 1980s, by which point developers had already filled many of the wetlands, prairies, and rice fields with town houses, condominiums, and suburban housing tracts. Each year, developers pushed closer to the coast and Galveston Bay. More than a million people had moved there since 2000. They now huddled in comfortable enclaves like Clear Lake and East Texas, along the fringes of the bay, and north through the Woodlands and west through Katy, two huge, prosperous suburbs, forming a nexus stretching more than five thousand square miles altogether. It was in every sense a perfect setup for a disaster: thousands of houses and low-lying coastal land laced with water. A hurricane with the right attitude might unfurl up the bay and make haste for Houston, flattening or drowning everything in its path.

\\\

For months, Jim Blackburn had been focused on the Ike Dike. He believed it was the wrong approach at the wrong time, and far too expensive. It was ironic, he added, that some of the state's most conservative politicians—Senators Cornyn and Cruz, and Governor Greg Abbott—embraced a Big Government solution to a local problem, and wanted to use the U.S. Treasury as their private bank.

"Texans like to take care of problems themselves," Blackburn said. "At least that's what they tell us all the time."

Blackburn contended it would be far cheaper to sell bonds or set up a special tax district and fund the work locally. It would also be quicker, and time was of the essence. A hurricane was now bearing down on the Texas coast. And while it was expected to make landfall 250 miles to the west, near Corpus Christi, it was only a matter of time until a catastrophic storm approached the upper coast and raced up the ship channel to Houston and all those oil refineries.

The SSPEED Center was proposing to place a levee forty miles up Galveston Bay, where the ship channel narrows into the landmass. The estimated cost was $2 billion to $3 billion—or about $12 billion less than the Ike Dike. "It is intentionally modest and could be built with local money. And it could be built fast, with virtually no environmental impact," Blackburn told me. Yet, it would provide nearly the same protection, especially for the refineries and chemical plants along the channel. "Those are critical. If a surge damages them, it would be the worst environmental disaster in American history," he said.

There were other differences between the two proposals. The SSPEED Center's plan didn't include a massive steel gate across the mouth of the ship channel at Bolivar Roads or a fifty-five-mile sand and clay levee along the spine of Galveston Island. "The question is, where do you put your big money? We achieve ninety-five percent of the benefits of Bill's plan for three billion dollars," Blackburn said.

The conversation ended with Blackburn fretting about whether Americans were prepared to make difficult decisions about their coasts. While the Houston situation was critical, he said, there was no shortage of other challenges: New Orleans, Mobile, Miami, Tampa, Jacksonville, Charleston, Norfolk, New York City, and Boston, among others.

"I don't think we are equipped as a society to make the kinds of decisions we are being asked to make about storms we haven't seen," Blackburn said. "Bigger storms and sea-level rise are going to come out. What is a reasonable storm to build to? It's hard. It's a really difficult policy decision. At what point do you not protect something? It's sort of like retreat from the coast is seen as a failure. But it may be a very rational thing."

\\\

Three days later, Hurricane Harvey raced ashore near the artists' colony of Rockport, not far from where Hurricane Carla had made landfall half a century earlier. The powerful winds and surge damaged thousands of homes and vacation retreats. But just as the meteorologists had predicted, Harvey was quickly squeezed by two cold fronts and rapidly lost strength. By the time it reached Houston, Harvey was spinning at a lazy 4 miles per hour, and relentlessly drenching the city and overwhelming its modest defenses.

By this point, Harvey was no longer a hurricane; it was a rain bomb. Parts of Southeast Texas were swamped with sixty inches of rain, more than in any storm in history. Houston itself was deluged with forty inches of rain over three days, according to the National Weather Service. Some neighborhoods were awash in four feet of water. The city's reservoirs bulged ominously. Two, known as the Addicks and Barker Reservoirs, had been placed on the old Katy Prairie, once a freshwater wetland but now filled with subdivisions, the *Houston Chronicle* reported. The Corps of Engineers was left with an impossible decision: risk having the reservoirs burst, or open the gates and intentionally flood neighborhoods. They made the latter choice, and were damned for it.

The Washington Post reported that Harvey dumped nine trillion gallons of water across the Houston metro area. "If that water were collected into a cube . . . it would cover an area of about four square miles and two miles tall," the newspaper said.

Harvey was the third torrential rainstorm in Houston in three years, following the Memorial Day floods in 2015 and the Tax Day floods in 2016. Many homeowners were still recovering from the year before when Harvey arrived at their doorsteps. The resulting damage was humbling. More than 700,000 people sought federal assistance. More than 300,000 houses and businesses were damaged. More than 91,000 homeowners filed claims with the federal flood insurance program. As of January 2018, they had received almost $9 billion in payments. That tied Harvey with Hurricane Sandy as the second-most-expensive flood in history, behind only Katrina. Altogether, the storm caused $125 billion in damage.

A surprising number of affected homes were located in places that weren't supposed to flood. The houses were in the so-called X Zones on the government's flood maps. In theory, they were outside the geography of risk. The owners weren't required to buy flood insurance, and most didn't. The homes were safe until water began to rush under their front doors. That was what had happened in 2001, when Tropical Storm Allison dumped thirty-five inches of rain, resulting in over $1 billion in damage, and what happened again in Harvey. Houston was now considered legendary, but not in a good way. It had the worst flood problem in the nation, even worse than New Orleans. And many believed it wasn't an act of God; it was an act of man.

"The tragedy of Houston is that the problems were well known prior to Harvey," said David Conrad, a former researcher with the National Re-sources Defense Council and now a private environmental consultant. "We produced an extensive report on Houston's flood problems way back in 1998. It talked about all of the same issues they're talking about now. I remember I talked with the state hazard mitigation officer at the time. I asked him how they could allow this. And he told me, 'They don't have zoning in Texas.' So, really, they're just spinning their wheels down there."

After the water from Harvey finally subsided, Jim Blackburn suggested that the federal government buy 75,000 flood-prone houses in the Houston metro area and leave the space empty. It was a grand idea and a fantastic number. Up to that point, FEMA had purchased only 45,000 houses in its entire forty-year history, and most of those properties were inland, along rivers, not at or near the coast. The annual federal budget for buying flood-prone property was millions, not billions. Assuming an average value of $200,000 per house, Blackburn's proposal would have cost $15 billion. As of July 2018, the Harris County Flood Control District had agreements to buy just one thousand flood-prone homes, or about one-tenth of 1 percent of the target homes.

That same month, Texas officials announced that they planned to use $5 billion in federal recovery funds for Harvey flood-control projects. Some of the money was earmarked to reimburse Houston for ongoing work. How-ever, most of the funds—$4 billion—were set aside to construct a levee along the southern Texas coast, where Harvey made landfall, hundreds of miles from Houston.

Governor Greg Abbott proclaimed the money would go "a long way toward future-proofing Texas against another hurricane and strengthening our infrastructure to withstand dangerous flooding." Apparently, Abbott didn't understand that a levee over a hundred miles away, at the coast, would do little if anything to prevent flooding from torrential rain events in Houston. Nor did the governor suggest tapping the state's rainy-day fund of $11 bil-lion to address flooding issues in the city.

Houston is years away from fully recovering from Harvey. Hundreds of families in low-income neighborhoods are still waiting for federal aid to help repair their damaged homes. In the meantime, city officials have been busy approving new development projects for hundreds of houses and condominiums. Under new building rules adopted after the hurricane, many of the houses will be required to be elevated. But surprisingly, one of every five new homes is being built in an old bayou, prairie, or floodplain likely to flood in the next torrential rain. More than six hundred building permits have been issued for tracts in the hundred-year floodplain, according to the *Houston Chronicle*. The projects include at least one Houston neighborhood a few miles upstream from where officials recently purchased houses that have flooded over and over. City council members defended their decision, saying there was nothing they could do to stop the subdivision.

\\\

In October 2018, the Army Corps of Engineers released a preliminary study on ways to defend the Texas coast. It did not include Jim Blackburn's idea. But it did include a bigger and costlier version of the Ike Dike that could cost up to $31 billion and take upward of fifty years to build. Among other steps, the plan would include a massive new levee protecting the rear of Galveston from bayside flooding. In effect, Galveston would now be a bowl, much like New Orleans, only smaller. Presumably, it would require massive pumps to drain any floodwaters into the bay. A surge gate would be built across the entrance to the Houston Ship Channel, as Bill Merrell originally envisioned. The study notes that Texas would probably have to share the extraordinary cost with the federal government, but no figures were provided.

The study still needs to be finalized. Blackburn told reporters that he continued to hope that the SSPEED Center's ideas could be incorporated into the plan. In an earlier newsletter to friends and colleagues, Blackburn had reminded them that "as bad as Harvey was, it was not the worst-case storm. Harvey should be considered as a warning shot that tells us that the storms of the future will not be like the storms of the past."

Harvey underscored how the risks at the coast are not limited to waves, storm surge, and wind. Torrential rainstorms fueled by rising temperatures and the oversaturated atmosphere are becoming increasingly common, and not only in Houston. Even if the engineers armor the nation's coasts, that won't save Houston, Charleston, Miami, or New York City when the next rain bomb stalls out there, unleashing the next epochal deluge.

That raised another question for me: What do you do when it's not one problem but many?

It was time for another trip.

15

Drowning Fast and Slow

JOHN TECKLENBURG HAD BEEN MAYOR of Charleston for less than a year. But the former oil company executive and amateur jazz musician had lived in the historic city long enough to know its weak spots. And so, when Hurricane Irma began pushing water into Charleston Harbor on the night of September 10, 2017, he knew exactly what to do. He needed to check to see if the city's historic seawall was holding back the flood.

The Low Battery was among the most revered landmarks in a city lush with historic churches, cemeteries, gardens, and military benchmarks. It was named for a Civil War barricade that protected the peninsula where the Ashley and Cooper Rivers merged to form Charleston Harbor. Early each morning, busloads of tourists decamped there to take photographs and admire the postcard-pretty antebellum neighborhoods behind the seawall, known locally as South of Broad.

For decades, the century-old rock-and-wood seawall had protected the city from storms. But rising water and a string of storms had undermined the battery in recent years, allowing water to pour through gaps onto the cobblestone streets. These days, the aptly named Low Battery was no longer high enough to keep water out of the graceful mansions behind it. Homeowners routinely found themselves bailing water and filing claims with the federal flood insurance program, millions altogether. By now, they were exhausted and frustrated. "I'm getting a couple of cyanide pills," one bitterly told the local newspaper after yet another flood. The homeowners wanted the city to fix the Low Battery—and fix it now.

Tecklenburg had a plan. In fact, it had been in the works for months and called for the city to spend upward of $100 million raising the seawall by several feet. Only a week or so earlier, a city worker had even placed a marker signaling where the new top would be.

But now when the mayor studied the battery, he saw something alarming. "The water was already higher than the spot where we'd put the marker. I couldn't believe it."

At its height, Irma generated a nearly ten-foot tide, four feet higher than normal, and nearly a foot higher than during Hurricane Matthew a year earlier, which also flooded the historic neighborhoods. Even more disturbing, Irma hadn't made direct landfall in South Carolina; it had swirled hundreds of miles offshore. Had it come closer, three-quarters of Charleston would have been wet or underwater, Tecklenburg told me.

It appeared the seawall would need to be higher than the city planned. But how much higher? Charleston is a tourist destination. Visitors come for the history, charm, and architectural gems. They want to see the water and take pictures.

"We can't wall off the city," said Laura Cabiness, the former director of public services for Charleston. "We can't put a twelve-foot wall around it. Visually, that would be unacceptable."

\\\

When you think about sea-level rise, you may think about Miami Beach, where the streets flood during full moons and king tides, and residents are occasionally trapped in their homes by rising water. Or you may recall Tangier Island, Virginia, in the Chesapeake Bay, which is eroding so badly it can barely keep its head above water. Or Annapolis, which has lost hundreds of thousands of dollars in business because of rising water. But nearly every coastal town and city along the Atlantic Ocean and Gulf of Mexico is wrestling with rising water to one degree or another, none more than Charleston. (Areas of the Pacific Coast are also sinking, but that is a different story.)

The small city famous for its preserved pastel row houses, horse-drawn carriages, and French Quarter is the very definition of risk. It is low and surrounded by water, with rivers on two sides and the harbor on the other. Most of the historic downtown sits in a bowl. Water gets in and has a hard time getting out. It pools on the streets near the minor-league ballpark, university medical complex, and low-income housing project, Gadsden Green, where moss and water stains are clearly visible on the concrete walls. Lockwood Drive, a major artery along the Ashley River, is often impassable in storms. The city has already raised the road several times. "But it looks like we may have to raise it again, and we may have to build a wall there as well," Tecklenburg said when I visited him in 2017.

Many of the city's current problems are the consequence of misguided planning in the past. Much of the Charleston peninsula was built on top of filled creek beds, salt marshes, and tidal exchanges, and is now either sinking or leaking—or both. Local experts estimate that 40 percent of the historic downtown was built on sawdust and fill. However, the actual figure could be higher. Some areas are over three hundred years old. Who knows if the maps are accurate?

As Charleston grew, annexing land across the rivers, its population trebled to about 150,000, including 40,000 who live in the historic downtown. It allowed developers to build subdivisions along flood-prone marsh and creeks. You can tell the houses that routinely flood because they are the ones with sandbags stored under the carports in anticipation of the next storm. The city has endured three 500-year floods in three years: Irma, Matthew, and an unnamed rain bomb in 2015. Homeowners have filed nearly $100 million in flood claims with the federal government. Some—like the West Ashley family with ten flood claims mentioned earlier—want to move to higher ground but can't sell their homes.

Yet, even as Charleston officials search for money for buyouts, they are approving thousands of building permits for new subdivisions and apartment complexes on or near coastal floodplains. And demand doesn't appear to be slowing. Developers have filed nearly 1,700 building permits since 2013, city data show; this, despite the repeated floods and growing concerns about rising seas.

\\\

There is little question that sea-level rise has played a major role in the recent flooding. The water level in Charleston Harbor has risen by about a foot in the last century, according to Douglas Marcy, one of the nation's experts on the subject. That elevates the platform for storm surge, tides, and waves to crest above the city's defenses. Levels vary by location and the physical characteristics of the coast—not to mention by season and decade. But Marcy, who is based at the National Oceanic and Atmospheric Administration's Coastal Research Center in Charleston, said, "I've been living here for twenty years, and I don't remember seeing anything like this."

Even ordinary high tides are becoming an issue, resulting in so-called "nuisance flooding," when water leaking into the city is high enough to interfere with traffic or shut down business. William Sweet, another NOAA researcher based in Maryland, has been studying nuisance flooding nationally for decades. According to his recent work, flooding from high tides is 50 percent more common today than it was twenty years ago—100 percent more common than it was thirty years ago.

"I think the underlying trend is quite clear," Sweet told reporters in 2017. "Records are expected to continue to be broken," he said.

According to federal data, Charleston averaged five days of nuisance flooding in the 1950s. By 2016, that number had swelled to about fifty days, a tenfold increase. Assuming the seas continue to rise, Charleston will likely have water on its streets more days than not by the middle of this century.

Charleston is also a magnet for rain bombs. According to the city's 2016

Sea Level Rise Strategy Report, four of the five highest rainfalls in state history have occurred around Charleston. In October 2015, nearly twenty-four inches inundated the peninsula with the equivalent of three billion gallons of water. *The Charleston Post and Courier* ran a photograph of residents paddle-boarding down the middle of a street. Some writers complained that government officials weren't moving quickly enough to address climate change, and noted that the county's 712-page hazard mitigation plan didn't even discuss sea-level rise.

Still, the city of Charleston has been singled out for national praise for its efforts to address flooding and, unlike some flood-prone communities, has detailed plans for addressing rising water. That was why I decided to travel there. What I learned was both inspiring and hugely disappointing. As much progress as Charleston has made, it isn't close to being waterproof. Storms and tidal floods continue to top its barricades, pouring into homes and onto streets. And as fast as the city pumps the water, more seems to flow in.

"I don't think anyone had any idea how quickly things would change," said Carolee Williams, a former city planner now working on flood issues for the nonprofit Conservation Voters of South Carolina. "Twenty or thirty years ago, we might be thinking about how do we handle a major hurricane. But no one was thinking how do we handle sea-level rise. It just wasn't part of the conversation. Now it is all we talk about."

\\\

Sea-level rise is easy to define but hard to see because it occurs in slow motion, and humans aren't particularly attuned to incremental changes. Rising water happens over hundreds, thousands, even tens of thousands of years—in other words, in geologic time, not according to human time scales. Occasionally, there may be a burst, a shift of tectonic plates or a volcanic eruption beneath the ocean. But more often, the changes are slow—a millimeter here, a millimeter there.

Long-term trends are tied to the waxing and waning of glaciers and ice sheets, as well as planet warming. When the planet is cold, water is removed from the seas and stored in the ice sheets in Greenland and Antarctica. When the planet warms, as it is doing now, water is released and surface levels rise. The rate of increase varies. Some years, there may be no rise at all, as though the oceans are on pause. But then the process resumes. It may even accelerate, as has happened since 1990, increasing at a rate that's threefold the historic average, or by about three millimeters a year, which also happens to correlate with the increase in ocean temperatures. In general, scientists say, the mean ocean sea level has risen between eight and twelve inches over the last century, which doesn't sound like a lot until you wake up one morning and realize that there is now water lapping at your doorstep.

That is more or less what happened to Billy Keyserling, the mayor of Beaufort, deep in the Low Country of South Carolina, about an hour south of Charleston. Keyserling likes to take his morning coffee by one of the waterways near his home. Over the years, he noticed something odd: The rungs of the ladder dipping down to the water were vanishing one by one. Then one morning he saw that they were completely covered. "That was my aha moment," he said. "That was when I truly understood what people meant when they talk about sea-level rise."

Keyserling may look like a wizard, short and rumpled, with a flowing white beard and bottle-glass-blue eyes, but he is a force of nature—a spark and a fulcrum. The mayor doesn't just run with ideas; he skips around town with them on a Vespa motor scooter. He is the son of a liberal New Yorker, Harriet Keyserling, who followed her physician husband, Herbert, to the bucolic port city after World War II and took up writing and politics. Harriet was the first woman to represent Beaufort in the South Carolina legislature and championed the arts and the environment. Billy followed suit, taking over his mother's seat for four terms. In 1984, he ran the presidential campaign of South Carolina's Fritz Hollings and jokingly tells visitors he is the reason why Hollings lost. Later, scrambling around for purpose, Billy ran for mayor and was elected in 2008, a Democrat in a deep-red state.

These days, Keyserling spends a lot of time thinking about water, or more accurately, how to live with rising water. Like his good friend John Tecklenburg, the mayor of Charleston, he is surrounded by challenges. The Intracoastal Waterway runs through his downtown. Beaufort's largest neighborhood, Royal Oaks, was built in the 1940s and 1950s and takes on water every time there is a storm or heavy downpour. The quaint bungalow-style homes are in a coastal floodplain. "We wouldn't allow that today," the mayor said. "If you look at where we have water problems, most of the areas are where we filled low-lying areas, if not wetlands."

Eventually, something is going to have to happen there, though it is too soon to know what that something will be. Meanwhile, Keyserling is busy setting aside land for open space, limiting big-box stores and national chain restaurants to one side of the highway leading into town, and designating the other side as a park where water can be stored during storms. Keyserling is lucky in that Beaufort County, which includes the popular Hilton Head resort, is one of the wealthiest in the state. So there is money available to help Beaufort adapt. "The idea is either to manage growth or create buffers or open natural vistas," he told me, "so the water has a place to go."

If you fly over Beaufort County at high tide, you'll notice that about 60 percent of the landmass is covered by water. There are copious amounts of swamp, salt marsh, and coastal forests, a good thing because they act like sponges. Unlike in Charleston, there are vast undeveloped spaces. A long area of coast between Beaufort and Charleston known as the ACE Basin—short for the Ashepoo, Combahee, and Edisto River drainage system—is owned by a nonprofit trust and largely virgin. It covers 300,000 acres, about twice the size of metropolitan Charleston.

Still, Keyserling understands that the water is going to keep rising. And the thirteen thousand citizens of Beaufort are going to have to learn to live with it—or retreat.

"When I give talks, I don't even mention climate change," he said. "I say my dock used to be here, and now it's there, under the water. People understand docks around here. Practically everyone has one. They get it if they can't use their dock because the water's too high."

\\\

Billy Keyserling's depiction of sea-level rise cuts across decades of complicated science to focus on the everyday experience. Nevertheless, a small amount of science is necessary to understand why the seas are rising. Water rises for different reasons, on different time scales, and differently in different places, as NOAA's Doug Marcy notes. It is affected by air and sea temperatures, ocean currents, lunar cycles, gravity, and something known as Milankovitch cycles. In the early 1900s, Milutin Milankovitch, a Serbian geophysicist, theorized that variations in the position of the earth's orbit around the sun were the primary drivers of the earth's climate. He concluded those cycles of heat and cold lasted for approximately one hundred years. Depending on the type of cycle, the sea would either rise or recede over a century.

Generally, water expands as temperatures increase. Expanding water takes up more space (volume), causing the sea to rise, or "fatten," a term I prefer. Over the last century, the average temperature in the United States has risen by 1.8 degrees Fahrenheit, according to NOAA. The Arctic, meanwhile, is warming at a rate twice as fast as the U.S. average, resulting in a dramatic loss of sea ice, spilling more water into the oceans. Alarmingly, the rate of loss appears to be accelerating, at a pace nearly four times what it was in 2003, according to a recent federal study that was nicely summarized by John Schwartz in *The New York Times*.

In 2012 alone, the ice sheets in Greenland shed an estimated 455 billion tons of ice into the oceans, according to data collected by NASA satellites. That added volume accounts for nearly two-thirds of the recent rise in sea levels, another recent report by the National Academies of Science noted. Yet another study warned that the accelerated rate of melting could add an additional half foot to sea-level rise by century's end. All of which spells trouble if you own property at the coast or are administering the federal flood insurance program.

In all, upward of eighty million Americans could be forced to flee the coasts by the end of the century. Over a billion dollars' worth of property on Hilton Head Island could be destroyed. And Amtrak's popular Northeast Corridor service, which carries twelve million passengers annually between Boston and Washington, could be continually inundated.

The June 2014 report *Risky Business*, prepared by a group co-chaired by the former New York City mayor Michael Bloomberg, estimated that between $66 billion and $160 billion worth of U.S. real estate could be below sea level by 2050—and up to half a trillion by the end of this century, as a result of rising seas.

In 2017, researchers for the real estate firm Zillow found that nearly 2 million homes at the coast worth almost $900 billion could be underwater by 2100. In Florida, the most vulnerable and heavily developed state, nearly one million homes could be swamped. The next most vulnerable state, New Jersey, would see nearly 200,000 houses inundated if the seas rise by six feet.

Even a modest rise will render many of the roads on Long Beach Island inaccessible, a 2015 study by the engineering firm HR Wallingford found. The low-lying barrier island is already plagued by nuisance flooding and drainage problems. During a speech in nearby Toms River, Harold Wanless, one of the nation's leading authorities on sea-level rise, told the audience that coastal homeowners face an impending disaster, as most of the barrier islands would be largely uninhabitable in fifty years.

Nevertheless, many members of the Trump administration don't believe in sea-level rise or human-induced global warming, including Trump himself, who mocks climate change as a hoax and often points to snowstorms as evidence that there is no global warming. Trump's former Environmental Protection Agency administrator, Scott Pruitt, spent much of his time undoing the climate-control efforts of his predecessors in the Obama administration. After resigning amid a cascade of ethical charges, Pruitt was replaced by Andrew Wheeler, a former lobbyist for the coal industry. In August 2018, Wheeler and the EPA proposed rolling back Obama's landmark 2012 agreement to increase fuel-efficiency standards and cut greenhouse gas emissions; this, even though cars, trucks, and SUVs are among the largest sources of planet-warming emissions in the United States, and lowering fuel standards would add hundreds of millions of tons of carbon dioxide into the already saturated atmosphere. The administration recklessly branded its proposal part of an initiative to "Make Cars Great Again."

In February 2019, the White House signaled that it was readying a panel to study the effects of climate change on national security. But an internal memo cast doubt on the government's own studies, which have identified rising temperatures and sea levels as looming threats to military installations in the United States, and a "worldwide risk to global stability." Trump dismissed the warnings and included a climate change denialist on his panel.

Of course, it is possible these maneuvers are a cynical ploy by the administration, as it promises to march the nation backward to a time when coal mining, steel plants, and other industrial giants filled the atmosphere with carbon dioxide and other pollutants. In effect, Trump is arguing that the short-term interests of the fossil fuel industry are more important than investing in a green economy that creates the jobs of the future and lowers dangerous emissions—another example of the Tragedy of the Commons.

In October 2018, the Intergovernmental Panel on Climate Change, the UN's scientific arm studying climate issues, painted an especially dire picture of the environmental and economic consequences of failing to address greenhouses gases and global warming. In a landmark report, the IPCC said that if greenhouse gas emissions continue at their current pace, the atmosphere will warm by 2.7 degrees Fahrenheit by 2040, much sooner than previously thought. Such a rise would inundate developed coasts, kill off coral reefs, accelerate droughts and crop losses, and result in widespread economic disruption. Preventing catastrophe will require "rapid and far-reaching" shifts in human and economic behavior on a level never seen before, the authors concluded.

Once more, the Trump administration responded with deafening silence. Meanwhile, conservative members of Congress continue to deny the seas are rising, scoffing at the scientists and offering explanations bordering on the bizarre. One member, Mo Brooks, a Republican member of a key House science committee, even blamed rising sea levels on falling rocks.

"What about erosion?" the Alabama congressman asked at a May 2018 hearing. "Every time you have that soil or rock or whatever it is that is deposited into the seas, that forces the sea levels to rise, because now you have less space in those oceans, because the bottom is moving up."

Philip Duffy, president of the Woods Hole Research Center in Massachusetts, advised Brooks, "I'm pretty sure that on human time scales, tumbling rocks are minuscule effects."

\\\

Over time, oceans rise and fall by hundreds of feet. For example, during the last ice age, roughly twenty thousand years ago, the New Jersey shoreline extended all the way to the continental shelf, or about one hundred miles from where it is today. Conversely, when the planet warms, the ice sheets release water and the coasts retreat inland. These paleo-shorelines are the geological equivalent of tree rings. They are everywhere, if you know where to look: a long, wavering ridge of sand covered by grass, or a steep, striated cliff along a drowned river estuary, such as the Croatan Sound in North Carolina, seventy miles inland from the Atlantic Ocean.

In theory, we should be entering a long-term cooling phase, climatologists note. Instead, the planet and oceans are warming, with eighteen of the warmest years in history in the last nineteen years. A majority of climate scientists attribute this to human-induced global warming and carbon dioxide concentrations in the atmosphere, which are at historic levels. These greenhouse gases are the wild card in future sea-level rise, the geologist Albert Hine told me. "The world is already awash in carbon. But if we continue like we are, it will only get worse."

According to government researchers, carbon dioxide concentrations—now more than 400 parts per million, or nearly double the rate they were in the late 1800s—could double or even triple by the end of the century, which would result in calamitous sea-level rise, leaving Charleston and other coastal communities no choice except to retreat to higher ground.

But projecting future sea-level rise isn't an exact science. To balance these uncertainties, researchers use computer models to provide a range of estimates. Generally, these models agree on an increase of one foot to three and a half feet of additional sea level by the end of this century. Some more aggressive models predict up to a six-foot increase. One recent NOAA model forecast a potential rise of two and a half meters, or about eight feet.

"It is a changing number . . . and changing science," said the NOAA's Marcy. Until relatively recently, scientists didn't have tools to study glaciers and ice sheets. Now they do. That knowledge critically adds to the inputs. "We come back with more information about ice sheets. We are starting to try new scenarios. It might be a low probability, but an upper range of two and a half meters is not out of the question."

Eight feet of additional water would pose an unprecedented physical and financial threat. Rising seas could also depress real estate values, resulting in staggering economic losses. One analyst recently likened coastal real estate to junk bonds, the high-yield, high-risk investments popularized by the 1980s financier Michael Milken. Meanwhile, credit rating agencies such as Moody's have begun warning coastal communities that a reckoning is coming.

"It's not something a lot of people are thinking about, but the potential consequences are huge," said John A. Miller, the floodplain manager in New Jersey, who studied credit issues as part of a master's degree at the University of Pennsylvania. As property values tumble, beach towns will face credit downgrades and higher borrowing costs, Miller found. Some beach towns may be stretched to pay back their loans.

There are signs that coastal investors are already beginning to factor risk in their purchasing decisions. A 2017 study in *The Journal of Financial Economics*, "Disaster on the Horizon: The Price Effect of Sea Level Rise," found that houses vulnerable to rising water were selling at a discount compared with houses considered safe. Meanwhile, in the Miami-Dade metro area, condos on upper levels are selling faster than condos at lower levels that are vulnerable to flooding.

Homeowners in Corolla, on the northern Outer Banks in North Carolina, are already seeing the economic impacts. The heavily developed vacation resort has flooded repeatedly in the last decade, including in July 2018, when a train of thunderstorms dumped a foot and a half of water over two days. The rains overwhelmed the stormwater system, with some vacationers reporting that the sewers were spilling into the lower floors of their pricey rental properties. County officials allowed a private contractor to pump the foul water into the ocean, warning swimmers to avoid the area.

"Property values have plummeted in the past few years," a homeowners' group noted in a July 2017 newsletter. "Sales of homes are continuing but at a reduced price."

In July 2018, a summer storm flooded the streets of Corolla, on the Outer Banks of North Carolina, with a foot and a half of water. Homeowners complain that frequent flooding is hurting sales and lowering property values.

(Photograph by the author)

＼＼＼

To address its metronomic flooding, Charleston has spent over $100 million on a new stormwater drainage system to keep the streets dry. It plans to spend another $150 million in the coming years as it adds to the maze of tunnels, drainage shafts, and pumping stations. Altogether, officials estimate they will need $2 billion to address all their water-related challenges, from elevating roads to repairing and building seawalls to buying homes that repeatedly flood. No one knows where all this money will come from, but undoubtedly the cost of owning a home in Charleston is going to be more expensive in the future.

Charleston is viewed as a national leader in dealing with sea-level rise. Reporters from influential newspapers and magazines routinely decamp in the

Low Country to interview officials and document the city's forward-thinking efforts. Along with Miami, Norfolk, and New York City, they single out Charleston as a community with an actual plan, not just hopes and dreams.

Much of the credit goes to Joe Riley, who served as Charleston's mayor for four decades. When Riley took over in the 1970s, Charleston was struggling with many of the same issues confronting other cities. "We were a poster child for the declining inner city," he said. "The real estate market was stagnant. People were leaving, not arriving. Too many buildings were vacant."

Riley set out to restore the city-center business and arts district and the historic neighborhood called South of Broad. The city also annexed large suburban tracts across the Ashley River, tripling in size. The larger tax base helped stabilize city revenue. Charleston began to collect accolades and awards.

The city had a long history of flooding, dating to the 1800s. Back then, Charleston's mayor, Henry L. Pinckney, offered a $100 gold medal to anyone who could come up with a good idea for keeping the water out. Apparently, he didn't lose a lot of money, because flooding only grew worse. Pointing to a yellowed map in his downtown office, Riley, an attorney, described a network of tidal creeks that early developers had buried in dirt, sawdust, and debris before building neighborhoods on top. "It was pretty much all fill," he said.

In 1984, city planners produced a master plan for managing stormwater. It was, Riley recalled, "a slow, complicated process." Not everyone was happy. Rain and tidal flooding continued. But little by little, the city began to make progress, digging tunnels and shafts to collect water, and building pumping stations to direct that water back into the rivers and harbor. One even won an award, which city engineers jokingly refer to as "our award-winning pumping station."

Now age seventy-five, Riley said that the city center is largely dry. Laura Cabiness generally agreed. "The system didn't prevent water in the recent storms," she told me in 2017, "but we were able to evacuate the water pretty quickly. And we never had a pump station go down."

Each of the pumping stations can move 160 million gallons of water a minute, Cabiness said. That's sufficient to handle the rainfall from a ten-year storm, a storm with a one-in-ten chance of occurring in a given year. The tunnels and shafts can be expanded to deal with larger rainstorms. But the drainage system isn't designed to handle a hurricane with massive surge. "We're not talking much about tidal surge," Cabiness said. "We can't pump storm surge."

Before Riley left office in 2016, the city unveiled a master plan for managing sea-level rise. It used a cautious estimate of 2.5 feet of additional water. However, it now appears that Charleston may need to raise that estimate by as much as a foot, the engineers told me.

"The technology is there to deal with the rising water," Riley said. "The capital investments over time will continue to be substantial. But there is no other choice. It is important to save historic cities like Charleston. I respectfully feel we were a leader in addressing this ourselves."

\\\

Not everyone is as pleased with the city's efforts.

"Ninety-eight percent of what you've heard about Charleston is wrong," said Dana Beach, executive director of the local nonprofit Coastal Conservation League. "For all of the accolades, there's frankly been almost no significant advancement of policies that will remove people out of areas hazardous to live in or to prevent new development in areas we know are hazardous."

Beach, who holds an MBA from Wharton, rattled off a list of the city's alleged failures. His most serious indictment appeared to be that the city wasn't moving quickly enough and wasn't taking advantage of various funding streams, including municipal bonds, to raise the vast sum required to save Charleston.

"The reality is, for forty years, and especially the last decade, we have been investing about eight million dollars a year in drainage improvement," Beach said. "At that rate, we can never keep up with sea-level rise. We're dealing with fifty days a year of nuisance flooding today. In the future, every third day on average would give us a flood."

"One of the graphics in the city's master plan says there are $1.7 billion in projects needed," Beach added. "Those are current projects meant to deal with the existential threats to survival of the city, including the Low Battery. People had three to four feet of water in their basements in Irma. And these are just the current threats, with no enhancements for hurricane intensity or frequency."

The last major hurricane to strike Charleston was three decades ago, in 1989, when Hugo pillaged parts of the South Carolina coast. Hugo was a Category 3 hurricane with 115-mile-per-hour winds. It did over a billion dollars in damage in Charleston. Yet, in some ways the city was spared. The dangerous right-hand quadrant of the hurricane, with the most powerful winds and destructive storm surge, smashed into the upscale Isle of Palms resort, north of the city.

"A Category 4 storm would wreck the city," Cabiness said. "We can't stop a hurricane, but I think we can put in engineered systems that minimize the risks and let people do reasonable things."

At the moment, Charleston is experiencing a building boom. A new apartment complex is rising along the Cooper River, not far from where cruise ships unload tourists. Tecklenburg pointed to the complex as an example of smart building. Even though it is next to the river, it is one block from one of the city's stormwater pumps. "So it's built in a place to accommodate thoughtful development," he said, "and would survive a once-in-a-blue-moon event."

I had a difficult time comprehending why it was smart to put people in the middle of a coastal floodplain. But maybe I was wrong. Maybe the tunnels and pumps were enough.

In late 2018, Tecklenburg led a Charleston delegation to the Netherlands to study its coastal defenses. The mayor told the *Post and Courier* he was struck by the giant pumps and surge gates, but even more impressed by the Dutch approach to managing risky development along the water.

But for now at least, Charleston has no plans to restrict building or offer buyouts in the historic but flood-prone neighborhoods behind the Low Battery.

"There may be parts of the city we decide at some point are no longer suit-able for future projects or developments," Tecklenburg told me. "But we aren't there yet."

\\\

After Charleston, I headed to Durham, North Carolina, to pick up Orrin Pilkey. We were on our way to meet another coastal geologist, Stan Riggs, in Greenville and take a two-day trip across Eastern Carolina, a mostly forgotten place, so flat, poor, and waterlogged that Riggs has taken to calling it NC Low.

"Most of the towns have less than one foot of elevation," Riggs had told me in an earlier telephone conversation. Almost all were encircled by riv-ers, sounds, and black-water creeks. The water leaked, trickled, and surged, flooding the houses and streets. One town had suffered three damaging floods in a handful of years. "It used to be dry. Now it has tides," he said. "All of these places are caught in the vise of rising water."

Now eighty, Riggs taught and conducted research at East Carolina Univer-sity in Greenville for fifty years, and is one of the state's best-known coastal geologists. Since retiring, he has worked closely with some of the small, old agricultural and fishing communities along the Inner Banks, directly behind the barrier islands, helping them prepare for what is coming.

A few years ago, Riggs formed a nonprofit, also called NC Low, to help fund his new mission. Most of the focus is along the greater Pamlico estuar-ies, spanning a distance of about two hundred miles, from Currituck County in the north to New Hanover County in the south. Many of these towns are drowning in slow motion as the sounds rise and face an uncertain future. NC Low is Riggs's vehicle to educate sometimes skeptical residents about the threat. It also helps them think about ways to take advantage of their history, culture, and environmental assets, especially the water, and create new econ-omies around tourism and ecology.

"The idea is to give them a fighting chance," Riggs said. "The towns out there on the barrier islands are fine, at least for now. But if only the rich can afford to build seawalls and widen beaches, that's not much of an adaptation. It's climate gentrification."

I'd been pestering Riggs for months for a visit. At first, he didn't seem interested, telling me he was too busy, but then he agreed, on one condition: I had to pick up his colleague and friend Orrin Pilkey. "Orrin's been bugging me for years for a tour of the Inner Banks. But he needs someone to drive him to Greenville. He doesn't like long drives anymore," Riggs said.

\\\

The coastal plain of Eastern North Carolina is a "big and subtle landscape characterized by complex geology and big bodies of water," Riggs explained as we started out near Washington in Beaufort County, a modest but well-kept town of ten thousand on the banks of the Pamlico River. Like most coastal plains, Eastern Carolina rolls gradually downhill, from higher ground near Riggs's home in Greenville to little or no elevation at the coast. Washington was somewhere in between: high enough for now but vulnerable to rising water in the future.

As Riggs drove down narrow two-lane blacktop roads, he began to tick off a list of flyspecked communities that probably won't survive the rising water in coming decades. After each name, he quietly added one word: "Gone."

The towns were tiny and poor. The dwindling populations ranged from the hundreds to a few thousand. Some had been formed by freed slaves who'd worked for decades on nearby farms. Others were fishing villages now trying to reinvent themselves as ecotourism destinations. They were filleted by black-water creeks and rivers. Water abounded in bogs, swamps, agricultural dikes, rivers, lakes, and sounds. Trees stripped of foliage and color haunted the landscape where saltwater had invaded fresh. "Ghost forests," Riggs said. A wharf that was once three feet above sea level was now two feet below. An abandoned gristmill verged on collapse from flooding. All were choking on tidal water rising up from the nearby estuaries and rivers.

In 2016, the remnants of Hurricane Matthew dumped twenty inches of rain on Eastern North Carolina, swelling the rivers and creeks, killing twenty-six people, and leaving over $1 billion in damage. For the town of Windsor, Bertie County, it was the third 500-year storm in three years. Water flooded the modest downtown, including a popular barbecue pit. Windsor had received federal funds to buy a few dozen flood-prone houses, and it was looking for more when we passed through. They were lucky, Riggs said: "Because they're high enough, they'll survive. They keep getting hammered, but they have some room to move."

Other towns weren't as lucky. "Columbia, Creswell, Princeville, the insides of Hyde, Dare, and Carteret Counties—they're all screwed," Riggs said.

Riggs was angry because no one was paying attention. Most of the focus of rising water was on the barrier islands, which was where

In 2017, Orrin H. Pilkey and Stan Riggs toured the Inner Banks of North Carolina, where rising water is threatening scores of small, poor communities. (Photograph by the author)

all the property and money was. "The issue isn't the Outer Banks," Riggs stressed. "They can take care of themselves until the water gets them. The politics ignores all of these small, poor places on the Inner Banks."

On the second day of our trip, we stopped at Columbia, the county seat of Tyrell County, population 891, and tumbling.

Columbia is a pleasant place, rich in history and Southern charm. It has a bed-and-breakfast and a good place for coffee. It also has a wrong side of the tracks, with run-down bungalows and trash-filled yards. Maybe if it didn't drown, Columbia would be able to reinvent itself as an ecotourist destination. That was the hope. It was surrounded by water: the Albemarle Sound to the north, the Alligator River to the east, and the Scuppernong River to the west. But all that water was rising, and so were the flood issues. A plaque at the end of Main Street noted that the Scuppernong River had crested at five feet above the flood stage during Matthew, a record. The local middle school had flooded ten times in recent years. A highway built by the state was adding to the misery. It was elevated above the flood stage and now functioned like a dike, spilling stormwater down onto a modest commercial strip.

"The water gets in and it can't get out," explained Karen Plough, a local resident who works with Riggs on Columbia water issues. "It's a real problem at the middle school. We have a lot more nuisance flooding. There's something going on."

But some residents of Columbia don't want to hear about sea-level rise. "They enjoy living here for the simple life and values and don't want to leave," Plough said. "Fishermen will tell you that they see it. But people fifty and younger don't believe it. I think part of it is that people are afraid of science. They don't understand it, or they don't trust it."

In North Carolina, it is practically a blood sport to attack scientists. A few years earlier, Riggs had quit a state panel on sea-level rise when state lawmakers rewrote the panel's report after being pressured by real estate and development interests. The original version had said sea levels could rise by nearly forty inches by 2100. But the lawmakers wanted to use a lower estimate, based on only a thirty-year time frame.

Until then, North Carolina had enjoyed a reputation as a national leader in coastal management, even embracing rules limiting oceanfront development. But after conservative Republicans took control of the state capitol, the politics turned ugly, and they began rolling back rules. In 2012, they criticized the committee's findings on sea-level rise as unfriendly to business and rejected the science as unproven estimates—even though the report closely mirrored the estimates of esteemed national panels. Riggs had seen enough. He was too old for mucking around with scabrous politicians, he said. "I decided I wanted to use whatever time I had left to do something good."

"What they did was an absolute disgrace," interjected Pilkey, who has also run afoul of developers and politicians in his long career. "It gave the state a terrible black eye. We haven't recovered, by the way. In fact, in my opinion, it has gotten worse. There's more building than ever on the coast, and the state is just going along with all of it."

Columbia has some time, Riggs said, but the residents need to act now.

"If sea level rises two feet, Columbia will have to move—period. If it rises three feet, it's gone."

It was getting late and we were falling behind schedule. Riggs stepped on the gas. He wanted to show us several other struggling communities before the sun dropped below the trees.

"The next couple of towns are destined for elimination," he said, as if beginning a lecture.

Then he added, more quietly, "Gone."

16

The Problem with the Bays

THE WIND HAD BEEN BLOWING HARD out of the northeast for days, a fitful knot that got under your collar and on your nerves. From the wheel of his boat, *Scholarship*, Dave Rinear gritted his teeth and ducked the froth and spray. Water came at the boat sideways, rolling it one way and then the other, scattering a cooler and some fishing gear. Dave eyed his companion, Jim Hutchinson. They had been friends and fishing buddies for half a century. Dave held a doctorate and had taught at a series of universities, including Trinity University in San Antonio, near his winter home. Hutch had taught Latin and coached football at the local high school, Southern Regional, in Manahawkin. Retired now, they spent as much time as possible fishing, especially in the fall when the stripers migrate down the coast. That explained why they were on Barnegat Bay in a bullying wind. It was the annual tournament, and they were desperate. They wanted to fill at least one cooler with fish before they quit.

Snotty weather wasn't unusual this late in the season, only days before Halloween, in 2012. But this was exceptional: sun, fog, and wind, day after day. The water was wrong as well. At 65 degrees, the bay was 5 or 6 degrees warmer than it should have been at this time of year. Some of their friends complained that it was holding back the stripers. The fish weren't migrating because they were confused and thought it was still summer.

Dave and Hutch fished for an hour or two near an old fish-processing plant off the southern tip of Long Beach Island, but they landed only one small striper, with iridescent skin and a pearly white bottom. It was pretty, but it wasn't going to win any awards, so they gave it back.

On the way home, the conversation shifted from fish to the storm working its way up the coast. Hutch said he was planning to move his computer and television up to the attic of his cape in Beach Haven West, just to be safe. Dave was debating whether to advise his wife, Sheila, a playwright, to leave. He didn't like to quit, but he didn't want to be stupid, either.

Most late-season hurricanes spin harmlessly out to sea by the time they reach New Jersey. But the weathermen were saying this one—Sandy—was different. A large high-pressure system parked to the north, near Greenland, was going to block the hurricane's path and steer it into the coast near Atlantic City, about fifteen miles to the south. That was a little too close for comfort for Dave. It meant that Long Beach Island and the communities along Barnegat Bay—Tuckerton, Mystic Island, Beach Haven West, Brick, Toms River, and a dozen other lagoon developments—would be on the wrong side of the storm, exposed to the worst wind and surge. It also worried Dave that the hurricane was so large, a thousand miles wide. The rule of thumb was, the bigger a storm, the longer its fetch. Dave's tiny cottage on Cedar Bonnet Island, near the bridge connecting the mainland and Long Beach Island, was at the end of a shallow cove with no defenses. If the wind turned south, the hurricane would push all that water his way.

"I had a bad feeling about the storm," Dave recalled years later. "I had stayed around for plenty of other storms in the past. But this one felt different. I told my wife I thought this was going to be the Big One people had been talking about since '62 [Ash Wednesday]. We agreed that she should pack up and leave, and I would catch up with her in San Antonio after I buttoned up the house."

\\\

Dave rode out the hurricane with another friend in Beach Haven West. Early the next morning, they took a boat up one of the lagoons to check on his cottage. The governor had closed the bay to regular boat traffic, and a marine police helicopter ordered them to turn around. Dave's friend had anticipated this moment and flashed a pass he'd secured from a local emergency official. The helicopter pilot waved them on.

The bay was eerily calm, the sky flawlessly blue, but the crossing was harrowing nonetheless. The water was cluttered with unmoored boats, parts of houses, fences, decks, outdoor showers, and aluminum siding. A couple of smaller boats were jammed beneath the bridge near Dave's cottage, forming a dam.

When they entered the cove, Dave saw a speedboat where his picture window used to be and groaned. Of all the boats in the world, he thought, why did it have to be a speedboat? Watermen loathed speedboats. The drivers roared up on you while you were fishing or clamming and then flipped you the bird if you complained. The hurricane was bad enough; finding a speedboat had crashed through the front of your bungalow only added insult to injury.

Dave's cottage was listing. One of the walls was blown out where the storm surge had rushed in and boomeranged back out. The interior was filled with sand, seaweed, and debris. Furniture and appliances were turned sideways or missing entirely. Dave opened drawers and pawed through trash, searching for the prized fishing journals he'd kept most of his life but had foolishly left behind in the rush to escape the hurricane. Now they were gone, washed away in the flood. That probably hurt the most. He could rebuild the cottage.

The journals contained his personal history, told through fifty years of fishing tales, and could never be replaced.

"I've been coming here most of my life. I got my first boat, a rowboat, when I was nine, so I could putter around on the bay. And I bought my own sixteen-foot Garvey when I was sixteen to clam out of. I spent so much time on the water, I felt like I knew every crack and hole and dent. And those journals were my history."

Dave's voice faded.

\\\

Dave Rinear's 700-square-foot cedar-shake bungalow was a total loss. But he never questioned whether he should rebuild. He lived on Cedar Bonnet Island seven months of the year and considered it home. The bay wasn't a hobby or a way to pass the time for him. It was his life. He was a waterman, one of a dwindling number of men who lived on and for the bay. He might have a degree in theater, he joked, but he had a doctorate in fishing and clamming.

Dave was luckier than some. He had federal flood insurance and also qualified for a state resettlement grant and a low-interest federal loan. He was able to rebuild in months, not years. The new home was elevated and had wonderful views of Barnegat Bay. It was 1,100 square feet, nearly twice as large as his old cottage, though modest compared with the lavish confections on the beach. Surprisingly, he did not buy more flood insurance.

"The way I look at it," he said, "if another storm takes out the new place, it will have to be one hell of a storm. And at that point, it won't matter. Everything will be gone."

\\\

Most of the media's focus after Sandy was on the oceanfront, including the memorable photographs of the Star Jet roller coaster tottering in the surf near Seaside Heights. But the epic hurricane did most of its damage along the bays and back sides of the barrier islands, pushing waves of water over the bulkheads and marsh.

In October 2012, a speedboat crashed into Dave Rinear's modest cottage during Hurricane Sandy. The cottage was destroyed, but Rinear rebuilt, though this time he didn't buy flood insurance. (Courtesy of Dave Rinear)

Nearly three-quarters of the damage in New Jersey—costing about $25 billion—occurred along the bays. Large towns, small towns, rich towns, poor towns: Sandy didn't discriminate. The Christie administration initially estimated that more than 300,000 houses had been severely damaged. But that proved to be wildly wrong. About 70,000 houses took on some water, including 45,000 that were inundated or wrecked. Half of those—22,000 houses—were in Ocean County, along the shoreline of Barnegat Bay, a shallow forty-four-mile funnel of water that has undergone relentless development in the past five decades.

Most of those houses had never flooded before, let alone endured three to six feet of water in their first floors and basements. Entire neighborhoods washed away. Families were left living in gutted bungalows for months with no heat or electricity. Others camped out in the basements of relatives and friends, waiting for help. As if to pour salt on their wounds, the two winters after Sandy were among the coldest in recent memory. Temperatures plummeted to the teens and snow swirled in the air.

In Beach Haven West, Herb and Jerry Shapiro's waterfront colony, 4,000 of the 4,500 houses flooded. Hundreds were destroyed, waterlogged, or filled with mold—"teardowns" in the parlance of zoning officials. Scores of elderly owners without flood insurance simply walked away. Others sold at bargain-basement prices. A township official kept a list of properties that, under the rules, would have to be elevated if they rebuilt—what FEMA calls "substantially damaged" properties with structural damage equal to 50 percent or more of the market value. The list quickly reached 1,000. However, the actual number was probably higher. "A lot of owners don't tell us, or they haven't been back to look at the damage," Bonnie Flynn, the former zoning officer, told me. "Their homes are sitting there with water and mold. Who knows what they'll find when they finally do open them?"

Other hurricanes had highlighted the risks of building along the nation's bays and sounds. In 2008, Ike had flooded most of the back side of Galveston Island, with billions in damage. But Sandy spotlighted the risks in new, surprising ways. For one, the scale of the damage was staggering. It shocked property owners, state officials, and insurers alike. It was too large, they said. The flooding was too extensive. In Union Beach alone, in North Jersey, the Raritan Bay had poured across the back of the small blue-collar enclave and into 1,400 homes, sweeping some into nearby wetlands. In a matter of hours, the town lost a huge chunk of its tax base.

For decades, mayors, state officials, and developers had been living inside a bubble, largely oblivious or indifferent to the surge of building along Barnegat Bay and other New Jersey coastal waterways. By the time Sandy struck, approximately 300,000 houses crowded the winding shorelines. Most had been built on top of salt marshes and other low-lying areas at the highest risk of flooding. Many bordered lagoons and canals, which funneled water into homes in the hurricane. But because their communities hadn't suffered a catastrophic flood in the recent past, the homeowners and officials shrugged off the risk.

Sandy quickly disabused them of that idea. Now, for the first time in decades, regulators and lawmakers began to consider the problem of the bays. Congress provided millions of dollars for studies of the bays in Maryland, New Jersey, and New York and tasked the Corps of Engineers with finding solutions. It quickly proved to be a daunting challenge. The engineers were good at repairing beaches and building jetties and seawalls. But they didn't have much experience protecting property along the bays. The bays and sounds were ragged and irregular, unruly and indented, full of curves, coves, and lagoons. Rock walls protected some of the inlets to the ocean. Others, including the Little Egg Inlet near the southern end of Barnegat Bay, were wild channels of sand prone to shoaling and dangerous currents.

The engineers set up "listening sessions" with mayors, property owners, and coastal planners. Then they drafted plans and reports and shared their ideas with their partners at the New Jersey Department of Environmental Protection. Publicly, they projected confidence, but privately they recognized that the task was formidable.

"The bays are a bigger fix [than the oceanfront]. There are a lot more pieces," said Jeff Gebert, the chief coastal planner in the Corps' Philadelphia District Office, which includes Barnegat Bay. "Will we come up with a solution? I'm sure we will. But will the solutions be something we can afford and Congress will fund? That's a much tougher question."

But it wasn't only Barnegat Bay. The problem of the bays was national in scope, and the sheer size of the challenge enormous. There were thousands of miles of shoreline stretching from the rocky cliffs of Maine to the low, murky waters of the southern Texas coast. The Gulf of Mexico alone included two hundred estuaries: the St. Lucie River estuary in Florida, Tampa Bay, Pensacola Bay, Biloxi Bay, Galveston Bay, and Corpus Christi Bay, among others.

Each was unique in its geography, environmental profile, and challenges. Some were long and shallow; others, wide and fat. Some were pristine. Others, such as the St. Lucie estuary, suffered from septic overflows, agricultural runoff, and constant algal blooms. All were rich ecological incubators and breeding grounds for fish and invertebrates; nutrient-rich sources for migratory fowl; sponges that absorbed floodwater in storms and filtered pollutants from industry and development. The engineers couldn't simply wall them off. Each decision was fraught with unique challenges, not the least of which was the explosive development along the water's edge.

As was the case with barrier islands, the nation's bays were now densely flanked by houses. There were tens of thousands of bungalows and homes in the high-risk flood zone in New Jersey alone. Meanwhile, 8 million people lived along the Long Island Sound, covering 110 miles from the Bronx to New Haven, Connecticut. As Houston had expanded, one million Texans had moved east, along Galveston Bay. What was once an empty coastal prairie was now one continuous suburb.

How did you defend so much shoreline and so many houses? You could begin by restoring the lost marsh and wetlands, as they were doing in Louisiana and Mississippi. You could elevate the houses and roads. Or you could try to prevent the water from getting into the bays by constructing huge steel gates and seawalls, as was currently being planned in Galveston and New York City. But the cost was enormous. A single gate in front of a small inlet could easily run $100 million, while the tab for a far larger wall, such as the proposed Ike Dike, could cost upward of $31 billion. The engineers could spin out their solutions. But someone was going to have to pay.

\\\

You can argue that Hurricane Sandy was a once-in-a-lifetime storm. After all, how many hurricanes have made a hard left-hand turn into the coast of New Jersey in late October? The answer is, not many. It took a series of meteorological quirks—a vaulting high-pressure system to the north, unusually warm water, a sudden shift in the wind—to create Sandy.

But that doesn't mean it can't happen again. Rising sea levels are making the bays more dangerous, expanding the reach for waves and storm surges to rush inland. "In the future," said Chris Huch, a coastal researcher and resiliency specialist who lives along Barnegat Bay, "even smaller storms will be able to cause the same level of damage that Sandy caused. That's why what's happening in the bays matters."

The shoreline in New Jersey is unusually low in elevation, Huch pointed out, and even lower and more vulnerable in densely developed Ocean County. Long Beach Island, with its $15 billion of real estate, is only seven feet above sea level, which explains why the back of the island, along Barnegat Bay, flooded so badly during Sandy. Even routine thunderstorms and nor'easters leave the island's streets impassable for hours. School buses occasionally have to wait for the water to recede to pick up and drop off students.

Many island homeowners blame the flooding on Sandy. They contend the storm changed the bathymetry of the bay and choked it with sand. But they're wrong. At least three studies have rebutted these arguments. One, by Jennifer L. Miselis and her colleagues at the United States Geological Survey, found that relatively little sand wound up in Barnegat Bay in Sandy. One reason: a barricade of vacation homes blocked the sand from reaching the bay. Instead, it piled up on the roads, side streets, and yards.

"It really was not much at all. In general, in terms of actually changing the volume of the bay, it really was not very significant," Miselis said in a 2016 interview.

Ideally, the beach towns should have left the sand where it blew, Huch said. That would have helped to elevate the middle of the low-lying island, adding protection. But the homeowners and politicians wouldn't stand for that. It was too messy. So they collected it and put it back on the beach.

\\\

"Hurricane Sandy was one of the most perfect scenarios for flooding," Chris Huch said. It was a big, slow-moving storm, which allowed plenty of time for the hurricane to push water into the back bays. A day before the storm even made landfall, Barnegat Bay was already at near-record levels.

The volume of water pouring through the bay's three inlets in Sandy also

was massive, according to researchers at Stockton University. It tripled the surface volume of Barnegat Bay and added over five feet of water on top of the salt
marsh. To raise the surface one foot requires the equivalent of 4 billion cubic feet of water, the researchers calculated. That meant, altogether, about 20
billion cubic feet of water gushed into the bay—or about 1.2 trillion pounds
of water, by my estimate.

Once all that water got in, it couldn't get out. One reason was that the wind
and waves blocked the water from retreating through the inlets. But Barnegat
Bay also has a long-standing plumbing problem. On average, it takes water
entering the bay about seventy days to find its way back out to sea. The slow
return cycle means water sits around longer, amplifying the volume and choking the circulation.

When Sandy started inland, the 40-knot wind field abruptly switched to
the south and pushed all the water impounded in Barnegat Bay on top of the
marsh and low-lying bulkheads into thousands of homes. "The wind was
like a seesaw," explained Thomas Herrington, a coastal scientist at Stevens
Institute of Technology and the coauthor of a research paper on Sandy and
Barnegat Bay. "The northeast wind had been holding the water back. But
then there was nothing to hold it back any longer, and it came roaring up
the bay."

\\\

After the flood, some of the mayors along Barnegat Bay decided they needed
to do more to protect their towns—none more so than John Spodofora, the former mayor of Stafford Township, which includes Beach Haven West.

"Before Sandy, I and all of the other mayors on the bay were somewhat
skeptical of sea-level rise," Spodofora told me in 2017, when he was still mayor.
"Now we're all on board. We've gone to the state Department of Environmental Protection and told them we need help. They are intent to spend a billion
dollars on sand dunes on Long Beach Island, but they're doing nothing for
the bay." (Actually, federal taxpayers are paying for the sand on Long Beach
Island.)

Spodofora grew up here hunting and fishing along the woods and tidal creeks and considers himself an environmentalist. Since Sandy, he has proposed a number of plans to protect Beach Haven West. Initially, he suggested building levees in the middle of the bay that would have acted like speed bumps blocking waves and surge approaching from the east. Then he suggested the state should use abandoned cranberry bogs in the nearby Pine Barrens to store flood water in storms. Neither of those proposals went anywhere. Later, Spodofora recommended building a dirt levee along the border of the Edwin B. Forsythe National Wildlife Refuge, where Sandy floodwaters surged across the marsh and into the neighborhoods of Beach Haven West.

In 2017, Spodofora met with the manager of the refuge, "who didn't like the idea. She thought it would hurt the wildlife." Another key issue involved the cost. Spodofora said Stafford couldn't afford the $10 million price tag for the levee. He wanted the state or federal government to pay. "It's a form of resilience," he told me, stressing the word du jour among coastal planners. "This is what they say we should be doing."

Since Sandy, Beach Haven West has undergone an astonishing transformation. Hundreds of old Shapiro-era bungalows have been replaced with large two- and three-story homes along the maze of lagoons connecting to Barnegat Bay. About 70 percent are second homes belonging to absentee owners. Not only has Stafford Township recovered $200 million in property values that Sandy destroyed; it has *added* another $200 million in value to its tax rolls, with millions more to come.

Even Spodofora seemed stunned by the changes. "Everything is so much bigger," he exclaimed one day as we drove around Beach Haven West. "The downside is, we've lost some of our senior citizens and retirees. The good news is, we have all of this. It's kind of amazing to me."

\\\

About ten miles down the bay, Mystic Island was also recovering. Sandy had flooded four of every five bungalows in the lagoon colony. But that had presented the blue-collar township with a rare opportunity to reinvent its waterfront community.

"I see this as a boom," the Little Egg Harbor administrator Garrett K.

Loesch told me in 2015. At the time, the recovery was just beginning. "We buy silver. We buy gold. We buy commodities. This is a commodity. Water is a commodity."

Loesch stressed that the new homes would be stronger. But he told me he didn't have the luxury of planning for thirty, forty, or fifty years in the future to accommodate rising water. He was too busy helping the community get back on its feet. The township had lost $100 million worth of property. The tax base was depleted. He needed as many homeowners as possible to return, the quicker the better.

One of those who never left was Lisa Stevens, a former social worker who'd retired to Mystic Island to live along the water. She and her partner, Kathy, had tried to ride out Sandy but had been trapped in their one-story ranch. The house was inundated. For two years, they camped out in their unheated house and a trailer they parked on their small lot. In 2017, after years of paperwork and battling state bureaucrats, they finally moved into a new, elevated house on their lagoon, largely paid for with a state grant.

"I'm thrilled," Lisa said when I visited. "The house is wonderful. But it was definitely a slog. Many times I wanted to pull out my hair. They made you feel like a criminal. I said, 'Wait, I'm not on trial, am I? Because that's the way I feel. I'm just trying to get a little help.'"

Lisa began attending township meetings to learn what officials were doing to prepare for the future. "The climate is changing, and the seas are definitely rising. I just wanted to know if they had any ideas," she said.

It turned out they didn't. Lisa began working with New Jersey Future, a nonprofit planning group, and studied the issues. She also ran for the town council and was elected. She tried to get the staff interested in flooding issues, she said, but didn't have much success.

Little Egg was one of dozens of coastal towns to receive a state grant to help guide development after Hurricane Sandy. As part of the grant, a professional planner, Leah B. Yasenchak, worked with township officials for about a year developing a plan. Meanwhile, researchers from New Jersey Future studied the potential impact of sea-level rise and future flooding on the township.

Unsurprisingly, the researchers identified rising water as Little Egg Harbor Township's biggest threat. By the middle of this century, they reported, a
third of the township—including more than one thousand properties—would
be inundated if the bay rose by just one foot. Most were in the Mystic Island
colony where Lisa lived.

Yasenchak and David Kutner, a planner for New Jersey Future, held a series of public meetings to share their findings and get feedback on possible
solutions. About seventy people showed up for the first session. But attendance
dropped sharply at subsequent sessions. I counted twelve attendees at a 2017
meeting to consider how to make the township safer.

The Shapiro shacks built in the 1960s in Beach Haven West have been replaced with towering second homes—with convenient access to the Route 72 causeway to Long Beach Island.
(Photograph by Ray Fisk / The SandPaper Inc.)

"There wasn't a lot of concern," recalled Yasenchak. "Nobody wanted to talk about hard solutions. They were afraid it was going to discourage investment . . . and to deplete their tax base, and send their real estate industry into a tailspin."

As part of a separate grant, David Kutner explored the possibility of buying flood-prone bungalows on Mystic Island lagoons and leaving the space undeveloped. But it was too late. By this point, Little Egg was busy rebuilding. It would eventually recover all of the $100 million in lost property values.

"The time for approaching people was right back after the storm before people started rebuilding," said Ray Gormley, Little Egg's current mayor. "The state had $300 million for buyouts then. But I can tell you we never heard from anyone. It was never mentioned in Little Egg."

The Christie administration used the $300 million to purchase houses that had flooded along inland rivers in Passaic and Middlesex Counties, far from the coast. Now, Gormley and Lisa Stevens were searching for funds to dredge the clogged lagoons. Lisa hoped the township could use the muck to fortify nearby wetlands. The primary beneficiaries of the dredging will be boat owners, Gormley told me. "It's to give residents quality of life. It's not part of rising water."

Little Egg officials also planned to use a grant to repair a heavily eroded shoreline along Iowa Court, bordering the bay. Sandy had obliterated a row of houses there. But when I asked Gormley how long he expected the sand to last, he shrugged. "We don't really have any other choice," he said.

Gormley, who is fifty years old, grew up in Little Egg. In his lifetime, the township has lost about two hundred feet of shoreline along the bay, he estimated.

"There's really not much we can do. What's done is done; what's built is built. Changing building codes and elevating is about all we can do. Lots of areas in future storms will not be able to build back—and probably for some, rightly so."

"I try to be hopeful," Lisa Stevens added. "Would I like to see us do more? Absolutely, I would. But what I am learning is, it's not easy. It's money, and it's politics, and it's trying to get people to pay attention."

\\\

In December 2016, the Corps of Engineers held a public meeting at Stockton University to solicit ideas for their study of the back bays, which included 450 square miles of flood-prone shoreline. It had been over a year since their study had been announced. But the engineers were still struggling to define exactly what they were studying.

Earlier meetings with coastal mayors and public officials had been inconclusive. Meanwhile, the engineers had pointed out a number of potential complications, including the high cost of walling off the bay, relentless development pressures, and what they artfully called "technical challenges."

One of the engineers' reports identified fourteen different ways to protect the bays. There were old standbys like seawalls, groins, levees, and breakwaters; as well as newer, Dutch-influenced ideas like floodgates. The engineers didn't indicate which approach they preferred, if any. It almost seemed as if they were waiting for someone to tell them the best approach, which possibly explained why they were holding so many meetings.

The Stockton auditorium was filled with anxious homeowners, politicians, and environmentalists. Many had seen their homes flood in Sandy. Others were worried that sea-level rise would swallow their homes in coming years. Water was already creeping ever closer to the attorney Pat Doyle's house in Lacey Township, Ocean County. After Sandy, the state had constructed a small rock wall to hold back the water. But every time there was a nor'easter, the waves scattered the rocks. "It doesn't work," Doyle said. "What we need is sand, a beach fill like on Long Beach Island." But there was no sand coming anytime soon. Doyle and the others were hoping to hear that the engineers had a plan—or, if not a plan, at least an idea.

J. B. Smith, a slight, earnest planner, was running the program for the Corps. He explained that the back-bay study was just getting started and would likely take three years. The goal was to have a "comprehensive, system-wide solution" that the engineers could then pass on to their bosses in the North Atlantic Division, in New York City. Assuming they approved, the plan would then go to Corps headquarters in Washington for another level of review.

How long is all this going to take? a homeowner wanted to know.

Years, Smith replied.

Murmurs of discontent gave way to anger and frustration, voices on top of voices.

Paul Jeffrey, a retired executive who lives on Barnegat Bay in Ortley Beach, Ocean County, one of the hardest-hit towns in Sandy, exclaimed that he and his neighbors would be dead by the time the engineers finished. "We won't live long enough to see it take effect," he said.

\\\

The following summer, I traveled to Philadelphia to get an update from Smith and his boss, Jeff Gebert. I was sympathetic. The engineers had a daunting assignment, and people living along the bays seemed to expect miracles. But I didn't sense any urgency on the part of the engineers. At the earliest, work wouldn't begin until 2026, Gebert said.

"We're still in the scoping phase," Smith explained.

"We haven't done any serious analytic work," added Gebert. "For example, we need to mesh the housing inventory with what is at risk. Do a serious inventory. We want to look at first-floor elevation . . . determine the still water plus waves. Basically, we have to do it all ourselves."

The engineers knew they would be blamed if another storm blew up the back bays, destroying homes. And they would be blamed for taking the time to get a fix right. Environmental groups and government agencies could toss around words like "resiliency" and "sustainability" all they liked. But there was no quick, easy, or cheap way to get there. Recently, New Jersey officials had asked FEMA for nearly $17 billion to address the state's resiliency needs. And that was only one state. Dozens of other coastal states wanted money.

During one of the Corps' earlier listening sessions, the engineers had handed out questionnaires. One of the questions they asked was, What was the best way to fix thousands of miles of broken, vulnerable shorelines?

One of the attendees, a Corps engineer no less, had scribbled across the top of his questionnaire "Stop spending money and leave."

Epilogue:
The Future Is Now

FOR MUCH OF THE 2018 HURRICANE SEASON, the Atlantic and Gulf basins were unusually quiet, with no hurricanes in sight. Some meteorologists even speculated that it might be a year with no storms. After the brutal season the year before, highlighted by Harvey, Irma, and Maria, this felt like a gift. Homeowners and businesses along the densely developed coasts might finally catch a break.

But in late August the run of good luck abruptly ended. A tropical wave emerging off the west coast of Africa organized into a hurricane and then rapidly grew into a Category 4 storm. Florence was big, explosive, and moody. And though it weakened as it approached the North Carolina coast near Wilmington, it remained dangerous, morphing into a rain bomb that flooded scores of small, poor inland communities without flood insurance or much of any other resources.

A few weeks later, a second hurricane formed in the Gulf of Mexico and raced toward the Florida Panhandle, near the resorts of Panama City Beach and Mexico Beach. It, too, rapidly intensified, exploding from an unexceptional storm into a Category 5 hurricane with winds topping 155 miles per hour. Only four hurricanes that powerful had ever made landfall in the continental United States. Michael's devastating winds and fourteen-foot storm surge obliterated the small resort of Mexico Beach, crumpling nearly every bungalow and house along the Gulf. Then it cut a narrow but catastrophic swath inland from Florida to Georgia, much like a tornado.

What had been an underperforming hurricane season was now an above-average season. Even more to the point, while the two hurricanes were vastly different, one a relentless rainmaker, the other a destructive wind machine, they highlighted the evolving nature of risk at the coast and the increasingly chaotic nature of hurricanes and climate.

Many of the hurricanes of recent years have intensified at alarming rates, strengthening from relatively small, even harmless storms into meteorological nightmares. Both Florence and Michael exploded from tropical depressions into major hurricanes in three days or less. Meanwhile, in the Pacific, Super Typhoon Yutu deepened from a tropical storm to a catastrophic hurricane in two days, smashing into the Northern Mariana Islands with 180-mile-per-hour winds. Only the 1935 Labor Day Hurricane that struck the Florida Keys was stronger.

Hurricane Michael accelerated as it made landfall, pushing a wall of water across Mexico Beach. As it moved inland, it razed smaller, rural communities in Florida and still packed major hurricane-force winds when it reached Georgia.

Florence, on the other hand, encountered wind shear and weakened. Then, like Hurricane Harvey had a year earlier, it stalled at the coast, allowing it to siphon heat and moisture from the ocean and morph into a rain bomb. That, too, appears to be one of the signals of the shifting nature of hurricanes: a propensity to linger in place for days, inundating communities with rain and flooding, rather than always sprinting inland or up the coasts. There are simply too many torrential rain events resulting in historic flooding for it to be a statistical glitch, researchers agree. Something is different. The climate is hotter and wetter, creating more favorable conditions for superabundant rainstorms.

"The record-breaking rainfall in Hurricane Florence (30 inches) and Hurricane Harvey in Houston (60 inches) is a long-expected outcome from a warming ocean," Orrin Pilkey wrote in October 2018, following the storms. Researchers also believe that the rate of warming may be accelerating faster than previously thought, adding enormous amounts of energy, not to mention potential fuel for future storms.

Florence made landfall near Wrightsville Beach, North Carolina, on September 14. It then slowed to a pedestrian 3 miles per hour, inching inland and flooding Wilmington, Fayetteville, Kinston, Lumberton, and scores of other communities dotting the coastal plains of Eastern North Carolina. The area is low, flat, and cleaved by rivers, creeks, and estuaries. Many of the towns were already saturated from earlier summer storms. The water tables had also risen by a foot or more in the last century.

"There just isn't as much room to accommodate the stormwater as there used to be," said Rob Young, the coastal geologist at Western Carolina University.

Much of Eastern North Carolina is poor. In Lumberton, nearly a third of the twenty thousand residents live at or below the poverty level. Almost no one can afford flood insurance. On average, just 10 percent of the residents in Eastern Carolina are covered. In some towns, as little as 1 percent are, records show.

It is too early to know the final cost of the 2018 hurricanes. Damage estimates for Florence range upward of $30 billion, including $2 billion to $5 billion in federal flood claims, most near the heavily insured coast. Hurricane Michael will likely cost less, but only because it cut a relatively narrow destructive path across the Florida Panhandle. A month after the hurricane, locals feared that Mexico Beach would be transformed from a modest beach town into a mile-long strip of high-rises and condos as developers scooped up damaged property on the cheap. "Those old beach cottage homes that have been passed down for generations? They're gone," Mayor Al Cathey told *The Washington Post*.

Much of Michael's damage was to public infrastructure, including the electric grid, toppled and bent by the hurricane's ferocious winds. The federal government will likely cover most if not all the cost of rebuilding the roads and utilities. Meanwhile, in North Carolina the congressional delegation already is busy lobbying for help. "It's critical they [victims] have fast access to the Federal Assistance they need and are entitled to," said Senator Richard Burr, a Republican.

Governor Roy Cooper has asked for $5 billion in federal aid. He has also called for a special legislative session to address the recovery, emphasizing that the plan should include buyouts. But after past storms, North Carolinians have been reluctant to retreat to higher ground. After Hurricane Matthew dumped two feet of water on Eastern Carolina in 2016, the state received $1 billion in federal aid. Just 10 percent went to buy houses that flood over and over, state records indicate.

After the recent hurricanes, then–FEMA head Brock Long expressed frustration that the nation appeared stuck in a costly loop of hurricanes, federal payouts, and more damage. "We repeat the same cycle over and over," he said at a press briefing. "If you want to live in these areas, you've got to do it in a more resilient fashion."

—February 2019

SOURCES

This is a work of reportage based on hundreds of interviews and thousands of pages of government studies, histories, hearings, data, newspaper archives, and personal e-mails. Where it makes sense, I included direct references to the people and sources. In most other cases, I have included a list of sources below. The scenes and stories depicted in the narrative were either witnessed directly by me or reconstructed from interviews, transcripts, and records.

Data on hurricane and coastal floods come from federal and state records, including but not limited to https://www.fema.gov/policy-claim -statistics-flood-insurance and https://www.ncdc.noaa.gov/billions/. Philip Klotzbach and his colleagues also compile useful historical data adjusted for population and inflations at www.iii.org/fact-statistic/facts-statistics -hurricanes#Catastrophic%20Hurricane%20Losses%20In%20The%20

United%20States,%202007-2016. Data for public assistance grants, mitigation, and other federal disaster spending come from FEMA and state datasets. All the analysis and calculations are the author's work.

Data on Army Corps of Engineers projects come from a variety of sources, including federal and state records, interviews with Corps officials, Freedom of Information Act requests for project work summaries, and historical datasets maintained by Andy Coburn at Western Carolina University, in North Carolina, at https://psds.wcu.edu/current-research/beach-nourishment/.

Finally, I collected and analyzed thousands of property records and land transactions dating back decades. The sources include county, state, and local tax assessors' offices, as well as county recorders of deeds.

Bibliography

Abbott, Patrick L. *Natural Disasters*. McGraw-Hill, 1999.

Bascom, Willard. *Waves and Beaches: The Dynamics of the Ocean Surface*. Anchor Books, 1964.

Bernstein, Peter L. *Against the Gods: The Remarkable Story of Risk*. John Wiley and Sons, 1998.

Blumberg, Alan, Thomas Herrington, Larry Yin, and Nikitas Georgas. *Storm Surge Reduction Alternatives for Barnegat Bay*. Stevens Institute, 2014. https://www.nj.gov/dep/docs/flood/final-studies/stevens-barnegat/stevens-barnegat-bay-flood-mitigation-study.pdf.

Brinkley, Douglas. *The Great Deluge: Hurricane Katrina, New Orleans, and the Mississippi Gulf Coast*. Harper Perennial, 2006.

Coyle, Gretchen F., and Deborah C. Whitcraft. *Beach Haven*. Arcadia Publishing, 2018.

———. *Tucker's Island*. Arcadia Publishing, 2015.

Davis, Jack E. *The Gulf: The Making of an American Sea*. W. W. Norton, 2017.

Emanuel, Kerry. *Divine Wind: The History and Science of Hurricanes*. Oxford University Press, 2005.

Hine, Albert C., Don P. Chambers, Tonya D. Clayton, Mark R. Hafen, and Gary T. Mitchum. *Sea Level Rise in Florida: Science, Impacts and Options*. University Press of Florida, 2016.

Hinshaw, Robert E. *Living with Nature's Extremes: The Life of Gilbert Fowler White*. Johnson Books, 2006.

Kahrl, Andrew W. *The Land Was Ours: How Black Beaches Became White Wealth in the Coastal South*. University of North Carolina Press, 2012.

Kaufman, Wallace, and Orrin H. Pilkey. *The Beaches Are Moving: The Drowning of America's Shoreline*. Duke University Press, 1983.

Kolbert, Elizabeth. *Field Notes from a Catastrophe: Man, Nature, and Climate Change.* Bloomsbury, 2006.

Kunreuther, Howard, and Erwann Michel-Kerjan. *At War with the Weather: Managing Large-Scale Risks in a New Era of Catastrophes.* MIT Press, 2011.

Kunreuther, Howard, and Richard J. Roth. *Paying the Price: The Status and Role of Insurance Against Natural Disasters in the United States.* Joseph Henry Press, 1998.

Moore, Peter. *Weather Experiment: The Pioneers Who Sought to See the Future.* Farrar, Straus and Giroux, 2015.

O'Neill, Karen M., and Daniel J. Van Abs. *Taking Chances: The Coast After Hurricane Sandy.* Rutgers University Press, 2016.

Pilkey, Orrin H., and J. Andrew Cooper. *The Last Beach.* Duke University Press, 2014.

Pilkey, Orrin H., and Katherine L. Dixon. *The Corps and the Shore.* Island Press, 1996.

Pilkey, Orrin H., William J. Neal, Stanley R. Riggs, Craig A. Webb, David M. Bush, Deborah F. Pilkey, Jane Bullock, and Brian A. Cowan. *The North Carolina Shore and Its Barrier Islands.* Duke University Press, 1998.

Pilkey, Orrin H., Linda Pilkey-Jarvis, and Keith C. Pilkey. *Retreat from a Rising Sea: Hard Choices in an Age of Climate Change.* Columbia University Press, 2016.

Platt, Rutherford H. *Disasters and Democracy: The Politics of Extreme Natural Events.* Island Press, 1999.

Savadove, Larry, and Margaret Thomas Buchholz. *Great Storms of the New Jersey Shore.* Down the Shore Publishing, 1993.

Shapiro, Herbert L. *Clamdigger, Tycoon and More: A Memoir of a Pioneer of Long Beach Island.* iUniverse, 2004.

Somerville, George B. *The Lure of Long Beach.* Long Beach Board of Trade, 1914.

Stafford Chronicles: A History of Manahawkin, New Jersey. Down the Shore Publishing, 2001.

Stick, David. *The Ash Wednesday Storm.* Gresham Publications, 1987.

Taleb, Nassim Nicholas. *The Black Swan: The Impact of the Highly Improbable.* Random House, 2010.

White, Jonathan, *Tides: The Science and Spirit of the Ocean.* Trinity University Press, 2017.

Primary Sources: Reports and Studies

American Shore and Beach Association. History. http://asbpa.org/history/.

Atlantic County (NJ). *Multi-Jurisdictional All Hazard Mitigation Plan,* 2016. www.atlantic-county.org/hazard-mitigation/plan-final.asp.

Barnegat Bay Partnership. *Economic Viability and Adaptation to Climate Hazards and Climate Change,* 2013. www.savebarnegatbay.org/wp-content/uploads/2014/05/Leichenko-March2013_FinalReport-with-logos.pdf.

Blumberg, Alan, Thomas Herrington, Larry Yin, and Nickitas Georgas, *Storm Surge Reduction Alternatives for Barnegat Bay.* Stevens Institute, 2014. www.nj.gov/dep/docs/flood/final-studies/stevens-barnegat/stevens-barnegat-bay-flood-mitigation-study.pdf.

Burby, Raymond J. *Are We Safe, Can We Be Safer.* University of North Carolina, Chapel Hill, 2005.

Burton, Ian, and Robert W. Kates. "The Floodplain and the Seashore," 1964. www .jstor.org/stable/pdf/212658.pdf?seq=1#page_scan_tab_contents.

Byrne, Brendan. "Proceedings of the Governor's Conference on the Future of the New Jersey Shore," 1979 (obtained from New Jersey State Library).

Byrne, J. Peter, and Jessica Grannis. "Coastal Retreat Measures: The Law of Adaptation to Climate Change," 2012.

Cape May County (NJ). *Multi-Jurisdictional All Hazard Mitigation Plan*, 2016. cape maycountynj.gov/DocumentCenter/View/4373/Final-CompleteVol-II?bidId=.

Center for Texas Beaches and Shores. www.tamug.edu/ctbs/.

Charleston, South Carolina. *City of Charleston Resilience.* www.charleston-sc.gov /DocumentCenter/View/15691.

Charleston, South Carolina. *Sea Level Rise Strategy*, 2015. www.charleston-sc.gov /DocumentCenter/View/10089.

Coastal Research Center, Stockton University. "Barnegat Bay Storm Surge Elevations During Hurricane Sandy." www.nj.gov/dep/shoreprotection/docs/ibsp-barnegat-bay -storm-surge-elevations-during-sandy.pdf.

Congressional Budget Office. "Potential Increases in Hurricane Damage," June 2016. www.cbo.gov/sites/default/files/114th-congress-2015-2016/reports/51518-hurricane -damage.pdf.

Congressional Quarterly. "History of Coastal Land Use Regulations," 1998.

Congressional Research Service. "Army Corps of Engineers Annual and Supplemental Appropriations: Issues for Congress," 2018. www.everycrsreport.com/reports/R45326 .html.

———. "Army Corps Supplemental Appropriations: History, Trends, and Policy Issues, 2012–2018." https://www.everycrsreport.com/reports/R42841.html.

———. "Federal Disaster Assistance Response and Recovery Programs," 2018. https:// fas.org/sgp/crs/homesec/RL31734.pdf.

———. "Federal Flood Insurance: The Repetitive Loss Problem," 2005. https://fas.org /sgp/crs/misc/RL32972.pdf.

———. "FEMA and Disaster Relief," 1998. https://www.hsdl.org/?view&did=15130.

———. "FEMA Disaster Cost-Shares: Evolution and Analysis," 2013. https://fas.org/sgp /crs/homesec/R41101.pdf.

———. "Stafford Act Declarations: 1953–2014," 2015. https://fas.org/sgp/crs/homesec /R42702.pdf.

Conrad, David R., and Edward A. Thomas. *Reforming Federal Support for Risky Development*, 2013. www.brookings.edu/research/reforming-federal-support-for -risky-development/.

CoreLogic. "Storm Surge Report," 2014. www.eenews.net/assets/2014/07/10/document _cw_01.pdf.

Corps of Engineers. *Barnegat Inlet to Little Egg Inlet Final Feasibility Report*, 1999. https://catalog.hathitrust.org/Record/100986247.

———. *Beach Changes at Long Beach Island, 1962–1973*, 1980.

———. *Beach Erosion Control Report* (NJ), 1958.

———. *Historical Origins*, 2004. www.iwr.usace.army.mil/Portals/70/docs/iwrreports /IWR04-NSMS-4.pdf.

———. *The History of the Beach Erosion Board: 1930–1963* (Mary Louise Quinn author), 1977. http://digitalcommons.unl.edu/watercenterpubs/28/.

———. *Hurricane Sandy Coastal Projects Performance Evaluation Study*, 2013. www .nan.usace.army.mil/Portals/37/docs/civilworks/SandyFiles/USACE_Post-Sandy _Coastal_Projects_Performance_Evaluation_Study.pdf.

———. *Long Beach Island Reconnaissance Study Engineering Analysis*, 1994. www .nap.usace.army.mil/Portals/39/docs/Civil/LBI/LBI_FeasRpt_Complete.pdf.

———. *Mississippi Coastal Improvements Program*, 2010. www.sam.usace.army.mil /Portals/46/docs/program_management/mscip/docs/MsCIP_DSEIS_02-27-14 _Final.pdf.

———. *National Shoreline Study*, 1973. https://catalog.hathitrust.org/Record/007178806.

———. *New Jersey Back Bays Coastal Storm Risk Management Feasibility Study*, 2016. www.nap.usace.army.mil/Missions/Factsheets/Fact-Sheet-Article-View/Article /490870/new-jersey-back-bays-coastal-storm-risk-management-study/.

———. *New Jersey Shore Protection Barnegat Inlet to Little Egg Inlet, Reevaluation Report*, 2014. www.nap.usace.army.mil/Missions/Civil-Works/Coastal-Storm-Risk -Management/.

———. *North Atlantic Coast Comprehensive Study*, 2014. www.nad.usace.army.mil/Comp Study/.

———. *Report on Operation Five-High: March 1962 Storm*, 1963. www.alamy.com /report-on-operation-five-high-march-1962-storm-was-issued-by-the-north-atlantic -division-of-the-us-army-corps-of-engineers-in-august-1963-and-it-describes-the -historic-storm-later-known-as-the-ash-wednesday-storm-and-the-corps-of-engineers -response-to-it-image187342149.html.

———. *Shore of New Jersey–Barnegat Light to Cape May Canal, Beach Erosion Control Study*, 1959.

———. *Shore Protection: History, Projects, Costs*, 2003. https://planning.erdc.dren.mil /toolbox/library/IWRServer/IWR03_NSMS_1.pdf.

———. *Shoreline Protection and Beach Erosion Control Study*, 1994. www.dtic.mil/dtic /tr/fulltext/u2/a343641.pdf.

———. "Site Visit Summary Post-Sandy, Long Beach Island," 2012 (document provided by Philadelphia District upon author's request).

———. *Survey Report Beach Erosion Folly Beach, South Carolina*, 1979.

CQ Almanac. Flood Insurance, 1956. https://library.cqpress.com/cqalmanac/document .php?id=cqal56-1349345.

———. Sandy Disaster Aid Bill Enacted, 2013. https://library.cqpress.com/cqalmanac /document.php?id=cqal13-1634-93328-2627902.

———. Senate Passes Omnibus Disaster Relief Bill, 1965. https://library.cqpress.com /cqalmanac/document.php?id=cqal65-1260010.

Crozier, George. "The Re-Re-Re-Redevelopment of the West End of Dauphin Island, Alabama," 2007. https://gsa.confex.com/gsa/2007AM/finalprogram/abstract_128384 .htm.

Crowell, Mark. "Impact of Climate Change and Population Growth on the NFIP," 2014. https://acwi.gov/climate_wkg/minutes/12sept2013/Mark_Crowell_NFIP_and _Climate.pdf.

Doggett, Tim. "The Growing Value of US Coastal Property at Risk." AIR Worldwide, 2015. https://www.air-worldwide.com/Publications/AIR-Currents/2015/The-Growing -Value-of-U-S--Coastal-Property-at-Risk/.

Dzieza, Josh. "Sand's End." *Verge*, 2016. www.theverge.com/2016/11/17/13660014/miami -beach-sand-erosion-nourishment-climate-change.

Emanuel, Kerry A. "Climate Science and Climate Risk: A Primer." https://eapsweb.mit .edu/sites/default/files/Climate_Primer.pdf.

Federal Register. *Establishing a Deductible for FEMA's Public Assistance Program*, 2016. www.federalregister.gov/documents/2017/01/12/2017-00467/establishing-a -deductible-for-femas-public-assistance-program.

Federal Emergency Management Agency (FEMA). *Costs and Benefits of Natural Hazard Mitigation*, 1997. www.fema.gov/media-library/assets/documents/3459.

———. *Mitigation Grants and Buyouts: Gulf of Mexico*, 2005 (FOIA request by author).

———. *National Strategy Recommendations: Future Disaster Preparedness*, 2013. www .fema.gov/media-library/assets/documents/35064.

———. Post-Sandy Buyouts and Elevation as of 2015, by town (FOIA request by author).

———. *State of New Jersey and Region II 10-Year Vision for Safer Homes*, 2017 (provided by Michael Moriarty).

FreddieMac. "Life's a Beach," 2016. www.freddiemac.com/research/insight/20160426 _lifes_a_beach.html.

Government Accountability Office (GAO). "Disaster Assistance, Information on Federal Costs and Approaches for Reducing Them." Testimony, 1998. https://www.gao.gov /assets/110/107360.pdf.

———. *Disaster Resilience*, 2014. https://www.gao.gov/products/GAO-14-603T.

———. *Extreme Weather Events*, 2014. https://www.gao.gov/products/GAO-14-364T.

———. *FEMA Emergency Preparedness*, 2016. https://www.gao.gov/products/GAO-16 -90T.

———. *Hurricane Sandy*, 2015. https://www.gao.gov/products/GAO-15-515.

Kenny, Nathaniel T. "Our Changing Atlantic Coastline." *National Geographic* 122, no. 6 (December 1962), with a focus on the Ash Wednesday Nor'easter.

Kinsey, David N. "CZM from the State Perspective: The New Jersey Experience."

Natural Resources Journal 25 (1985). https://digitalrepository.unm.edu/nrj/vol25/iss1/7/.

Klotzbach, Philip J., and William M. Gray. "Causes of the Unusually Destructive 2004 Hurricane Season," 2006. https://journals.ametsoc.org/doi/10.1175/BAMS-87-10-1325.

Kousky, Carolyn, and Roger Cooke. "Adapting to Extreme Events: Managing Fat Tails," 2010. http://www.rff.org/files/sharepoint/WorkImages/Download/RFF-IB-10-12.pdf.

Kousky, Carolyn, and Michel Erwann-Kerjan. "Hurricane Sandy, Storm Surge and the National Flood Insurance Program." Resources for the Future, 2012. https://www.publicadjuster.com/Portals/hurricane-sandy-insurance-claim-adjuster/Blog%20Articles/SandyNFIPReport.pdf.

Kousky, Carolyn, and Howard Kunreuther. "Addressing Affordability in the National Flood Insurance Program." University of Pennsylvania, 2014. https://repository.upenn.edu/cgi/viewcontent.cgi?article=1110&context=bepp_papers.

Kousky, Carolyn, and Leonard Shabman. "Price Flood Insurance: How and Why the NFIP Differs from a Private Insurance Company." Resources for the Future, 2014. www.rff.org/files/sharepoint/WorkImages/Download/RFF-DP-14-37.pdf.

Kunreuther, Howard C., and Gilbert F. White. "The Role of the National Flood Insurance Program in Reducing Losses and Promoting Wise Use of Floodplains," 1994.

Little Egg Harbor Township. *Vulnerability and Exposure Analysis*, 2015. www.njfuture.org/wp-content/uploads/2017/02/LEHT-VE-Assessment-Final-Report-3-15.pdf.

Long Beach Township (NJ). *Master Plan*, 2018. https://www.longbeachtownship.com/wp-content/uploads/2018/01/master_plan_final_011018.pdf.

Mather, John R., Henry Adams III, and Gary A. Yoshioka. "Coastal Storms of the Eastern United States," *Journal of Applied Meteorology*, 1964.

Mattingly, Kyle S., Jordan T. McLeod, John A. Knox, J. Marshal Shepherd, and Thomas L. Mote. "A Climatological Assessment of Greenland Blocking Condition Associated with the Track of Hurricane Sandy," 2014. https://rmets.onlinelibrary.wiley.com/doi/full/10.1002/joc.4018.

McCallum, Bryan E., et al., *Monitoring Storm Tide and Flooding from Hurricane Sandy*. U.S. Geological Survey, 2013. https://pubs.er.usgs.gov/publication/ofr20131043.

Michel-Kerjan, Erwann. "Catastrophe Economics: The National Flood Insurance Program," 2010. https://create.usc.edu/sites/default/files/publications/catastropheeconomics-thenationalfloodinsuranceprogram_0.pdf.

Miller, H. Crane. "The Barrier Islands: A Gamble with Time and Nature." *Environment*, no. 23, 1981.

Miller, John A. "Credit Downgrade Threat, Barrier Islands and Sea Level Rise Adaptation." Master's thesis, University of Pennsylvania, 2017.

Miselis, Jennifer L., Brian Andrews, Neil Ganju, Robert Nicholson, and Zafer Defne. "Mapping, Measuring, and Modeling to Understand Water-Quality Dynamics in Barnegat Bay." USGS Sound Waves, 2013. https://soundwaves.usgs.gov/2013/02/.

Miselis, Jennifer L., et al. "Evolution of Mid-Atlantic Coastal and Back-Barrier Estuary Environments in Response to a Hurricane," 2015. https://pubs.er.usgs.gov/publication /70159495.

Monmouth County (NJ). *Multi-Jurisdictional All Hazard Mitigation Plan*, 2009. www.visitmonmouth.com/documents/29/1%20MONMOUTH%20Mar09 %20Final%20Main%20Text.pdf.

Moore, Willis L. *Moore's Meteorological Almanac and Weather Guide*, 1901. https://catalog .hathitrust.org/Record/100523710.

Moss, David A. "Courting Disaster: The Transformation of Federal Disaster Policy Since 1803," 1999. www.nber.org/chapters/c7954.

Munich, R. E. "What's Going On with the Weather," 2015. www.munichre.com/site /mram/get/documents_E-1959049670/mram/assetpool.munichreamerica.wrap/PDF /2014/MunichRe_III_NatCatWebinar_01072015w.pdf.

National Association of Insurance Companies and the Center for Insurance Policy Research. *Flood Risk and Insurance*, 2014. www.naic.org/documents/cipr_study_1704 _flood_risk.pdf.

National Flood Insurance Program (NFIP). Actuarial Rate Review, 2011. www.fema .gov/national-flood-insurance-program-actuarial-rate-review.

———. *AECOM Climate Change* (Divoky Report), 2013. www.aecom.com/fema-climate -change-report/.

———. American Institutes for Research. *A Chronology of Major Events Affecting the National Flood Insurance Program*, 2005. www.fema.gov/media-library/assets /documents/9612.

———. American Institutes for Research. *The Developmental and Environmental Impact of the NFIP*, 2006. www.fema.gov/media-library-data/20130726-1602-20490 -5762/nfip_eval_dei_summary_report.pdf.

———. Association of State Floodplain Managers. Gilbert F. White Flood Policy Forum, 2013. www.asfpmfoundation.org/ace-images/forum/2013_Forum_Participant _Papers.pdf?pagename=forum/2013_Forum_Participant_Papers.pdf.

———. Association of State Floodplain Managers. *The Nation's Responses to Flood Disasters*, 2000. www.floods.org/PDF/hist_fpm.pdf.

———. Association of State Floodplain Managers. "Reducing Flood Losses: Is the 100 Year Flood Standard Sufficient?" www.nrcs.usda.gov/Internet/FSE_DOCUMENTS /16/nrcs143_009401.pdf.

———. *Efforts to Delay the Gradual Elimination of Flood Insurance Premium Subsidies.* CRS, 2014. www.everycrsreport.com/reports/R43395.html.

———. *Estimate of US Population Living in 100-Year Coastal Flood Hazard Area.* FEMA, 2009. www.floods.org/PDF/JCR_Est_US_Pop_100y_CFHA_2010.pdf.

———. *Financial Soundness and Affordability.* CBO, 2017. www.cbo.gov/publication /53028.

———. Flood Insurance Claims Process in Communities After Sandy, 2014. www.gpo

.gov/fdsys/pkg/CHRG-113shrg91460/pdf/CHRG-113shrg91460.pdf. Also June 2015. Serial No. 114-28.

———. Floodplain Management, 1966–1994. USACE, 2014. www.iwr.usace.army.mil /Portals/70/docs/iwrreports/2014-R-02_AppendixB.pdf.

———. *Floodplain Management in the United States.* Federal Interagency Floodplain Management Task Force, 1992. www.fema.gov/media-library/assets/documents/432.

———. GAO. *Comprehensive Reform Could Improve Solvency*, 2017. www.gao.gov /products/GAO-17-425.

———. GAO. "Flood Insurance: More Information Needed on Subsidized Properties," 2013. www.gao.gov/products/GAO-13-607.

———. "The 100 Year Flood Myth." FEMA. https://training.fema.gov/hiedu/docs /hazrm/handout%203-5.pdf.

———. Kates, Robert W. "Gilbert F. White, 1911–2006: Biographical Memoir." NAS, 2011. www.nasonline.org/publications/biographical-memoirs/memoir-pdfs/white -gilbert.pdf.

———. Knowles, Scott G., and Howard Kunreuther. "Troubled Waters: The NFIP in Historical Perspective," 2014. http://opim.wharton.upenn.edu/risk/library/J2014JPH _Troubled-Waters_Knowles+Kunreuther.pdf.

———. Moore, Rob. "Flood, Rebuild, Repeat: The Need for Flood Insurance Reforms." National Resources Defense Council, 2016. www.nrdc.org/experts/rob-moore/flood -rebuild-repeat-need-flood-insurance-reforms.

———. Murphy, Francis C. "Regulating Flood-Plain Development," 1958.

———. National Academies of Sciences. "Affordability of NFIP Premiums," 2015. www.nap.edu/catalog/21709/affordability-of-national-flood-insurance-program -premiums-report-1.

———. Office of the Inspector General. *FEMA Does Not Provide Adequate Oversight of Its NFIP Write Your Own Program*, 2016. www.oig.dhs.gov/assets/Mgmt/2016/OIG -16-47-Mar16.pdf.

———. Policy and Claims Statistics. www.fema.gov/policy-claim-statistics-flood-insurance.

———. PricewaterhouseCoopers. *Study of the Economic Effects of Charging Actuarially Based Premium Rates for Pre-FIRM Structures*, 1999. https://biotech.law.lsu.edu/blaw /FEMA/NFIP-1999-finalreport.pdf.

———. "Private Flood Insurance and the National Flood Insurance Program." CRS, 2018. https://fas.org/sgp/crs/homesec/R45242.pdf.

———. Reuss, Martin. "Interview with Gilbert F. White," 1985. http://ponce.sdsu.edu /interview_with_gilbert_white.pdf.

———. Significant Flood Events. FEMA. www.fema.gov/significant-flood-events.

———. "The State of the National Flood Insurance Program: Treading Water or Sinking Fast?" *Journal of Insurance Regulation 33*, no. 5 (2014). www.naic.org/documents /prod_serv_jir_JIR-ZA-33-05-EL.pdf.

———. U.S. House of Representatives Committee on Homeland Security. Statement of W. Craig Fugate, February 28, 2017. https://docs.house.gov/meetings/HM/HM12 /20170228/105585/HHRG-115-HM12-Wstate-FugateW-20170228.pdf.

———. U.S. House of Representatives Subcommittee on Housing and Community Opportunity. *Review and Oversight of the National Flood Insurance Program*, 2005. https://www.loc.gov/item/2006415148/.

———. U.S. House of Representatives Subcommittee on Housing and Insurance. Testimony of R. J. Lehmann, June 7, 2017. https://2o9ub0417chl2lg6m43em6psi2i -wpengine.netdna-ssl.com/wp-content/uploads/2018/04/HFSC-Testimony-6-7-2017 -1.pdf.

———. U.S. House of Representatives Subcommittee on Housing and Insurance. Testimony of Roy E. Wright, March 9, 2017. https://www.fema.gov/media-library -data/1489685302278-528f910fa1819506f313a623b99dd7a0/WrightTestimony _NFIPReauthorization-3.9.17_FINAL.PDF.

———. U.S. Senate Committee on Banking, June 22, 2015, Majority Staff Report, "Assessing and Improving Flood Insurance Management and Accountability." www .banking.senate.gov/imo/media/doc/Majority%20Staff%20Flood%20Insurance%20 -Report2015.pdf

———. U.S. Senate Committee on Banking, Housing, and Urban Affairs. Testimony of Larry Larson, Association of State Floodplain Managers, May 4, 2017. www.floods .org/ace-images/ASFPMTestimonySenateBanking_May2017.pdf.

———. U.S. Senate Committee on Banking. *Report: Federal Disaster Insurance*, 1956. Also National Flood Insurance Act of 1967, https://library.cqpress.com/cqalmanac /document.php?id=cqal67-1313369 and Hearing S.1405, 1994.

———. U.S. Task Force on Federal Flood Control Policy, 1966. www.loc.gov/law/find /hearings/floods/floods89-465.pdf.

———. *Value of Properties in the National Flood Insurance Program*. CBO, 2007. www .cbo.gov/publication/18774.

National Geographic. Cool It: The Climate Issue, 228, no. 5 (November 2015).

———. *Our Changing Atlantic Coastline*, 122, no.6 (December 1962).

National Highway Safety Administration. Environmental Impact Statement, July 2018. www.nhtsa.gov/sites/nhtsa.dot.gov/files/documents/ld_cafe_my2021-26_deis_0.pdf.

National Hurricane Center. Tropical Cyclone Report, Hurricane Harvey, 2017. www .nhc.noaa.gov/data/tcr/AL092017_Harvey.pdf.

———. Tropical Cyclone Report, Hurricane Ike, 2009. www.nhc.noaa.gov/data/tcr /AL092008_Ike.pdf.

———. Tropical Cyclone Report, Hurricane Irma, 2017. www.nhc.noaa.gov/data/tcr /AL112017_Irma.pdf.

———. Tropical Cyclone Report, Hurricane Ivan, 2004. www.nhc.noaa.gov/data/tcr /AL092004_Ivan.pdf.

———. Tropical Cyclone Report, Hurricane Sandy, 2012. www.nhc.noaa.gov/data /tcr/AL182012_Sandy.pdf.

National Oceanic and Atmospheric Administration (NOAA). *Global and Regional Sea*

Level Rise Scenarios, 2017. https://tidesandcurrents.noaa.gov/publications/techrpt83 _Global_and_Regional_SLR_Scenarios_for_the_US_final.pdf.

———. *Hurricane Charley*, August 9–15, 2004. www.weather.gov/media/publications /assessments/Charley06.pdf.

———. *The Gulf of Mexico at a Glance*, 2011. https://sero.nmfs.noaa.gov/outreach _education/gulf_b_wet/applying_for_a_gulf_b_wet_grant/documents/pdfs/noaas _gulf_of_mexico_at_a_glance_report.pdf.

———. *U.S. Billion-Dollar Weather Disasters 1980–2018*. www.ncdc.noaa.gov/billions /events.pdf.

National Research Council. *Beach Nourishment and Protection*, 1995. www.nap.edu /catalog/4984/beach-nourishment-and-protection.

———. *Reducing Coastal Risk on the East and Gulf Coasts*, 2014. www.nap.edu/catalog /18811/reducing-coastal-risk-on-the-east-and-gulf-coasts.

Neal, William J. "Why Coastal Regulations Fail." *Journal of Ocean and Coastal Management*, 2017. www.researchgate.net/publication/317129581_Why_coastal_regulations _fail.

New Jersey Climate Adaptation Alliance. "Assessing New Jersey's Exposure to Sea-Level Rise," 2016. https://njadapt.rutgers.edu/docman-lister/conference-materials/167-njcaa -stap-final-october-2016/file.

New Jersey Department of Community Affairs. Sandy Disaster Recovery Action Plan, 2013. www.nj.gov/dca/divisions/sandyrecovery/action/.

New Jersey Department of Environmental Protection. Assessment of Dune and Shore Protection Ordinances, 1984.

———. Coastal Storm Hazard Mitigation, 1985.

———. Disaster Resilience Competition, 2015.

———. Inventory of the New Jersey Coast, 1975.

———. *New Jersey Coastal Hazard Management Plan*, 1996. www.gpo.gov/fdsys/pkg /CZIC-gb648-13-n5-p34-1996/html/CZIC-gb648-13-n5-p34-1996.htm.

———. *New Jersey Shore Protection Master Plan*, 1981. www.gpo.gov/fdsys/pkg/CZIC -tc224-n5-n47-1981-v-3/html/CZIC-tc224-n5-n47-1981-v-3.htm.

———. Section 309 Coastal Assessment, 2006.

New Jersey Future. *In Deep: Helping Sandy-Affected Communities*, 2015. www.njfuture .org/research-publications/research-reports/in-deep/.

New Jersey Senate Environment and Energy Committee. Sandy Recovery Hearings, August 2013 and October 2013. Transcripts. www.njleg.state.nj.us/legislativepub/pubhear /senaen08152013.pdf, www.njleg.state.nj.us/legislativepub/pubhear/senaen10212013 .pdf.

New Jersey State Legislature Energy and Natural Resources Committee. New Jersey Dune and Shorefront Protection Act Hearings, July 14 and 21, 1980. Transcripts (obtained from State Archives). Also, Dune and Shorefront Protection Act, Assembly No. 1825, June 1980.

New Jersey State Legislature Senate Budget and Appropriations Committee. Sandy

Recovery Hearings, 2012 and 2013, Transcripts. www.njleg.state.nj.us/legislativepub/pubhear/sba11262012.pdf, www.njleg.state.nj.us/legislativepub/pubhear/sba02112013.pdf.

New Jersey Water Resources Research Institute. Survey of Estuarine Site Development Lagoon Homeowners: Ocean County, New Jersey, 1973. https://rucore.libraries.rutgers.edu/rutgers-lib/34639/.

Nordhaus, William D. "The Economics of Hurricanes and Implications of Global Warming," 2009. https://pdfs.semanticscholar.org/e1f3/fcc2194ae7f921d89b3e789dba6c1abf9796.pdf.

North Carolina Department of Public Safety. *North Carolina Enhanced Hazard Mitigation Plan*, 2018. www.ncdps.gov/document/north-carolina-enhanced-hazard-mitigation-plan.

North Carolina Department of Transportation, Currituck County, Outer Banks Access, May 1982.

Ocean County (NJ). *2014 Multi-Jurisdictional All Hazard Mitigation Plan*. www.co.ocean.nj.us/WebContentFiles/ecb2ccb3-1d14-4c12-8ef8-4936909e864d.pdf.

Ocean County Planning Board. *Comprehensive Master Plan*, 2018. www.planning.co.ocean.nj.us/frmSROceanCountyComprehensiveMasterPlan.

Ocean County Recovery and Resiliency. Tim Hart slide presentation, 2015.

Pielke, Jr., Roger A., et al. "Normalized Hurricane Damage in the United States: 1900–2005," 2006. www.nhc.noaa.gov/pdf/NormalizedHurricane2008.pdf.

Planning Healthy Communities Initiative. *Mystic Island Voluntary Buyout Assessment*, 2015. http://phci.rutgers.edu/mystic-island-voluntary-buyout-hia/.

Platt, Rutherford H. "Congress and the Coast." *Environment* 27, no. 6 (1985). www.tandfonline.com/doi/abs/10.1080/00139157.1985.9931279.

Rankin, J. K. *Development of the New Jersey Shore*, 1952.

Richard Stockton Coastal Research Center. "NJ Shoreline Protection and Vulnerability." https://stockton.edu/coastal-research-center/njbpn/protection-vulnerability.html.

Risky Business Project. *The Economic Risks of Climate Change in the United States*, 2014. https://riskybusiness.org/site/assets/uploads/2015/09/RiskyBusiness_Report_WEB_09_08_14.pdf.

Rockefeller Foundation. *Structures of Coastal Resilience*, 2014. http://structuresofcoastalresilience.org/wp-content/uploads/2014/06/SCR_Phase_2_Summary.pdf.

Scientific American. "The Oceans: Will Melting Ice Flood the Lands?," 9, no. 3 (November 1998).

Severe Storm Prediction, Education, and Evacuation from Disasters Center. Hurricane Harvey Reports. Rice University. www.sspeed.rice.edu/harvey-reports.

———. *Learning Lessons of Hurricane Ike*, 2010. Rice University. http://doctorflood.rice.edu/sspeed/learned_IKE.html.

Siders, Anne. "Managed Coastal Retreat." Columbia Law School, 2013. https://web.law.columbia.edu/sites/default/files/microsites/climate-change/files/Publications/ManagedCoastalRetreat_FINAL_Oct%2030.pdf.

Southeast Florida Regional Compact. *A Region Responds to Climate Change*, 2012. www
.southeastfloridaclimatecompact.org/wp-content/uploads/2014/09/regional-climate
-action-plan-final-ada-compliant.pdf.

State of New Jersey. Ocean County General Tax Rates, 2017. www.state.nj.us/treasury
/taxation/pdf/lpt/gtr/Ocean17.pdf.

———. *2014 Hazard Mitigation Plan.* http://ready.nj.gov/mitigation/2014-mitigation
-plan.shtml.

*Strategies for Flood Risk Reduction for Vulnerable Coastal Populations Around Barnegat
Bay.* Qizhing Guo, Yunjie Li, Michael J. Kennish, Norbert P. Psuty, Richard G. Lath-
rop, and James L. Trimble, Rutgers University, 2014. www.nj.gov/dep/docs/flood
/final-studies/rutgers-hackensack/hackensack-river-study-area-flood-mitigation-final
-report.pdf.

Sweet, William, Chris Zervas, Stephen Gill, and Joseph Park. *Hurricane Sandy Inundation Probabilities Today and Tomorrow*, NOAA, 2013.

Texas General Land Office. *Texas Coastal Resiliency Master Plan*, 2017. www.glo.texas
.gov/coastal-grants/projects.

Thornthwaite, C. W. *The Shores of Megalopolis: Coastal Occupance and Human Adjust-
ment to Flood Hazard*, 1965. www.gpo.gov/fdsys/pkg/CZIC-gb459-s5-1965/html
/CZIC-gb459-s5-1965.htm.

Titus, James C. *Greenhouse Effect, Sea Level Rise, and Barrier Islands: Case Study
of Long Beach Island, New Jersey.* www.tandfonline.com/doi/abs/10.1080/089207
59009362101.

United Nations Intergovernmental Panel on Climate Change. "Summary for Policymakers of IPCC Special Report on Global Warming of 1.5°C Approved by Governments,"
2018. www.ipcc.ch/news_and_events/pr_181008_P48_spm.shtml.

U.S. Census. Population files, showing declines in beach town year-round populations.
Also, Median and average square feet for housing, 1973–2010.

U.S. Geological Survey. *Hydrologic Analysis of Hurricane Sandy.* Report 2016-5085.
https://pubs.er.usgs.gov/publication/sir20165085.

U.S. Global Change Research Program. *Climate Science Special Report: Fourth National
Climate Assessment*, 2018. www.globalchange.gov/nca4.

U.S. House of Representatives Subcommittee on Economic Development. Hearing: Rebuilding After the Storm, 2015. https://docs.house.gov/Committee/Calendar/ByEvent
.aspx?EventID=102854.

U.S. Senate Subcommittee on Appropriations, Sandy Hearing, 2013.

Valacer, Jeffrey. "Thicker Than Water: America's Addiction to Cheap Flood Insurance."
Pace Law Review, 2015. https://core.ac.uk/download/pdf/46713389.pdf.

Ventry, Dennis J. "The Accidental Deduction: A History and Critique of the Tax
Subsidy for Mortgage Interest," 2013. https://scholarship.law.duke.edu/cgi/view
content.cgi?referer=https://www.google.com/&httpsredir=1&article=1561
&context=lcp.

Walker, Nan D., et al. "Hurricane Prediction: A Century of Advances." *Oceanography*

18, no. 2 (2006). http://tos.org/oceanography/article/hurricane-prediction-a-century -of-advances.

Wallingford, H. R., *North Atlantic Coast of the USA: Sea Level Change Vulnerability and Adaptation Measures*, 2014. www.dtic.mil/dtic/tr/fulltext/u2/a597481.pdf.

Interviews

Adams, Keith: Former analyst, New Jersey Department of Environmental Protection and Sandy Recovery, 2015.

Anderson, John: Geologist, homeowner, Galveston, 2017.

Beach, Dana: South Carolina Coastal Conservation League, 2017.

Beaty, Tom and Elizabeth: Homeowners, Long Beach Island, 2015, 2016.

Bernstein, George: Former Administrator, National Flood Insurance Program, 2016.

Blackburn, James: Environmental attorney, Severe Storm Prediction, Education, and Evacuation from Disasters Center, Rice University, 2017.

Bohan, David: Homeowner, Long Beach Island, 2015.

Bramlett, Jared: Engineer, Charleston, South Carolina, 2017.

Buchholz, Margaret: Author, former publisher, *The Beachcomber*, 2015.

Buckhorn, Robert: Mayor, Tampa, 2017.

Burby, Ray: Researcher, National Flood Insurance Program, 2005.

Caddell, Hank: Attorney, 2017.

Collier, Jeff: Mayor, Dauphin Island, Alabama, 2017.

Colmer, Nathan: Real estate agent, Long Beach Island, 2015.

Conrad, David: Environmental consultant, 1998, 2017.

Crozier, George F.: Former director, Dauphin Island Sea Lab, 2017.

DeCamp, Willie: Save Barnegat Bay, 2017.

Doyle, Patricia: Attorney, homeowner, Lacey Township, 2016.

Egan, Kenneth: Owner, Kubel's Too, Long Beach Island, 2016.

Eisenberg, Steve: Owner, Terrace Tavern, Long Beach Island, 2016.

Emanuel, Kerry: Climatologist, hurricane expert, MIT, 2017.

Farrell, Stewart: Stockton University Coastal Research Center, 2012, 2013, 2015.

Flanigan, Maryann: Attorney, New Jersey Legal Services, 2016.

Flynn, Bonnie: Former floodplain manager, Stafford Township, 2014, 2015.

Fraser, Mary Edna: Artist, Charleston, 2017.

Fugate, Craig: Former administrator, FEMA, 2017.

Ganju, Neil: U.S. Geological Survey, 2016.

Gebert, Jeffrey A.: Army Corps of Engineers, 2014, 2015, 2016, 2017.

Gleghorn, Jenny: Tuckerton Borough, 2015.

Glorsky, Maxine: 2016.

Goldshore, Lewis: Attorney, 2015.

Gormley, Ray: Mayor, Little Egg Harbor Township, 2017.

Griffin, Chuck: Homeowner, Mystic Island, 2015, 2016.

Hair, J. Brady: Attorney, 1998.

Halsey, Susan D.: Environmental consultant, 2016.

Haney, Bernie: Tax assessor, 2015, 2016.

Hart, Timothy: Historian, Ocean County, 2015.

Hazelton, Jason: Stafford Township, 2015.

Herrington, Thomas: Stevens Institute of Technology, 2015.

Hine, Albert: Geologist, 2017.

Honeycutt, Maria: National Oceanic and Atmospheric Administration, 2017.

Houghtaling, John: Attorney, 2015.

Huch, Chris: Coastal resiliency expert, 2017.

Hughes, Thomas: Owner, Sea Shell Resort, Long Beach Island, 2015.

Husenbeck, William: Mayor, Ship Bottom, 2015, 2016.

Hutchinson, James: Homeowner, Beach Haven West, 2015, 2016.

Kaloudis, Yanni: Homeowner, Long Beach Island, 2017.

Kelly, Willo: CEO, Outer Banks Association of Realtors, 2017.

Keyserling, Billy: Mayor, Beaufort, South Carolina, 2017.

Kinsey, David N.: Former head of coastal programs, New Jersey Department of Environmental Protection, 2015.

Klotzbach, Philip J.: Hurricane expert, 2017.

Kopp, Robert: Sea-level expert, Rutgers, 2017.

Krimm, Richard: Former assistant administrator, National Flood Insurance Program, 2016.

Krynowski, Edward and Carol: Homeowners, Beach Haven West, 2015.

Kutner, David: New Jersey Future, 2015, 2016.

Larson, Larry: Former director, Association of State Floodplain Managers, 2017.

Leacy, Gail and John: Homeowners, Dauphin Island, Alabama, 1998, 2005.

Lee, Buck: Former general manager, Pensacola Beach, 2005.

Lin, Ning: Princeton University, 2015.

LoBiondo, Frank: U.S. Congressman, 2015.

Loesch, Garrett: Administrator, Little Egg Harbor Township, 2015.

Mahoney, James: Homeowner, Long Beach Island, 2015, 2016, 2017.

Mancini, James A.: Tax assessor, Stafford Township, 2017.

Mancini, James J.: Former mayor, Long Beach Township, 1998, 1999.

Mancini, Joseph H.: Mayor, developer, Long Beach Township, 2015, 2016, 2017, 2018.

Mangino, Joseph: Homeowner, activist, Beach Haven West, 2015, 2016.

Mannchen, Brandt: Sierra Club, Texas Chapter, 2017.

Marcy, Douglas: Sea-level expert, National Oceanic and Atmospheric Administration, 2017.

Markoski, Dawn: Homeowner, Long Beach Island, 2016.

Marticek, Susan: Ocean County Long Term Recovery Group, 2015.

Merrell, William: Galveston, 2017.

Michaels, Nancy: Homeowner, Long Beach Island, 2016.

Miller, John A.: New Jersey Association of State Floodplain Managers, 2016, 2017.

Miller, Kenneth: Rutgers University, 2015.

Mohn, Jerry: Homeowner, Galveston, 2017.

Moore, Robert: National Resources Defense Council, 2017.

Moran, James: Administrator, Stafford Township, 2015, 2016.

Moriarty, Michael, Mitigation Specialist, FEMA, New York City, 2017.

Muriello, Mark: Former administrator, New Jersey Department of Environmental Protection, 2015.

O'Brien, Margaret: Homeowner, Long Beach Island, 2013.

Osbahr, Robert and Jaclyn: Homeowners, Long Beach Island, 2015.

Paul, Jeffrey: Homeowner, Ortley Beach, 2016.

Pilkey, Orrin H.: Coastal geologist, 1998, 1999, 2005, 2013, 2017, 2018.

Plunkett, Richard: Owner, Wizard of Odds, 2015.

Psuty, Norbert P.: Marine scientist, 2016.

Quinn, Doug: Homeowner, Silverton, Ocean County, 2015.

Ratzenberger, John: Commissioner, Town of Nags Head, NC, 2017.

Reed, Phil: Construction official, Tuckerton Borough, 2015.

Riggs, Stanley: Geologist, East Carolina University, 2017.

Riley, Joseph: Former mayor, Charleston, 2017.

Rinear, Amanda: New Jersey Organizing Project, 2015, 2016.

Rinear, David: Homeowner, Cedar Bonnet Island, 2015, 2016, 2017.

Robles, Romeo: Owner, Tuckerton Bar and Grille, 2016.

Rochette, Stephen: Public Affairs Office, Army Corps of Engineers, Philadelphia District, 2014, 2015, 2016, 2017.

Rulli, Joseph: Owner, Joeys' Pizza, 2016.

Ryan, Michael: Architect, 2016.

Santos, Mike: Council member, homeowner, Tuckerton, 2015.

Shapiro, Herbert: Developer, 2014, 2015, 2016, 2017.

Shearer, Douglas: Homeowner, Long Beach Island, 2015.

Smith, Brady: Tampa Bay Regional Planning Council, 2017.

Smith, J. B.: Planner, Army Corps of Engineers, 2016, 2017.

Soladz, Scott: Homeowner, Long Beach Island, 2016.

Sorrentino, Joseph: Homeowner, Little Egg Harbor Township, 2016.

Spodofora, John: Former Mayor, Stafford Township, 2015, 2016, 2017.

Stevens, Lisa: Homeowner, council member, Little Egg Harbor Township, 2015, 2016, 2017, 2018.

Tallon, Joanne: Construction officer, Long Beach Township, 2014, 2015.

Tecklenburg, John: Mayor, Charleston, 2017.

Titus, James: Sea-level expert, EPA; homeowner, Long Beach Island, 2017.

Ventry, Dennis J.: Tax law expert, University of California, Davis, 2016.

Verdino, James: Homeowner, Long Beach Island, 2015, 2016.

Waldner, Jeffrey S.: U.S. Department of the Interior, 2016.

Watkins, Nancy: Project leader, National Flood Insurance Program Modeling, Milliman, 2017.

Watson, Keith D.: Army Corps of Engineers, 2014, 2015, 2016.

Weingart, John: Former coastal manager, New Jersey Department of Environmental Protection, 2015.

Weisberg, Robert H.: Oceanographer, University of South Florida, 2017.

Wentworth, Leonard: Galveston, 2017.

Wetmore, Spencer: Administrator, Folly Beach, South Carolina, 2017.

Whitcraft, Deborah: Former mayor, Beach Haven, 2015.

Williams, Carolee: Conservation Voters of South Carolina, 2017.

Yasenchak, Leah: Environmental consultant, 2015, 2016.

Young, Robert S.: Geologist, Western Carolina University, 2017, 2018.

Zanni, Mark: Chief economist, Moody's Analytics, 2017.

ACKNOWLEDGMENTS

I first saw the unrivaled power of the ocean in 1962 while living in a tiny bungalow in the then sparsely developed dunes of Long Beach Island. It was just a few months after the Great Ash Wednesday Storm, and broken houses still straddled the oceanfront and bay. But it wasn't until Sandy wrecked the entire New Jersey coast fifty years later that I decided to write this book. In those interceding years, many friends and colleagues helped me better understand the history, geology, and culture at the beach, including Tom Dolan, Jim Salvano, Steve Balbo, Robert Kirn, and Paul Schoenberger. Special thanks to Anthony R. Wood, one of the most insightful writers on weather and hurricanes anywhere. In the late 1990s, Tony and I worked on a series of articles about the coasts for *The Philadelphia Inquirer*, and I never had more laughs or learned more.

Herb Shapiro generously spent hours with me re-creating the early days of the modern coast and his family's critical role on Long Beach Island. Similarly, Joe Mancini, the mayor of Long Beach Township, provided important insights and perspectives on the politics and business of coastal development, as well as the role of his family on the island. Joe and Herb may disagree with some of my conclusions, but I suspect they will acknowledge the relentless pace of my research.

I also owe a deep debt of gratitude to John Anderson, Dana Beach, Tom and Elizabeth Beaty, George Bernstein, Jim Blackburn, Margaret Buchholz, Bob Buckhorn, Jeff Collier, George Crozier, Willie deCamp, Kerry Emanuel, Stew Farrell, Jeff Gebert, Maxine Glorsky, Lewis Goldshore, Ray Gormley, Bernie Haney, Tim Hart, Jason Hazelton, Al Hine, Chris Huch, William Husenbeck, Jim Hutchinson, Billy Keyserling, David Kinsey, Dick Krimm, David Kutner, Ning Lin, Jim Mahoney, Mark Mauriello, Bill Merrell, John Miller, Orrin Pilkey, Stan Riggs, David and Amanda Rinear, Joe Rulli, J. B. Smith, John Spodofora, Lisa Stevens, John Tecklenburg, Keith Watson, John Weingart, Leah Yasenchak, and Rob Young. Special thanks to Bruce Clark for generously sharing some historical photographs and newspaper advertisements.

I can't thank Art Carey and Frank Corrado nearly enough for their careful insights and suggestions. Art and Frank were early readers, and their comments and criticisms greatly helped to shape the final book.

My editor at Farrar, Straus and Giroux, the inestimable Sarah Crichton, was always empathetic but equally tough. Her suggestions pointed the author in exactly the right direction. Thanks to Laird Gallagher for guiding me through the final steps and to Ben Rosenstock for his invaluable assistance. Of course, *The Geography of Risk* wouldn't exist without the important input of the copyediting, design, production, and marketing teams. Finally, thanks to my agent, Barney Karpfinger, for seeing the value in my idea and successfully bringing it to market.

As always, love to my wife, Cathy, for her support.

INDEX

Page numbers in *italics* refer to illustrations.

A NOTE ABOUT THE AUTHOR

Gilbert M. Gaul was awarded Pulitzer Prizes in 1979 and 1990, and has been short-listed for the Pulitzer four other times. He is the author of three previous books, including *Billion-Dollar Ball: A Journey Through the Big-Money Culture of College Football*, which was named one of the best sports books of 2015. He lives and surfs in New Jersey.